DATE DUE

DE 21 02			

DEMCO 38-296

The New Hampshire Primary and the American Electoral Process

The New Hampshire Primary and the American Electoral Process

NIALL A. PALMER

Foreword by Stuart Rothenberg

PRAEGER

Westport, Connecticut
London

Library of Congress Cataloging-in-Publication Data

Palmer, Niall A.
   The New Hampshire Primary and the American electoral process /
Niall A. Palmer ; foreword by Stuart Rothenberg.
       p.   cm.
   Includes bibliographical references and index.
   ISBN 0-275-95569-9 (alk. paper)
   1. Primaries—New Hampshire.   2. Political culture—New Hampshire.
3. Presidents—United States—Nomination.   I. Title.
JK2075.N42P35   1997
324.2742′0154—dc21   96-50322

British Library Cataloguing in Publication Data is available.

First published in 1997

Praeger Publishers, 88 Post Road West, Westport, CT 06881
An imprint of Greenwood Publishing Group, Inc.

Printed in the United States of America

The paper used in this book complies with the
Permanent Paper Standard issued by the National
Information Standards Organization (Z39.48–1984).

10 9 8 7 6 5 4 3 2

Copyright Acknowledgments

The author and publisher gratefully acknowledge permission for use of the following material:

Excerpts from a letter from Joseph F. Keefe to William Gardner, reprinted with permission of Joseph F. Keefe; excerpts from a letter from Basil Bettaglia to Governor Wilson, reprinted with permission of Basil Bettaglia; comments by Emmett L. Buell, Jr., about the 1984 primary reprinted with permission of Emmett L. Buell, Jr.; and excerpts from memos by Martin L. Gross reprinted with permission of Martin L. Gross.

For My Father and Mother

Douglas 1940–96
Valerie 1940–89

Contents

Tables

Foreword

Only death and taxes are inevitable, says the old saw. To those two markers in our lives, I would add a third and a fourth: the New Hampshire primary and criticism of that quadrennial event. In spite of repeated attempts to preempt and overshadow it, the New Hampshire primary has remained a political constant. It is still the first primary of each election year and the most-covered, most-discussed event of the nominating process. And it continues to play a critical role in the selection of the nation's presidential nominees.

Niall Palmer (as an Englishman) brings needed distance and detail to the study of the New Hampshire primary in the first major examination of that event since Charles Brereton's *First in the Nation: New Hampshire and the Premier Presidential Primary* (1987), and Dayton Duncan's *Grass Roots: One Year in the Life of the New Hampshire Presidential Primary* (1991). But while Duncan's journalistic approach reported on a single primary, 1988, and Brereton's book was largely a narrative of the state's primary battles from 1952 to 1984, Palmer goes much further as he both updates New Hampshire through the 1996 primary and brings the analytical eye of a political scientist and academic to the spectacle and to the charges of critics.

Palmer understands that any primary process is going to advantage some candidates and disadvantage others, and he recognizes that each election cycle is different. That means that tinkering with the process often produces different results than anticipated. While the delegate selection process was "front-loaded" in 1996, advocates argued that it would minimize the likelihood of long, drawn-out (and frequently divisive) battles for delegates. But "front-loading" the process tends to benefit candidates who begin with national stature, who can compete in a number of states simultaneously, and who can raise mountains of cash. In 1996, the front-loaded schedule helped win the Republican nomination for the front runner, Bob Dole, but it didn't prevent Dole from being battered by attacks from fellow Republicans or from running out of money during the delegate selection phase, thereby eroding his already bleak general election prospects.

Palmer documents the ways in which the national parties have sought to pressure New Hampshire and other states to follow a pre-ordained schedule, and he gives us a behind-the-scenes look at the maneuvering in 1996 by Arizona and Delaware to challenge New Hampshire's position as first among equals and the Granite State's efforts to keep their prized position at the front of the primaries. New Hampshire is undoubtedly the only state that could demand the candidates pass up other primaries, and the state's Republican voters helped destroy the presidential ambitions of Texas senator Phil Gramm when he refused to support a seven-day window between the New Hampshire and Delaware primaries.

Not merely a cheerleader for the Granite State, Palmer defends the state against the now routine attack on its "representativeness." He argues that in many ways —including the racial makeup of its citizens, its tax structure and anti-tax obsession, its partisanship and its size—New Hampshire does not mirror the rest of the country. But he notes that there is no consensus on which state should replace New Hampshire at the front of the pack, and he makes it clear that New Hampshire voters take their responsibility for winnowing the field of presidential hopefuls very seriously.

Palmer does an excellent job dealing with the way technology has changed the state's primary. While everyone else focuses on (and, according to Palmer, exaggerates) the impact of the notorious *Union Leader*, he also devotes much-needed attention to WMUR, the state's influential television station. Palmer, of course, echoes the view of others that "retail politics" remains a staple of the primary, but he notes that WMUR's influence "has come to rival that of the *Union Leader*." And he asserts that the station is "at the center of every media strategy" of every serious presidential primary campaign.

Part of our fascination with the Granite State's primary stems from the strange way in which victory and defeat are judged. Unlike the general election or the ballots during presidential nominating conventions, the winner in New Hampshire isn't necessarily the candidate who receives the most votes, as Edmund Muskie found out in 1972. That's because the primary is all about expectations, and expectations change during the months before the election and from cycle to cycle. In 1992, for example, Paul Tsongas's victory in the Democratic race was overshadowed by Bill Clinton's performance, which suggested to reporters, pundits and party insiders that the Arkansas governor was still a credible candidate even after significant questions had surfaced about his private life.

Palmer explains the "expectations game" as the result of the timing of the primary and the uncertainty surrounding the entire process. "Largely because it occupies a key place in the early weeks of the electoral cycle," he writes, "New Hampshire campaigns are difficult to report and especially vulnerable to competing interpretations, speculation and the attendant phenomenon of 'pack' journalism." Until the results are in, the presidential nominating process "has no clearly defined context, leaving candidates and reporters greater leeway for subjective claims and counter-claims."

Will the New Hampshire primary continue to receive the attention it has in the past? Probably, at least in the months before the 2000 primary. Most of the momentum for "front-loading" the primary calendar has dissipated, and New Hampshire proved in 1996 that it is more than willing to fight for its place as the first primary. While there will always be talk about creating regional primaries or even one national nominating primary, there is no evidence that those sorts of systems would produce "better" nominees or that support for changing the current system has reached anything close to critical mass.

Of course, critics of the status quo will note that Bill Clinton in 1992 and Bob Dole in 1996 won their party's nomination even though each placed second in the New Hampshire primary. Part of the reason the media and politicians have paid so much attention to the state is New Hampshire's record for selecting the eventual nominees. If that should change, it could affect coverage and clout.

Fundamentally, however, New Hampshire is special because it is first. After months of speculation and prediction, it offers a true test of candidate appeal, and as long as it is the first stop in the winnowing process that ultimately gives the electorate two nominees who will vie for the presidency, the Granite State will remain the focal point of presidential politics. Niall Palmer has helped us understand the state's role—and appreciate it.

Stuart Rothenberg
Editor, *The Rothenberg Political Report*

Acknowledgments

In the arduous process of converting my doctoral thesis into book form I have had much valuable assistance and would like to take the opportunity to thank those people who have given me so much advice and help. Mrs. Anne Merriman put in much painstaking work transferring the original text to disk. How she managed to negotiate a way through my scribbled notes I shall never know, but her determination and interest were an inspiration. Professor Richard Hodder-Williams, of the University of Bristol, supervised my original doctoral thesis, and I am happy for the chance to thank him for his support and advice. Likewise, I benefited greatly from the advice of Professor Emmett H. Buell, Jr., of Denison University, Ohio, another political scientist fascinated by the New Hampshire primary. Closer to home, I would like to express my appreciation to Dr. S. J. Kleinberg and Brunel University College for its support in the completion of this work and to the Nuffield Foundation and the U.S. Embassy and British Academy for their generosity in financial assistance for the project.

My frequent visits to New Hampshire have enabled me to make many contacts and many new friends. Notable amongst the latter are Representative Natalie Flanagan, Representative Susan McLane, former Representative Larry Elliott, Mrs. Aileen Katz, Skip and Gloria Calley, John Duval and freelance writer Charles Brereton. To each I wish to extend my thanks and appreciation and the hope that they will find this book of some interest. The campaigns I have witnessed have now receded into history, but I retain fond memories of the energetic "Gephardt For President" crowd, particularly Mark Fusaris and Mark Longabaugh, and of Bush coordinator Will Abbott and Kerrey strategist Al Rose. I hope they will come across this book at some point in the future. Thanks also to Lee Ann Steiner, Paul Young and Joe Grandmaison for their valuable insights into New Hampshire politics and to Professor Charles Cutter at San Diego State for some memorable cultural experiences!

Most importantly, I wish to thank New Hampshire's long-serving secretary of state, William M. Gardner, who has shown so much interest and enthusiasm for my project and has given me help and encouragement every step of the way. Access to his files concerning the primary proved immensely important for my research, as did his acute observations and knowledge of the elections over which he has presided for twenty years. I hope he finds this work to be a fair and balanced assessment of the state and its primary.

I am grateful to James Dunton and Marcia Goldstein, my editors at Greenwood, and to Martin Lasater for his work in copyediting and typesetting. Thanks, finally, to David Hornsby, to Paul Frayne for the Sitwell quote, and especially to Stuart Boydell for all his encouragement.

Introduction

But the see-saw crowd sent the Emperor down
To do the howling dust—and up went the clown.
—Edith Sitwell, "Said King Pompey," *Collected Poems*,
Macmillan & Co., Ltd., London, 1957, p. 117

One of the dominant themes of American election politics for much of the twentieth century has been the inexorable decline of partisan structure and linkage. This decline has been manifest in the changes that occurred in the presidential nominating process after the introduction of the presidential primary as a means of candidate selection. The primary was intended to foster a new, more "open" and "representative" system through which the nation's leaders could be chosen. The New Hampshire primary, first held during the 1916 election cycle, was one of the first of the new contests. As the popularity of electoral reform waned in the 1920s and 1930s, New Hampshire retained the position it had first gained in 1920—the lead-off competition for convention delegates. This position, however, held no real clout, and the state was not considered an important factor in a process still decided by convention bartering and compromise.

With the advent of television after 1948, primaries in general and New Hampshire in particular began to receive more attention from candidates and reporters. The year 1952 witnessed the birth of the modern era of televised campaigning, and the New Hampshire primary gained significant attention in the same year. This was partly due to a change of format since previous Granite State contests had been mere delegate selection events while 1952 saw the first use of the presidential preference ballot. The greater concentration on candidate personality that resulted from this change was magnified by television coverage. Reporters seized on New Hampshire as the first in a series of popularity polls which, though not decisive, certainly propelled Dwight Eisenhower toward the Republican nomination and assisted in Harry Truman's rapid withdrawal from the race. Almost overnight, the once insignificant New Hampshire contest became important for candidates wishing to develop a "bandwagon" to the conventions.

Since 1952, New Hampshire's first-in-the-nation primary has become one of the most well-known and notorious landmarks of the presidential election calendar, as well-known a fixture as the convention acceptance speech and Labor Day rally.

The size and character of the Granite State has been analyzed by media pundits, while campaign strategists have pored over polling data and pumped thousands of dollars into what became, by the late 1960s, a must-win contest. In its share of media coverage and candidate attention, New Hampshire has come to dwarf larger states with greater delegate yields such as Ohio or New York. It has also acquired the reputation as a burial ground or near-fatal hurdle for presidents and front-runners such as Harry Truman, Lyndon Johnson, Edmund Muskie, Walter Mondale and Robert Dole. Conversely, it has proved a vital jump-off point for low-budget, low-profile candidacies such as those of Eugene McCarthy, George McGovern, Jimmy Carter and Gary Hart. Each scored victories or near-victories that overturned conventional pundit wisdom and threw the nomination process into at least temporary turmoil.

In this role, New Hampshire enjoyed considerable popularity during the 1960s and early 1970s, but in more recent years it has come increasingly under attack from observers and candidates who question the representative quality of its verdict and resent its alleged influence over other states. As the primary marathon lengthened in the 1970s and 1980s, New Hampshire's perceived influence appeared increasingly out of proportion to its actual delegate yield. Criticism of the primary as anachronistic and perverse found echoes in congressional committee rooms and in the offices of national party organizations. During the 1980s, members of the House of Representatives and of the Democratic National Committee made several determined attempts to rein in New Hampshire's influence. Individual states also became resentful of their neighbor's high profile, claiming New Hampshire denuded the candidate field and left later states with no real candidate choice. Thus began the phenomenon of "front-loading" primaries as states moved their dates closer to New Hampshire's limelight.

This hostility has augmented New Hampshire's importance. The state's politicians have become adept at protecting their most treasured possession, repeatedly outmaneuvering members of Congress, national party officials and other state representatives in the endless status wars that have dogged nomination politics over the last ten years. Using a combination of guile and state law, the Granite State has successfully fought off or nullified challenges from Delaware, Arizona and other states, laying claim in the process to a vacuum-sealed position in the primary calendar. This position, after Iowa's caucuses and before any other delegate selection event, has become the most hotly disputed turf in American electoral politics. The battles surrounding it have come to symbolize, to many, the problems besetting the modern nominating system. For supporters, however, the first primary stands as a last bastion of "retail" politics—a unique electoral environment in which voters have a chance to meet and question candidates and presidents at close quarters. This opportunity has already been lost to larger states in which campaigns consist of televized debates and adverts, mass rallies and motorcades.

This book attempts to fill a gap in campaign literature. Despite its notoriety, relatively few books exist that offer an in-depth analysis of the first primary. Many election texts confine themselves to detailed accounts of specific campaigns. When mentioning New Hampshire, most of these tend to restrict themselves to fairly stereotypical and outdated observations concerning the socioeconomic character of the state and its quirky electorate. The work undertaken here represents a small step in filling this gap. Chapter 1 offers an historical review of New Hampshire campaigns since 1952, with specific emphasis on those primaries most important in contributing to the primary's notoriety. Thus the defeats of Truman and Dole are considered alongside the moral victories of McCarthy, McGovern and Buchanan. In this way, campaign techniques as applied to the peculiar environment of the Granite State can be observed and placed in perspective.

The second chapter comprises a socioeconomic and political profile of the state and its voters—a profile designed to address and, occasionally, correct some long-held but essentially outdated views of New Hampshire's character. A major criticism has long been that the state's citizens are isolated, conservative and ignorant of the social and economic problems that face urban America, making them ill-qualified to render judgment on presidential aspirants. A serious consideration of these charges is long overdue. In addition, the chapter discusses and seeks to invalidate a major weapon in the arsenal of the primary's critics —namely, that the first primary should be representative of the wider electorate and national political sentiment. The flawed premise underlying this claim is examined.

In Chapter 3, New Hampshire's primary is placed within the context of the wider nomination system, and the link between weakening party cohesion, television and the increasing importance of primaries as vehicles for popular political expression is explored. This contextualization helps promote understanding of New Hampshire's relatively sudden rise to prominence and the nature of its impact.

Chapter 4 deals with media coverage of the primary and assesses the relationship between candidates, reporters and voters in the highly charged and exceptionally volatile atmosphere of the early election period. Do reporters place too much stress on the first primary, galvanizing candidates into risking everything on the first throw, or does the election system itself dictate an unbalanced, trivia-oriented style of coverage?

The fifth chapter sets the first-in-the-nation contest in national political perspective, utilizing case studies to observe the ways in which New Hampshire state and party officials have battled to maintain first place in the primary calendar against apparently insuperable odds. Three separate arenas of conflict are examined involving the national Democratic party organization, interstate disputes over primary scheduling and consideration of regional primary proposals in the U.S. House of Representatives. These disputes throw into sharp relief the resentments, claims and counterclaims that have been created by the expanding use of presidential primaries and related reforms introduced since the 1960s. As a symbol to critics of much that is wrong with nomination politics, New Hampshire has become a target for reform or abolition, yet much of the criticism leveled at the state and many of the proposals for its replacement are flawed and based on idealistic and unworkable visions of a fair and representative selection system. These criticisms and the practiced arguments employed by Granite State representatives in countering them appear repeatedly in all three of the case studies presented.

In conclusion, this book summarizes the major points to be retained from the analysis and asks whether or not New Hampshire does indeed make a unique contribution to nomination politics or whether, instead, it is overzealous in its self-defense and has fallen victim to a hubris that cannot countenance the possibility that its primary does more harm than good in choosing among aspirants for the White House.

Granite State Watersheds, 1916–1996

What is it about New Hampshire and how do you go about winning there?
— Michael Kramer, *Time*, July 31, 1995, p. 33

BACKGROUND

New Hampshire held its first presidential primary in 1916. As in other states, candidate selection procedures had been reformed by the antipartisan impulse of the Progressive movement. An open primary, a contest open to voters from any or no declared party, had been instituted in 1910 by future governor Robert P. Bass.[1] The influence of the Boston and Maine Railroad Company, a powerful controlling influence in turn-of-the-century Granite State politics, had prevented this measure from being expanded to include presidential races in 1912. The new Democratic majority in New Hampshire's House and Senate (collectively known as the General Court) after 1912 permitted passage on May 21, 1913, of an Act to Provide for the Election of Delegates to National Conventions by Direct Vote of the People. Candidates for delegate were required to declare their candidacy not more than sixty days nor less than eighteen days before the primary. A ten dollar fee or two petitions of one hundred names of registered voters were to be submitted to the secretary of state. No provision was made for the separate declaration of personal candidate preference by voters; ballots were for delegate choice alone.

At the next biennial session of the General Court, on April 11, 1915, the laws were revised. The primary date had been originally set for the third Tuesday of every fourth May, but this was now moved to the second Tuesday in March to coincide with Town Meeting Days. Legislators calculated that March was more convenient for the large rural population, much of which would be engaged in ploughing in late April.

The next change in the primary format represented the first recognition of its increasing importance to the electoral process. In 1916 the primary had taken place one week after Indiana's and on the same day as Minnesota's. New Hampshire gained first position in 1920 when these states either moved or abandoned their primaries as the Progressive reform impulse weakened across the nation. By May 1949 primaries were undergoing something of a renaissance. Richard Upton, speaker of the New Hampshire House of Representatives, secured the passage of an Act to Provide for a Presidential Preference Primary enabling voters to state their preference between contenders for the White House. Under this revision, candidates for delegate status could run as favorable to a candidate without being committed to him. Any name could be placed on the ballot, provided sufficient signatures were collected. An explicit disclaimer of presidential ambition would be necessary for removal of a name. Upton later recalled his motives for introducing a piece of state legislation that was to have significant consequences for the presidency of the United States in future years. Interviewed nearly four decades later, he admitted that parts of the eventual bill had been scribbled on the back of an envelope and that then-governor Sherman Adams had been reluctant to commit himself to the changes. Upton also attributed part of his inspiration for the reform to an extant Oregon law permitting voters to vote directly for presidential candidates.[2] The legislation went through the House because, as Upton explained, "It was largely due to dissatisfaction with the system we had at the time. . . . It wasn't a very meaningful process. . . .The turnout wasn't so great either. . . . So I thought I would personally try to do something about it."[3] The attention attracted by the revamped primary after 1949 ensured that Upton's innovation would remain on the New Hampshire statute books. No further substantial changes were made to the primary until June 28, 1971, when a new law raised the signature requirement on petitions from 50 to 500 per congressional district. Entry onto the preference ballot was made subject to a $500 fee. Also in 1971, the primary date was moved to the first Tuesday in March.[4] Later changes updated primary procedures. In 1977 the selection of convention delegates and alternates was removed from the ballot, leaving only the names of presidential candidates for voters to consider, and in 1983 the petition requirement was abolished altogether, with the filing fee raised to $1,000.[5]

With the burgeoning primary system now dominating presidential nomination races, New Hampshire came under increasing pressure during the 1970s to take part in a regional New England primary. As a result of this pressure, combined with attempts by Florida and Massachusetts to move their primary dates ahead of New Hampshire, the Granite State legislature approved a bill on May 29, 1975, ensuring that its primary would precede all others in the election calendar.[6] The measure, introduced into the state House of Representatives by Representative Jim Splaine, required that New Hampshire's primary be held on the second Tuesday in March or on the Tuesday immediately before the date on which any other New England state should hold a similar election. The ambiguity of this provision was not to become apparent, either to the state legislature or other state governments, until the front-loading disputes of the 1990s moved Splaine to push through a revision of his statute, which specified that the intended gap between the first primary and all others was to be seven full days, was signed into law by Governor Stephen Merrill in June 1995. This revision, and New Hampshire's interpretation of the original statute, were to prove highly controversial.

By the close of the twentieth century, the famed first-in-the-nation primary had become one of the major centers of controversy in nomination politics and New

Hampshire had become almost perpetually embroiled in acrimonious disputes with other states over its privileged status. Reform elements within the U.S. Congress, together with politicians, academics and journalists, have added their voices to the growing clamor for a new, standardized nomination procedure in an effort to eradicate some of the instabilities and inequities of the primary system. The Granite State has been wary of such calls, detecting in them the covert intention to remove its first-in-the-nation tradition. Its determination to safeguard this tradition has been reinforced by state law and intraparty maneuvering and has, for the most part, been successful. Part of the state's defense, and the underlying cause of its primary's fame, stems from its image as a graveyard of presidential ambitions, a down-to-earth indicator of public opinion, a leveler and winnower of the candidate field. This chapter provides a selective history of New Hampshire contests since 1952, the year in which the primary first grabbed national attention and impacted on the nominating process. Through this narrative it is possible to distinguish the changing nature of the primary and of electoral politics generally and to explore the myths and realities that have been utilized by the primary's supporters in their efforts to prove that the contest offers a unique and valuable contribution to the presidential nominating process.

EARLY CAMPAIGNS: EISENHOWER, KEFAUVER AND LODGE

The first New Hampshire primary to feature a preference ballot came at an auspicious time for the Republican party in its efforts to end twenty years of Democratic dominance in Washington. The GOP's conservative wing favored Ohio senator Robert Taft for the presidential nomination, an outcome feared by those of the more moderate wing who believed that the isolationist Taft would take the party to its sixth successive election defeat. Their favored nominee, General Dwight Eisenhower, supreme commander of NATO, was still stationed in Europe at the beginning of 1952 and had yet to declare his political sympathies. The general had been targeted by draft movements of both the Republican and Democratic parties but had thus far accepted only the presidency of Columbia University.

In the knowledge that an impressive showing on the new preference ballot could furnish the spark for a nationwide draft-Ike movement, the general's suitors began a coordinated campaign. Massachusetts senator Henry Cabot Lodge and New Hampshire businessman Robert Burroughs established a rudimentary campaign organization and persuaded New Hampshire governor Sherman Adams to openly declare his support on September 30, 1951.[7] This in itself was something of a leap in the dark since Adams's own discreet inquiries to the Kansas County Clerk's Office had brought the answer, "Mr Eisenhower has never voted in this county as far as I know. . . . I don't think he has any politics."[8]

Lodge, frustrated at Eisenhower's apparent reluctance to give his sanction to the movement despite this encouragement, took matters into his own hands. He realized, as Herbert Parmet recorded, that a good performance in the first primary "held a valuable psychological reward for the winner, which was more important than merely winning the state's fourteen convention delegates."[9] This boost was essential. Although Eisenhower was nationally known and popular, Taft retained the loyalties of many party activists and potential delegates, and his poll ratings lagged only slightly behind those of the general among party voters.

On January 6, 1952, Lodge held a press conference to declare that Eisenhower had privately confirmed his Republican partisanship and his willingness to be drafted. Stephen Ambrose reports that Eisenhower himself was furious at this attempt to force his hand and spoke of his "bitter resentment" at Lodge's presumption.[10] Lodge had another motivation, however. A Democratic party official in Grafton County, New Hampshire, had decided to smoke out Eisenhower's political loyalties by putting his name forward for the Democratic party ballot. Since the 1949 state law had stipulated that any man petitioning to place a name on the ballot must be of the same political party as the proposed candidate, Eisenhower would then have been forced to make a negative declaration of intent by removing his name, possibly from *both* party lists.[11] In the event, Eisenhower allowed himself to be persuaded to run. Sherman Adams later recalled explaining the problem of the New Hampshire statute to Henry Cabot Lodge, "who went to NATO headquarters in Paris and talked with Eisenhower about it. The General announced on January 7, 1952 that he was, indeed, a Republican. Our problem was solved."[12]

Eisenhower's managers soon faced an unforeseen predicament. Their candidate remained an absentee, while Bob Taft had decided to commit himself to a three-day tour of the Granite State during the campaign's final week. With the backing of the omnipresent and acerbic Manchester newspaper, the *Union Leader,* and its outspoken owner, William Loeb, the Ohioan threatened to snatch the initiative and momentum from the Eisenhower camp. Charles Brereton observes that, with this development, the outlines of a New Hampshire campaign that would one day become all-too familiar began to take shape:

Taft's tour had wiped the grin off the faces of the Eisenhower backers. . . . Their earlier incautious remarks that the state was "in the bag" allowed Taft to claim a moral victory. . . if he collected even one delegate. . . . The great "expectations game" that would cause such consternation in many a New Hampshire primary henceforth was underway.[13]

After a panicked effort to reduce expectations of the general's performance, Ike's supporters succeeded in defeating Taft anyway. The senator failed to carry one New Hampshire county and took only one of its twelve cities—Manchester, home of the *Union Leader.* None of the fourteen elected delegates was pledged to Taft, and he trailed Eisenhower in the popular vote by over 11,000 votes. Having demonstrated the power of his popular appeal, even when absent from the country, after New Hampshire Dwight Eisenhower was on the road to the White House.

Ironically, although the Republican primary had inaugurated the forty-year tradition that no man would reach the presidency without first winning in New

Hampshire, it was the Democratic contest that produced the first shock result of the primary's modern era.

Estes Kefauver, a Tennessee senator who had made his name investigating political corruption and racketeering during the 1940s, embarked on an open challenge to incumbent President Harry Truman. Truman, ever the intense partisan, disliked the Tennessean (whose name he persistently mispronounced as "Cow Fever") for the trouble his investigations had caused the Democrats. Though unpopular in the polls, Truman still retained the clout of incumbency and by March 1952 had not announced his intention to run or retire. Questioned about Kefauver's New Hampshire bid during a White House press conference, the president remarked that "all these primaries are just eyewash when the convention meets, as you will find out."[14]

Truman was nonetheless surprised to find his name had been entered on the Democratic ballot and was reportedly on the point of instructing national party chairman Frank McKinney to withdraw it. McKinney changed Truman's mind, arguing that an early show of support could help the beleaguered administration. Another motivation for allowing his name to remain might have been provided by a telegram from William Loeb which said that rumors of his withdrawal suggested that "in your autumn years your courage is turning distinctly yellow."[15]

Truman's backers in New Hampshire were slow to marshal their resources and measure the president's support, sharing their boss's low opinion of primaries as vehicles for public opinion. Kefauver, however, became the first in a long line of public officials to appeal for help from local politicians and activists. Brereton regards Kefauver's personal, grass-roots approach as the secret to his success: "He had a great instinct for working the ground level of politics, he ambled along countless main streets, greeting shoppers and clerks, worked the assembly lines in factories, attended teas in private homes."[16]

Alarmed at the senator's ability to attract media attention and at his growing popularity within the Granite State, Truman supporters swung into action, distributing leaflets, airing radio ads and placing others in newspapers across the state. Turnout, particularly in the smaller communities where Kefauver was particularly strong, would be influenced by Town Meeting Day, but the Truman camp was finally lulled into a false sense of security by national polls giving him a comfortable edge over the Tennessean.

According to Brereton, Kefauver's nine percentage point victory over the president, as well as his clean sweep of the delegate slate, surprised the senator as much as his opponents. He had intended to shake what he perceived to be the administration's lax attitude to cronyism but had never contemplated outright victory. As Kefauver feared, his humiliation of the president gained him dangerous enemies within the Democratic party hierarchy, who still controlled the major part of the presidential nomination mechanism. The odds against ultimate success had been lengthened, not shortened, by the New Hampshire primary. It was a pyrrhic victory.

On March 29, 1952, addressing the annual Jefferson–Jackson Day dinner at Washington's National Guard Armory, Truman announced his intention not to seek a further term in office. Subsequent histories tend to record this as a "first scalp" for New Hampshire's primary, but evidence suggests that the president had more or less decided *not* to run by January 1952 and was actively engaged in seeking alternative candidates, including Chief Justice Fred Vinson and Illinois governor Adlai E. Stevenson, well before the beginning of the administration's half-hearted New Hampshire campaign.[17]

The events of both primaries set a new course for the first-in-the-nation primary. By delivering a stunning rebuke to one president and providing the first electoral endorsement for another, the state came to be recognized by politicians and journalists alike as an early and useful testing ground. It had yet to become the must-win event of future elections. The new medium of television had not yet come to dominate campaigning, and the nomination system itself was sixteen years away from the dramatic events of 1968 which would redistribute its dynamics and increase the state's electoral clout. Nonetheless, the 1952 New Hampshire campaigns marked the end of one political era and the gradual emergence of a new one, a role it was to play many times in the future.

The nomination contests of 1956 and 1960, while not devoid of incident, kept development of the Granite State's reputation on hold. Adlai Stevenson's reluctance to campaign openly for a second nomination in 1956 handed another victory to Estes Kefauver, but, as before, the convention balloting nullified New Hampshire's verdict. Stevenson drew a lesson from his loss in the first primary and campaigned energetically in later primaries, securing victory at the national convention on the first ballot. President Eisenhower's recovery from his heart attack in September 1955 and his subsequent decision to seek reelection terminated any discussion of an open Republican race, although the New Hampshire contest was notable that year for a small-scale effort by local Republicans to dump Richard Nixon from the vice-presidential slot on the party ticket.

In 1960 Nixon stormed to the nomination with little real opposition, taking care to utilize the primaries in order to prove the depth of his public appeal. On the Democratic side, John F. Kennedy faced little serious opposition in New Hampshire, the sole contender being Illinois businessman Paul Fisher. The crucial contests with Minnesota senator Hubert Humphrey were fought in the Wisconsin and West Virginia primaries later in the spring. Another potential candidate, Senate majority leader Lyndon B. Johnson, chose to sit out the primaries in the belief that convention strategy would deliver him the nomination. This was to be one of the last instances in which a presidential contender seriously underestimated the new power of the primary system.

In the aftermath of John Kennedy's assassination, the Democrats made a gift of the nomination to the new incumbent, Lyndon Johnson. Competition that year focused on the Republican race. The 1964 primary in New Hampshire witnessed another milestone in the state's growing reputation and another victory for a candidate *in absentia*. This was, in many ways, a more remarkable feat than the

Eisenhower win. Unlike the popular general, Ambassador Henry Cabot Lodge did not go on to win the nomination. His win in the Granite State was achieved by a write-in campaign organized by zealous volunteers. That year's major announced contenders were Nelson Rockefeller of New York and Barry Goldwater of Arizona. Both invested substantial amounts of personal time and campaign money in New Hampshire but were defeated by a U.S. ambassador to South Vietnam who, like Eisenhower, had not made any firm declaration for the presidency.

The Lodge victory was a consequence both of the determination and skill of his grass-roots activists and of the weaknesses inherent in the Rockefeller and Goldwater campaigns. The New York governor had been politically weakened by his divorce and remarriage to the wife of one of his officials in 1963. Charges that Happy Rockefeller had signed custody of her children over to her ex-husband, thus abandoning them, meant that Rockefeller encountered considerable public opprobrium during his campaign appearances, worsened by editorials in the *Union Leader* in which Bill Loeb issued vitriolic accusations, labeling the governor a "wife-swapper" and "home-wrecker."[18] Entering the campaign, Rockefeller was behind Goldwater by margins of 4–1.

The Arizona senator himself remained critically vulnerable. He faced three basic difficulties. First, as Brereton notes, dissension was rife among his in-state campaign team. Second, there was insufficient coordination or direction from the national campaign, headed by F. Clifton White, which was busy waging guerrilla warfare in the caucus states.[19] Finally, and most significantly, Goldwater's tendency to shoot from the hip in his public pronouncements was causing considerable political embarrassment. Theodore White described the senator as possessing "the completely unrestrained candor of old men and little children."[20] In the weeks prior to the primary, Goldwater was quoted advocating the sale of the Tennessee Valley Authority (TVA), withdrawal of diplomatic recognition from the Soviet Union, the abolition of a graduated income tax, voluntary Social Security contributions and withdrawal from the United Nations if China were admitted. Together with hints at the use of nuclear weapons in Vietnam, such outbursts made national headlines and undermined the senator's credibility as a serious contender. In New Hampshire, even conservatives were disturbed. A disillusioned Concord industrialist, who had been active for Goldwater, quit the campaign declaring: "If he doesn't mean what he says, then he's just trying to get votes; and if he does mean what he says—then the man is dangerous. So I quit."[21]

The avenue was open for a third candidate able to exploit the vulnerabilities of the front-runners. Boston lawyer David Goldberg and business executive Paul Grindle identified Henry Cabot Lodge as the ideal candidate. The scion of a noted political family and Richard Nixon's 1960 running mate, Lodge had the background necessary for a plausible nominee. Unfortunately, his position as ambassador in South Vietnam meant that he was prevented under the rules of Foreign Service from issuing political statements. He would therefore be unlikely to declare his candidacy without a firm indication from the electorate that the commitment would prove worth the risk. Goldberg and Grindle moved to Concord and opened a ramshackle headquarters with a skeleton staff and little office furniture. The decision to mount a write-in campaign was taken from political necessity, but its execution was a daunting task. It required far more voter motivation and a more intensive voter education effort by Lodge activists for the strategy to work. Consciously ignoring the choices on the ballot and writing in a different name required a degree of political awareness and commitment on the part of New Hampshire voters which could not be guaranteed. Misspelling the candidate's name or writing it on the wrong part of the ballot sheet would automatically spoil the paper.

Nonetheless, the Lodge movement had certain advantages. The candidate could be portrayed as a loyal citizen on active service in a dangerous land, awaiting the call to duty—a ploy borrowed from the Eisenhower campaign of 1952. In addition, the absence of the candidate left Goldberg and Grindle free to plan their New Hampshire operations without interference from a national organization or from the candidate himself. Finally, the gap between Rockefeller and Goldwater was being slowly whittled away as Goldwater's off-the-cuff comments sank him into ever-deeper waters. By mid-February, polls indicated Goldwater margins of only 3–2.[22]

The Lodge group played its hand with consummate skill. A pledge card operation was initiated whereby 96,000 homes received an invitation to pledge their support to Lodge by returning their cards to the Concord headquarters.[23] This device was not new in election campaigning, but it enabled the Lodge organization to roughly gauge the strength of their position. The first response to the mailshot—8,600 replies—was surprisingly high, and a second was immediately set up. This time respondents were urged to pick up two more votes. The Lodge campaign hoped that, if this was achieved, the ambassador's performance might top 27,000 votes, far above his media-projected performance.[24]

Goldwater, meanwhile, continued to hamper his own campaign progress with ill-advised comments. Brereton sarcastically noted, "Goldwater was a disaster during his first sustained and intimate contact with the national press corps. They kept printing what he said, not what he really meant to say."[25] Later, journalists would become more sympathetic to the senator's awkward honesty, but his comments that Eisenhower had "stolen" the 1952 nomination from Bob Taft and that governments could not stop depressions, only start them, had reporters running for the phones with alarming frequency.

The Lodge managers, aware of the former general-president's clout, compiled a five-minute film profile of their candidate in heroic stances and included some favorable comments from Eisenhower himself. The film was shown thirty-nine times in the Manchester area.[26] They were able to capitalize on an atmosphere of suspense generated by rumors that Lodge was on the point of formally announcing his candidacy. The deadline for candidates filing for the Oregon primary would fall only hours before the first votes were cast in New Hampshire. Oregon's secretary of state was legally entitled to place on the ballot any declared or undeclared candidate unless the man in question *specifically* instructed him that he was not in the race. Robert Mullen, a public relations adviser to the Lodge camp, casually announced that it was the general assumption that the ambassador *would* formally announce if New Hampshire's voters so demanded. George Lodge, the ambassador's son, confirmed that his father's name would remain on the Oregon ballot.[27] Such pronouncements ensured that the Lodge write-in campaign held media attention in the last few days before the Granite State primary vote.

The polls closed at 7.00 P.M. EST on Tuesday, March 10. At 7.18 P.M., Walter Cronkite of CBS had called the election for Lodge.[28] The absentee ambassador had taken 35 percent of the vote, leaving Goldwater more than ten points behind and Rockefeller an embarrassing third at 21 percent. This result immediately entered the New Hampshire hall of fame, but its aftermath was not the media-generated bandwagon that would often accompany primary results in later years. Lodge went on to further victories in New Jersey on April 21 and Massachusetts on April 28, but primary outcomes did not yet control the nomination decision.[29] Goldwater's organizational strength and concentrated efforts in the caucuses ultimately delivered him the party nomination. New Hampshire's role in 1964 was therefore not that of arbiter but of the incubator for an experiment in grass-roots democracy, what White described subsequently as a "madcap adventure."[30]

Brereton reveals that the Lodge managers later admitted to joining the race more for the excitement and challenge than from any deep-seated political principles. In a fascinating passage, he describes a weekend meeting of Paul Grindle and Nelson Rockefeller at the home of Pennsylvania governor William Scranton during which Rockefeller jokingly inquired how much it would have taken for him to "get the hell out of New Hampshire." Grindle reportedly replied that the campaign team had been waiting for just such a bribe and would have decamped almost immediately. Rockefeller was dumbstruck and asked if Grindle was serious:

Grindle: Absolutely I am. I've never been bribed to do anything in my life. I've always wanted to be bribed. I always expected you to do it. We'd have closed up shop for ten grand.[31]

CLASSIC CAMPAIGNS: McCARTHY, McGOVERN, CARTER AND HART

At the beginning of 1968, President Johnson was considered a virtual certainty for renomination, if not reelection. In a situation closely mirroring Harry Truman's in 1952, Johnson was unpopular as the result of war policies in Southeast Asia but considered to have complete control of the party machinery and therefore the nomination. The Republican field was similarly solid. Former vice-president Nixon appeared to have the party endorsement sewn up after years of careful cultivation of political IOUs among national party representatives and officials. The only major challenge at the outset of the race came from Michigan governor George Romney and New York governor Nelson Rockefeller. Since Rockefeller ran only a write-in campaign in New Hampshire and Romney had damaged his prospects with an ill-advised confession to having been "brainwashed" during a tour of South Vietnam, Nixon faced no serious problems in New Hampshire and utilized the first primary as a launch pad toward an inevitable second nomination.

Johnson's path was not to prove as smooth. His sole serious challenge in New Hampshire came from a senator considered a maverick by many in his party. Minnesota senator Eugene McCarthy had launched his crusade in late 1967 for open, honest government and an end to involvement in Vietnam. The bid was considered futile by most reporters since polls indicated that only New York senator Robert Kennedy had any chance of beating Johnson. McCarthy's candidacy had been slow to materialize. Although he had formally declared for the presidency on November 30, 1967, McCarthy was reluctant to make his opening bid in New Hampshire. He believed that the state was too right-wing and hawkish to provide him with the crucial first boost he desperately needed. Two of his Granite State organizers, David Hoeh and Gerry Studds, fervently believed that the senator's aloof nature and dry wit would appeal directly to similar qualities in the New England state. In a thousand-word memo to McCarthy they stressed, "If we are to move, we must get going yesterday."[32] They had the nucleus of an experienced campaign already in place and believed there would be substantial help from student volunteers who could be bussed in cheaply from neighboring states. Moreover, the proximity of Massachusetts made the campaign more cost-effective since the two could be treated as a package. Finally, they noted, a good early start could pay the highest dividends in media recognition, something McCarthy desperately needed. A Gallup poll of December 6, 1967 revealed that 58 percent of those questioned had never heard of the senator and of those who had, 42 percent preferred Johnson for the nomination.[33]

The campaign developed rapidly from this point into the prototype of New Hampshire longshot, grass-roots efforts—a model for many to follow in future elections. McCarthy organizer Ben Stavis recalled that only twenty-eight days before the March 12 vote the McCarthy headquarters in Concord was still not fully operational.[34] Maps were quickly obtained from the State Highway Department, and these were duplicated, divided into sections and marked with routes for canvassers. Democratic and undeclared voters were located and listed alphabetically for each city and town. The size of the student volunteer movement that descended on New Hampshire surprised even the campaign managers. Hundreds arrived at the Concord headquarters until many had to be turned away. Those accepted were quickly divided into groups according to physical appearance. Those with beards and long hair were encouraged to shed both or were put to work in offices where they would be out of the public's sight. Clean-shaven and neatly dressed volunteers were assigned as canvassers. McCarthy's people were only too aware of possible negative reactions to the hippy image associated with antiwar protestors. The slogan "Neat and Clean for Gene" and a framed front-page headline recalling Kefauver's defeat of Truman were signs of the volunteers' faith that New Hampshire would again prove fertile ground for an insurgency.

Stavis later noted that this method of grass-roots politicking was not new. It had been an accepted tool of big-city party machines and bosses since the nineteenth century. What *was* novel about the New Hampshire effort was its amateur style, applied on a statewide basis and using outside resources:

No one had ever thought of actually canvassing personally all the voters in a state and pulling all favorable voters. But no campaign had had the thousands of people willing to do precinct work and the dozens of diligent office and field workers to organise such a massive effort. We had created, on an amateur basis, a super-machine capable of being moved from state to state.[35]

The campaign used film stars such as Paul Newman, Myrna Loy, Dustin Hoffman, Lauren Bacall and Jason Robards to publicize their efforts. Sample ballots were distributed throughout New Hampshire demonstrating how to register a McCarthy vote. The senator himself made numerous campaign appearances, trailing in and out of shops and restaurants, standing outside factory gates to greet workers coming off shift and even playing a brief game of ice hockey in Concord.

The state's Democratic governor, John King, was a firm Johnson backer, but this did not impede the insurgents since the diffuse nature of political power in New Hampshire ensured that the lack of official endorsement was not a crippling blow to any campaign. The student volunteer effort, nicknamed the Children's Crusade in the press, accepted and conformed to established political rules in their primary campaign. Only later, embittered by McCarthy's defeat and by the death of Robert Kennedy, would many turn to violence on the streets of Chicago to register their protest against the establishment candidacy of Hubert Humphrey.

McCarthy was helped to some extent by the perception that he was a one-issue candidate. This enabled the students to set the agenda for the primary and to focus attention on the senator. They were assisted by the Johnson campaign itself, run by Governor King, Senator Thomas J. McIntyre and former federal official Bernard Boutin, which proved a study in complacency and miscalculation. Brereton believes that the president's decision to allow his name to go forward as a write-in candidate in New Hampshire was a serious mistake, overestimating both the clout of the state Democratic party and the administration's popular support, much as Frank McKinney had overestimated Truman's in 1952.[36] Voters and Johnson workers resented the president's reluctance to campaign in person. The Johnson camp decided to emulate the 1964 Lodge pledge card tactic, with disastrous results. The plan was developed to send thousands of cards to individual voters with the message: "President Johnson. I pledge my support to you and will WRITE IN your name on my ballot in the 12 March New Hampshire presidential preference primary."[37]

Returned cards entitled their senders to free portraits of the president and first lady and the possibility of a personal phone call from the president to thank them for their support. The McCarthy camp had little difficulty portraying this strategy as Big Brotherism and promptly printed posters reproducing the pledge card and asking "Whatever Happened to the Secret Ballot?" An embarrassed White House eventually denied it had received any cards at all. King compounded the error with vehement attacks on McCarthy, impugning his patriotism. A radio commercial aired in the last days of the campaign blared the message, "The Communists in Vietnam are watching the New Hampshire Primary. . . . Don't vote for fuzzy thinking and surrender."[38]

When the governor publicly asserted that a vote for McCarthy "would be greeted with cheers in Hanoi," even McIntyre felt obliged to state that he did not support such tactics. King's comments, he said, did the Minnesota senator "a very great injustice because his patriotism, his loyalty to his country, is as good as yours or mine any day of the week."[39] McIntyre was subsequently compelled to retract his criticisms of King, adding to the image of a campaign in disarray.

Media attention focused almost entirely on the Children's Crusade. Robert Kennedy had quashed a nascent bid to draft him in New Hampshire, and Richard Nixon was a runaway favorite in the Republican race. This left the Johnson–McCarthy feud as the only show in town for reporters. Early predictions of the senator's strength were low as he made his first forays into the Granite State, averaging between 10 and 12 percent.[40] Even as late as the last week of February 1968, *Time* reported a Roper poll giving McCarthy only 11 percent of the vote.[41] As the president's campaign faltered, however, its leaders made a spirited attempt to head McCarthy off by raising expectations of his performance to levels he could not reasonably be expected to match. The process of benchmarking—setting performance target levels for candidates—had begun in earnest and would feature prominently in the future strategies of both candidates and reporters.

Throughout the night of March 12–13, President Johnson's lead over his challenger remained slim. McCarthy's supporters gathered at Manchester's Wayfarer Inn and became ecstatic as their candidate's tally passed the 40 percent mark. In the final result, with Republican write-ins added, McCarthy came close to defeating Johnson. The president actually *lost* the delegate selection battle itself. Twenty-four slots were available on the slate for the national convention, but because write-in candidates were not permitted control over whose names would compete for these places, forty-five pro-Johnson names had battled it out between them. McCarthy's camp ran only one delegate per slot and thus won twenty delegates to the president's four.[42]

For Lyndon Johnson the result was a disaster since the media focus was almost entirely on the success of the crusade. McCarthy was labeled the moral victor of the New Hampshire race so frequently that many observers retained the impression that the Minnesotan had actually won the contest outright. For an unpopular president to achieve 49.6 percent of the vote in a badly run campaign with no personal appearances was in fact a remarkable feat in itself, but this was largely ignored in the rush to bury the president's political reputation. Faced with defeat in Wisconsin, Johnson unexpectedly withdrew from the race on March 31, 1968, leaving the field to his vice-president, McCarthy and New York senator Robert

Kennedy who, gaining the strength of McCarthy's convictions, had finally jumped into the fray.

The year 1968 represented a milestone for New Hampshire's primary. Its result on the Democratic side had reinforced the lessons of 1952 and 1964 regarding grass-roots campaigns. The state had claimed, at least in the minds of many reporters, a second presidential scalp and could no longer be lightly dismissed as an irrelevant or optional contest. More importantly, however, it was the last New Hampshire primary to be conducted under the old rules of engagement. Denied the nomination of McCarthy and presented instead with Hubert Humphrey who entered no primaries but simply harvested delegates away from public scrutiny in the caucuses, thousands of Democratic party activists would press for reform of the whole nomination procedure during the summer of 1968. This would be granted by party bosses in an effort to restore unity. These reforms would result in a root-and-branch overhaul of the system and in the redistribution of power from party bosses to local activists, from caucus states to primary states, from backroom deals to open debates, from politicians to reporters and television cameras—in sum, from the old politics to the new.

By 1972 New Hampshire's primary would head a changed system, one of nearly thirty primary contests that together dictated the outcome of the nomination race. The Granite State verdict would no longer be advisory. Henceforth it would become the most critical stage of the entire campaign, capable of creating momentum for successful candidates or of sending even well-established and well-funded names down to defeat.

President Nixon faced the 1972 Republican nomination cycle with as much confidence as he had in 1968. His challengers, California's Representative Paul "Pete" McCloskey from the GOP left and Representative John Ashbrook of Ohio from the right, were both little-known longshots, and California governor Ronald Reagan was not willing to enter the lists and divide the party. His most dangerous potential Democratic challenger, Senator Edward Kennedy, had been politically crippled by Chappaquiddick, and the remaining candidates were about to embark on a bitter fight for their party's nomination. Nixon's major fear was that his failure, thus far, to end the Vietnam War could be exploited by Maine senator Edmund Muskie, Hubert Humphrey's 1968 running-mate and almost certainly the man to face off against Nixon in November.

In the early months of 1972, the nomination of Muskie appeared close to a racing certainty. Yet Muskie's victory in New Hampshire proved to be one of the most contentious of the Granite State's verdicts and failed to secure his nomination. It was later claimed that adverse media coverage sank Muskie's candidacy, but a large portion of the blame for his ultimate failure rests with fundamental weaknesses in the senator's organization and tactics. Muskie's backers failed to appreciate the new dynamics of the nomination race and continued to place great stress on locking up the support of key political figures in the state. George McGovern, senator form South Dakota and Muskie's main rival in New Hampshire, was better placed to understand the new rules. As the first chairman of the McGovern–Fraser rules review body, he had been deeply involved in converting the Democratic party to a more open, participatory nominating process.

McGovern was also aided by student volunteers, liberal in political stripe and committed to change in politics and ending the war in Vietnam. A tightly run organization developed in the state, headed by J. Joseph Grandmaison and directed by national coordinator, Gary Hart. Both were able to exploit the sentiments of protest politics. Hart later recalled the enormity of the challenge:

It was here in New Hampshire that the McGovern Army was born. The purpose of a political organization is to contact voters. . . . It is possible to get elected without an organization; if a candidate is widely-known or can afford expensive media. . . . But McGovern was practically unknown and had no money.[43]

McGovern was scheduled to spend twenty-four days in the state, against Muskie's thirteen. His supporters attempted to maximize the benefits of travel by ensuring that a press conference or media event would be scheduled for each stopover in Boston en route for New Hampshire. Such events were heavily covered, free of charge, in the Boston media, much of which reached across the border into New Hampshire's southern counties. This free media was crucial, but Muskie, Hart noted, had no stopovers planned.[44]

Where Muskie was circumspect, McGovern was ubiquitous. Brereton notes the astonishment of one reporter, who commented, "I have shaken his hand four times, talked with him at length twice. The guy's everywhere!"[45] Muskie's entourage did not appear particularly concerned about their candidate's light schedule, believing he might lose three or four percentage points from his victory margin at worst. The forecast was accurate but, as it transpired, unhelpful. The Muskie campaign appeared to lack organizational and thematic cohesion. Theodore White quotes the New York campaign manager who observed, "To this day I don't know what the campaign was all about. We never had a theme."[46]

Conversely, McGovern's liberal social stance and antiwar rhetoric struck a chord in the more liberal sections of the primary voting population in New Hampshire. His appearances and policies began to pay dividends. In the closing days of the campaign, Hart first noticed a change in public attitude during a tour of the J. F. McElwayne Shoe Company in Manchester, later recalling that "for the first time in more than a year of campaigning, workers got up from their seats all over the plant when they saw McGovern. . . . They wanted to shake his hand, to offer their support. . . . Momentum was with us."[47]

The emerging picture was potentially disastrous for the Muskie camp. It bore all the hallmarks of an upset win by the outsider candidate, or at least a surprising showing that could steal the limelight from a Muskie victory. Overestimating its own strength, however, and confident that McGovern's left-of-center politics could not find a substantial following in this New England state, Muskie's managers sat on their hands.

The events that sealed the fate of the Maine senator centered on the role of the news media, both national and local. By 1972 the setting of a benchmark percentage for candidate performance had become accepted practice. Muskie had been tireless in his efforts over the years to help New Hampshire state Democrats strengthen their organization and was presumed therefore to have an inbuilt advantage. Fred Emery, a commentator for the BBC, claims that R. W. Apple of the *New York Times* originally came up with 50 percent as a marker for Muskie, while James Perry cites both David Broder of the *Washington Post* and John Becker of the *Boston Globe* as its source.[48] But Muskie's staff and the candidate himself contributed to the legend. Campaign aide Maria Carrier jokingly claimed that she would blow her brains out if the senator failed to win 50 percent of the vote, while Muskie admitted to reporters that "The significance of the victory may depend upon the size of the vote."[49]

The 50 percent marker quickly became Muskie's phantom opponent. McGovern strategists had tried and failed to tag him with a 65 percent lower limit, but the new limit would serve them just as well. Muskie was now vulnerable. Simple numerical victory was not necessary for his opponents to declare their result a triumph. For Muskie, however, it would not be enough. Sensing the danger ahead, Muskie attempted to pin the responsibility for his difficulties on the media with the assertion that New Hampshire was only important to his candidacy "because you gentlemen of the press have undertaken to make it important, in order to test me."[50] To some, this statement carried proprietorial overtones, an impression of Muskie that remained with J. Joseph Grandmaison, McGovern's 1972 state coordinator, who later observed that Muskie had already elected himself president in his imagination and "spent a lot of time worrying about ambassadorial appointments he was going to make as President. In the end it didn't make much difference!"[51]

One late gaffe was needed for the McGovern camp to come within striking distance; it was furnished by the candidate himself. For some weeks he had been taunted remorselessly in the columns and editorials of the *Union Leader*. In the first incident, a letter was published purporting to describe a Muskie visit to The Seed—a drug rehabilitation center in Florida—during which the senator supposedly laughed when someone referred to French-Canadians by the derogatory term Canucks. The letter, whose author was never found, was followed up by Bill Loeb's own comments:

We must remember that this is the same Senator who had the gall to . . . say that the publisher of this newspaper didn't understand northern New England. . . . WE HAVE ALWAYS KNOWN THAT SENATOR MUSKIE WAS A HYPOCRITE BUT WE NEVER EXPECTED TO HAVE IT SO CLEARLY REVEALED IN THIS LETTER.[52]

The editorial was potentially damaging since French-Canadians made up 50 percent of the total vote in Manchester, which itself made up one-half of the state's Democratic party support. In the second instance, Loeb reprinted a *Newsweek* article that had taken bitchy sideswipes at the unguarded behavior of the candidate's wife. "On the Bus with Jane Muskie" included revelations that she chewed gum, had two drinks before dinner and a creme de menthe afterwards but couldn't mix her drinks because "I get a headache and have little dreams."[53]

Standing on a flatbed truck before the *Union Leader* offices on the freezing morning of February 26, 1972, Muskie became so outraged in defense of his wife that he appeared to choke and stutter with tears. He attacked Loeb personally, adding that it was just as well the publisher had stayed at home in Massachusetts that day. This image contrasted poorly with pictures on the main network news programs that day of President Nixon touring China, every inch the statesman.[54]

Muskie's victory on primary day was insufficient to gain him the vital momentum needed for the rest of the primary season. With 46.4 percent he had failed to breach the psychologically crucial barrier, while McGovern exceeded expectations and walked away with the laurels of victory in the national media.[55] Even in Manchester, where the South Dakota senator had not been expected to do well, he came within 600 votes of the front-runner. McGovern himself was disappointed at the result, having privately entertained hopes of outright victory. His irritability on election night, Hart recalled, reduced some of his exhausted young New Hampshire staffers to tears.[56] After realizing the import of his performance, however, he wasted no time in claiming a moral victory, which the media were not slow to recognize. The road to the nomination lay open.

By the mid-1970s, the reforms of the McGovern–Fraser and Mikulski commissions had been largely digested by the Democrats, and a record number of presidential primaries now faced candidates in both parties. New campaign finance laws and the introduction of proportionate allocation of delegates in some contests added a new volatility to the process. Outsiders generally appeared to have benefited most from this uncertainty, and their focus on the earlier events in the nomination calendar grew more intensive. The first-in-the-nation primary was no longer an optional experiment but an electoral imperative. By now, reporters were cosily familiar with the small state, its towns and communities, its activists and local press, its restaurants and hotel bars. Logistically, it was an easy state to cover.

The former governor of Georgia, James Earl Carter, Jr., had reached a similar conclusion. Carter had no national name recognition to compete with other potential runners in a crowded Democratic field. Fred Harris had been party chairman, Hubert Humphrey had been vice-president under Lyndon Johnson, Henry Jackson and Birch Bayh were senators and Morris Udall was a respected member of the House of Representatives. Carter needed an early boost to attract media attention in order to gain new volunteer support and badly needed donations. The famous memorandum prepared for him by his chief aide, Hamilton Jordan, in November 1972 had stressed the Granite State as the pivotal contest:

As you know, New Hampshire's primary traditionally has been a place where sure winners have stumbled and the dark horses like Eugene McCarthy and George McGovern have established themselves as serious contenders. New Hampshire is a small state which is rural and independent and given to the kind of personal campaign that you and your family are capable of waging.[57]

Enjoying the benefits of unemployment, the ex-governor made regular visits to New Hampshire beginning in 1974, while other campaigns conserved their energies. There was a possibility that the first primary might not "be allowed to be the whole ballgame," being preempted by the Iowa caucuses, held in January 1976.[58] To account for this eventuality, Carter covered the caucus state with the same determination.

The Carter campaign in New Hampshire operated from a sidestreet building in Manchester which also housed a gymnasium. Staffers compiled a 50,000-card index of voter telephone numbers, and National Telephone Advertisers of New York were hired to conduct a canvas.[59] Volunteers worked door-to-door in Manchester, Nashua, Concord, Bedford and virtually all other towns, returning to the headquarters to write personal thank you notes. From early 1976 over 200 volunteers worked almost 70 percent of New Hampshire's Democratic households.[60] Carter and his family worked the state with prodigious energy. The former governor stood for hours on many mornings shaking hands with workers coming off the factory night shifts. Secretary of State William Gardner later recalled the future president's early anonymity. "Jimmy Carter spent a lot of time in and around the State House. I remember him sitting in the State House cafeteria early in the morning having breakfast—all alone, many times. . . . Early in the campaign he wasn't given much chance at all, but he persisted."[61]

Carter's poll ratings remained low, but he was helped by the decision of Washington State's Senator Henry Jackson to avoid New Hampshire since he could not commit the necessary time to mount a serious campaign. This left Carter as the only nonliberal candidate in the field, with the liberal field divided between Udall, Bayh, Harris and Sargent Shriver. Bayh's campaign manager, James M. Friedman, discovered from polls taken in January that Carter had effectively sewn up the entire right-wing Democratic vote. In addition, he had begun airing radio commercials during the first week of the year, while Bayh at this point had not even appointed his media consultant.[62]

The closest challenge to Carter came from the Udall camp. Organizers David Evans and Maria Carrier conducted thorough surveys to pinpoint Udall's strongest bases of support. The Arizona veteran was unused to waiting at factory gates, however. New Hampshire staffer Joanne Symons recalled Udall's evident discomfort during a tour of a paper mill in Groveton, when the candidate asked plaintively, "Why do I have the right to stop these people from their work?"[63]

Iowa also helped Carter. Udall's managers had belatedly decided to try to counter Carter's strength in the caucus state, dividing badly stretched resources between two states to no effect. Symons called the strategy "stupid," adding, "We were all screaming, 'What's he doing in Iowa? Get him back here because we can win here.'. . . If he'd won here, if he'd beaten Jimmy Carter, I think Carter would have been dead."[64]

Although Carter came in second in Iowa, he was the highest-ranked candidate to the uncommitted vote. This, combined with growing media interest and months of assiduous campaigning paid off in New Hampshire. His victory started the momentum for what soon became an unstoppable bandwagon. Jackson's entry into the race in Massachusetts one week later became an irrelevancy. Jackson triumphed in a state with ten times the number of delegates carried by New Hampshire, but the news media's headlines and magazine covers carried Carter's pictures. The challenge for the loyalties of southern voters presented by former Georgia governor George Wallace was easily pushed aside. Bids from Idaho senator Frank Church and California governor Jerry Brown during the latter weeks of the primary season came too late to deny Carter an outright majority of convention delegates.

The 1976 campaign that carried Carter to the White House came to be regarded as a model for future New Hampshire efforts. The former governor, with no national political standing, had demonstrated the potential of the first primary for creating a cycle of dollar-generating media interest which could bring the smallest, most poorly resourced campaign through the lengthy series of primary tests. This bandwagon effect carried Carter through to the New York Convention in July 1976.

The first primary did not prove nearly so smooth for Republican president Gerald Ford, who had replaced Richard Nixon eighteen months earlier and now faced a serious challenge for the nomination and control of the party from Ronald Reagan. Both candidates recognized the importance of New Hampshire to their nomination prospects since their support within Republican ranks was so finely balanced that an early victory for either could prove decisive in the longer term. Reagan went into New Hampshire with a poll lead, but his campaign suffered from careless remarks concerning tax and spending policies made by the candidate himself and by his New Hampshire champion, conservative GOP governor Meldrim Thomson. Thomson also made a serious mistake in giving reporters an estimate of the percentage of votes Reagan needed to be able to claim a moral victory. The estimate, far too high under the circumstances, robbed Reagan of whatever credibility he might have taken away with him from the Granite State. A determined and high-visibility campaign by Ford, combined with a last-minute error by Reagan's managers, who flew him out of the state to campaign in other contests on the final, crucial weekend, allowed Ford to gain a narrow victory. It was not to be the end of the Reagan challenge, but in later discussions, the former governor's campaign advisers held firmly to the belief that victory in New Hampshire would have delivered them, and not Ford, the nomination in Kansas City. Reagan was not to underestimate New Hampshire's potential again.

In 1980, with the Democrats in the White House, incumbent President Jimmy Carter faced Edward Kennedy in the first Democratic primary. Unfortunately for Kennedy, a lackluster interview performance on television the previous November had slowed the shift of public opinion in his favor. Moreover, the seizure of the United States Embassy in Teheran by fanatical students loyal to the Ayatollah Khomeini soon gave the American public reason to rally behind the president, at least for the moment. Carter easily deflected Kennedy's challenge in a state the Massachusetts senator might once have been expected to win handily. The Republican race had quickly singled out two main candidates, Ronald Reagan and former ambassador to China, George Bush. After the Iowa caucuses delivered an upset win to Bush, Reagan's candidacy was in deep trouble heading into New Hampshire. The candidate abandoned the low visibility, above-the-fray tactics that had damaged his Iowa support and campaigned in the Granite State with a vigor that belied his age. The poll gap between Reagan and Bush began to close up almost immediately. Reagan's support among New Hampshire's conservative Republican communities was far more substantial and reliable than the more centrist voters generally attracted to Bush. Like Nixon before him, Reagan had a natural constituency in New Hampshire and worked it effectively. The event that sealed Bush's fate, and ultimately the outcome of the GOP 1980 race, was a debate sponsored by the Nashua *Telegraph*. This was originally to have been a confrontation between the top two contenders, but the Reagan camp had contrived to have the other candidates, including Illinois congressman John Anderson and Kansas senator Bob Dole, invited to share the rostrum. Faced with this *fait accompli* on stage and before live television, Bush adamantly refused to allow the participation of the other candidates while Reagan, drawing on his long acting career, protested forcefully when debate moderator Jon Breen attempted to cut off the power to his microphone in an effort to stop the former governor from turning the confusion into a publicity stunt. The effort failed. Reagan's protests that "I am *paying* for this microphone, Mr Green [sic]" and Bush's frozen visage turned public opinion in Reagan's favor. After a convincing New Hampshire victory, Reagan barnstormed to the nomination and on to the White House.

The Republican primary in 1984 provided one of the most one-sided New Hampshire primaries since the Eisenhower and Johnson walkovers of 1956 and 1964. There was no prospect of competition on the Republican side, as the GOP prepared President Reagan's coronation at the Dallas Convention. Media attention therefore focused entirely on the Democratic race. A *Newsweek* cover in January 1984 had presented a portrait of a smugly confident former vice-president under the caption "Can Anyone Stop Mondale?"[65] Since the withdrawal of Senator Edward Kennedy in 1982, Mondale had been the acknowledged front-runner. An initial challenge from former astronaut-turned Ohio senator John Glenn had rapidly faded by late 1983. Employing a run everywhere strategy, laden with heavy financial support and public endorsements from union leaders, Mondale's strategists aimed to flatten competition early in the race, leaving the party united and free to focus opposition to the phenomenally popular President Ronald Reagan. In October 1983, *Newsweek* reported that while "there's plenty of time for surprises," it had begun to look unlikely that the feats of outsiders McCarthy, McGovern and Carter would be matched in 1984's primary season since "the brutal mechanics of raising money and next year's dramatically compressed primary and caucus schedule make it increasingly difficult for a little-known candidate suddenly to emerge from the pack."[66]

The creation of Super Tuesday, a one-day marathon of thirteen presidential primaries, had effectively raised the stakes in both Iowa and New Hampshire. Candidates now faced a choice of strategies—to bypass the small early contests to concentrate fire on the bigger delegate harvest in March, or to step up activities in Iowa and New Hampshire in the hope that an impressive showing would reap financial and electoral rewards in time for Super Tuesday. Almost all candidates chose the second option. Underfunded outsiders such as Glenn, Colorado senator Gary Hart, California senator Alan Cranston and a newly ambitious George McGovern had no real choice but to risk all in the two early contests. Their budgets and levels of volunteer support would not sustain a long campaign. By tradition, New Hampshire in particular represented their first and last best hope.

The Mondale camp was uneasy about their Granite State strength as early as 1982, when they had initially backed efforts to downgrade its influence. In July 1983, Brereton records, Mondale pollster Peter Hart discovered a virtual tie among respondents between Mondale and Glenn, 37 percent to 36 percent.[67] As the Glenn campaign faltered, however, they feared that the media would seek to anoint a new challenger to maintain the race's competitiveness. This fear was realized on February 21, 1984, when Gary Hart captured 15 percent of the vote in the Iowa caucus, a full 30 percent behind Mondale and only 2 percent ahead of McGovern, his former boss. Surveying news reports for the period, William Mayer discovered that Hart received far more coverage for his "by any reasonable standard . . . unspectacular" showing than Mondale.[68] The result catapulted Hart into the role of challenger. The media had become bored by the inevitability of Walter Mondale, and the New Hampshire race took on an eerie echo of the Muskie–McGovern battle.

The Hart strategy was based on the Carter model of early surprises inducing media coverage and stimulating campaign finances. Only Mondale could count on victories in the Super Tuesday states regardless of his New Hampshire showing. During October 1983, the breakthrough strategy was implemented with door-to-door canvassing of over 28,000 Democratic households (comprising over 40,000 registered voters) while radio ads aired continually. Senior New Hampshire staffer Susan Casey recalled that the media had paid little attention to Hart until the late fall of 1983 when "a story here and there" began to appear, "And the story was that, while the other candidates and the press were counting the straw poll votes in Maine, Hart was out talking to the voters in New Hampshire."[69]

The Iowa boost was the key to Hart's plan. His groundwork in the Granite State meant that the campaign was now in a position to take full advantage of the tide that appeared to be running his way. The surge, Casey wrote, was palpable between the Iowa caucus and the February 28 primary. Media interest, minimal for fourteen months, skyrocketed overnight:

Great masses of movement were documented through the ABC/Washington Post polls, which saw Hart's "surge". . . . It wasn't just in the polls. . . . You could feel it on the streets, hear it at our phone banks, experience it in every local headquarters. And, most importantly, you could watch it on television. . . . Overnight we made believers out of almost everyone.[70]

Hart campaigned intensively, spending fifty-seven days in the state during the run-up to primary day, against Mondale's fifty-one and Glenn's thirty-seven. The former vice-president, confident that his strategy would pay off, failed to turn up to join other candidates in addressing the State Employees Association at the National Guard Armory in Concord, one of the largest events of the campaign just four days before the primary. Mondale also repeated the error made by Ronald Reagan in 1976 and George Bush in 1980 by allowing himself to be bustled out of New Hampshire on the final weekend. This once-regular practice had been utilized by state campaign managers to give themselves and their staffers free rein to concentrate on getting out the vote.[71] In all three cases, the tactic proved a blunder which their challengers remained behind to exploit.

The final result proved to be one of the most remarkable upsets in modern election campaigning. Hart defeated Mondale by the largest margin ever accorded a Democratic primary victor. For a few weeks afterward, rumors would abound that Mondale was on the point of quitting the race. His initial strategy, however, enabled him to fight on through Super Tuesday using much of the resources carefully husbanded during the New Hampshire campaign. Mondale was able to capitalize on the new superdelegates (Democratic party officials and representatives with automatic access to the convention and pledged mainly to the Minnesotan) and on months of painstaking work cultivating contacts and building up delegate slates. Hart, though well-prepared for the early stages of the contest, had not established a sufficiently broad organization across the states to enable him to convert his Iowa–New Hampshire momentum into solid victories. The former vice-president regained his balance and eventually forced Hart out of the race before the summer convention met in San Francisco.

The 1984 Democratic primary thus added a new slant to the New Hampshire legend. Hart had fulfilled the criteria required of an outsider candidate, had copied the textbook grass-roots efforts of McGovern and Carter and had triumphed. The fact that he failed to win the nomination provided an object lesson in the status of the first-in-the-nation primary. While always influential and sometimes decisive, it could not guarantee success in the nomination contests of the 1980s if the candidate benefiting from its result failed to maintain his momentum or sustain his message. Unlike McGovern, Hart did not back up his candidacy with a strong platform of policy proposals. Unlike Carter, he did not face a weak and divided field of opponents. The Mondale camp had the resources and the will to fight back, and with the derailed front-runner back on track, speculation arose that the system had finally got the measure of the New Hampshire primary.

CONTEMPORARY CAMPAIGNS: BUSH, CLINTON, BUCHANAN AND
DOLE

The result of the 1988 New Hampshire primaries served only to confirm the
state's reputation as a presidential benchmark. Both eventual party nominees,
Republican vice-president George Bush and Democratic governor of Massachusetts
Michael Dukakis, received their first boost from the Granite State. Both had
previously lost the Iowa caucuses to rival candidates, a fact that served to weaken
that state's hold on candidate attentions. Richard Gephardt, the Democratic victor
in Iowa, was compelled to withdraw from active contention after the Super
Tuesday contests due to financial constraints. Dukakis was expected to perform
well in his own backyard, and this expectation diminished the impact of the first
primary. Only with the Super Tuesday regional primary the following month was
the governor able to establish himself as the leading contender, with Tennessee
senator Al Gore, Jr., and Reverend Jesse Jackson following closely behind. New
Hampshire, in this instance, had indicated the direction the nomination struggle
would take but did not prove conclusive.

On the Republican side, George Bush's campaign to succeed his boss, President
Reagan, after two terms as vice-president was fought in a general atmosphere that
was "short on content, long on bile." Bush secured victory in New Hampshire after
an upset defeat in Iowa at the hands of Senate minority leader Bob Dole. This
much-needed boost to the Bush campaign was achieved largely with the active
support of New Hampshire's Republican governor John Sununu, whose impressive
state organization was pressed into service for the vice-president.[72] Bush had been
working the state assiduously for several years during the 1980s, using the political
action committee Fund for America's Future as a front organization for fund-
raising. Bush strategist, later national party chairman, Lee Atwater was reported to
have told the New Hampshire Bush coordinator Will Abbott that hopes of
constructing a strong base in the South would be dashed if New Hampshire was
lost and that "if we win there, we're going to win the nomination."[73] Despite Dole's
rising poll ratings, the senator was unable to match the fund-raising abilities and
impressive get-out-the-vote drive of the Bush camp. Governor Sununu persuaded
local television station WMUR to bend its normal regulations regarding campaign
commercials and to air a last-minute attack ad against Dole. Entitled Senator
Straddle, it purported to show Dole's reversal of position on various key issues,
notably taxation. This final wave of negative advertising may have contributed to
Bush's margin of victory. On primary night, Dole responded to Bush's suggestion
that they bury the negative commercial hatchet by snarling that the vice-president
should "stop lying about my record." The New Hampshire result ended Dole's
brief surge of momentum, and Bush, dominating the remaining primaries and
caucuses, proceeded at a leisurely pace to the New Orleans Convention.

In February 1991, with victory in the Gulf War against Saddam Hussein
achieved, President Bush seemed content to bask in the success of Operation Desert
Storm; his reelection prospects were secure and his administration was enjoying

unprecedented levels of public support. At first, the onset of recession in 1990 had not appeared to threaten this golden scenario, but by the fall of 1991, the president was in serious trouble. He had been forced to renege on his pledge not to raise taxes, cutting a budget deal with the Democratic Congress which outraged the GOP's right wing and prompted a nomination challenge from Patrick Buchanan, a former staffer in the Nixon and Reagan White Houses. The White House appeared unable to offer a coherent program for tackling the rising unemployment and business failure rates, and the president himself compounded a severe image problem by vomiting into the lap of the Japanese prime minister during a trade-boosting trip to Tokyo in January 1992.

According to Tom Rosenstiel, Bush ran the hardest campaign of any incumbent in a New Hampshire race, galvanized by his much-noted absence from the state for the entire period since his 1988 victory. The president reached out to the Granite State electorate via drive-time radio shows, phone or satellite interviews on local media and teleconferences, hoping to instill confidence in New Hampshire's hard-hit business community and increasingly resentful voters. The strategy was intended to bypass the more hostile and challenging organs of the national media, but, in Rosenstiel's view, the president could not escape "the invisible gears that drive politics—economics, ideology and character."[74] On all three, the administration had become increasingly vulnerable. Attempting to soothe the angry, volatile electorate, the president stressed in an interview with WMUR-TV reporter Jack Heath, "I signed a good jobs bill that will mean $200 million to New Hampshire over the next couple of years. That means jobs for New Hampshire. I hope that got through to the people there."[75]

The Buchanan campaign attempted to follow the traditional strategy for challengers, appealing to grass-roots activists and scheduling frequent personal appearances. Buchanan's message, that Bush had betrayed the Granite State electorate through his abandonment of the "no new taxes" pledge, played well in key areas such as Manchester and its environs, but the challenger himself was dogged throughout his visits by protestors alleging anti-Semitism and racism in Buchanan's staff and in the writings of the candidate himself. These protests added an unsavory dimension to a candidacy that many New Hampshire voters found too conservative for their taste. Nonetheless, polls indicated that, as the sole real challenger to the incumbent, Buchanan would reap the benefit of state voters' anger with George Bush. On polling day, Buchanan took seven of Manchester's twelve wards, although the president took a larger percentage of the area's total popular vote. The insurgent campaign damaged its own cause, committing a classic blunder by indulging in speculation with journalists over the performance required for Buchanan to be able to claim a moral victory. Although the candidate came close to the 40 percent mark, falling short did nothing to improve his prospects. In addition, Buchanan appeared to lack a substantial base beyond New England, and his campaign did not possess the resources required to carry him through the onrushing Super Tuesday contests. Not for the last time, the dynamics of a front-loaded primary calendar worked against the challenger. Republican voters would ultimately draw back from rejecting their own president, but the damage had been done. Bush had improved on his 1988 showing, but his margin of victory substantiated neither his claims to have strong public support nor Buchanan's claims to be on the point of sparking a full-fledged middle American revolution. The *Boston Herald* claimed the result inflicted "humiliating damage" to Bush's reelection chances, noting that the president had been rejected by close to half of New Hampshire's GOP primary voters.[76] For its part, the *Union Leader* printed the banner headline, "Read *Our* Lips," on the morning after the primary and attempted, unconvincingly, to argue that the result was "stirring serious recollections" of the Kefauver and McCarthy campaigns.[77]

The Democratic race of 1992 proved considerably more muddled in conduct and outcome than the GOP race. By the fall of 1991, despite plummeting administration poll ratings, many eligible senior Democrats, including New Jersey senator Bill Bradley, Georgia's Sam Nunn and New York governor Mario Cuomo, could not be lured from the sidelines. The power of incumbency, combined with the still-potent legend of Desert Storm, represented formidable obstacles to a party that had not fought a successful presidential election in sixteen years. The candidates who eventually entered the race, including Arkansas governor Bill Clinton, former Massachusetts senator Paul Tsongas, former California governor Jerry Brown, Nebraska senator Bob Kerrey and Iowa's Tom Harkin, were universally regarded as inferior challengers capable of inspiring neither the Democratic party nor the general electorate. Clinton had several advantages, however, not least of which was the superiority of his organization and funding. By the end of the campaign, with Clinton securely in the White House, Federal Election Committee contribution reports showed the Arkansan had netted $25,105,044 in individual contributions alone, ahead of Brown by almost 5–1.[78] These had enabled him to secure an early endorsement in the September 1991 Florida straw poll and permitted the news media to confirm his status as front-runner on the strength of a clear victory in that season's invisible primary.[79] Further advantages lay in the candidate's southern base, his youth, his experience as chairman of the National Governors Association and his tenure as chairman of the centrist Democratic Leadership Council. The Council, which Clinton helped found in 1985, had worked assiduously to move party policy away from its traditional liberal roots, encouraging it to adapt to the environment of Reagan-era conservatism.

The image of electability that the governor had been carefully cultivating was nearly derailed during the New Hampshire primary of 1992. Facing a stiff challenge from Paul Tsongas, whose Massachusetts base lent him the aura of favorite son, Clinton came under simultaneous attack for alleged adultery, draft-dodging during the Vietnam War and pot-smoking. In normal circumstances, any one of these charges might have been sufficient to cripple his campaign. Clinton's poll ratings sank rapidly as primary day neared, and the candidate and his wife expended much valuable campaign time refuting or downplaying the allegations. Tsongas quickly assumed front-runner status and campaigned almost entirely on economic issues, presenting a detailed action plan for reviving the recession-hit economy and ensuring his proposals were widely available to voters through local libraries. Tsongas's rising ratings may have suggested to media pundits that 1992 voters were less interested in allegations of sleaze than in positive action to remedy unemployment and mortgage defaults. A WMUR-sponsored debate on January 20 drew a statewide audience of 140,000. According to Rosenstiel, New Hampshire citizens paid "astonishingly close attention" to the alternative solutions proposed by candidates and asked "remarkably sophisticated" questions.[80] Clinton's advisers had reacted swiftly to the success of Tsongas's point-by-point policy approach and soon made public their own plan for economic recovery and deficit reduction, including specific targets for tax hikes on high-income earners and a comprehensive national healthcare scheme.

As the focus began to switch away from the former front-runner's personal probity and toward the prospect of Democratic defeat with Tsongas as nominee, Clinton's poll ratings began to rise slowly. By finishing a clear and unexpectedly strong second, the Arkansan could claim a moral victory over the media and promptly dubbed himself "the Comeback Kid." The stay of execution granted by New Hampshire was all the Clinton camp required. Tsongas had neither the appeal nor the financial capacity for a sustained battle beyond the confines of New England. Clinton's powerful organization had plentiful supplies of both. With only the weak candidacies of Kerrey, Harkin and Brown in real contention, the governor swiftly regained first position with the Super Tuesday primaries and swept to victory at the New York Convention. The Democrats were heading back to the White House for the first time in twelve years.

The 1996 election season began with one of the closest and most notable New Hampshire primaries in memory. For the first time since 1964, an incumbent Democratic president faced no serious primary opposition as 1996 began. President Clinton did not enjoy the same popularity ratings as the last incumbent to enjoy this luxury, Ronald Reagan, but the negative ratings of the Republican Congress, elected in the fall of 1994 and deeply unpopular for the perceived unfairness of its social and fiscal policies, discouraged potential Democratic challengers from rocking the party boat. Media attention focused on the Republican race and a candidate field dominated by conservatives. The acknowledged front-runner, Senate majority leader Bob Dole had led the field in poll ratings, fund-raising and political endorsements since 1995, when the candidate courted by every Republican except those on the far right, General Colin Powell, refused to enter the race. By February 1995, the front-runner had secured the backing of twenty-four of thirty-one Republican state governors and had accumulated a war chest of nearly $25 million. Pat Buchanan resurrected his 1992 crusade against high taxes, big government and internationalist foreign and trade policies and was regarded as the only possible threat to Dole's stately progress. Also in the field in the fall of 1995, Texas senator Phil Gramm, Indiana senator Richard Lugar, millionaire publisher Malcolm "Steve" Forbes, former Tennessee governor and Bush education secretary, Lamar Alexander, former UN ambassador and talk-show host Alan Keyes, California governor Pete Wilson, Pennsylvania senator Arlen Specter, California congressman Bob Dornan and millionaire businessman Morry Taylor. This large and diverse field was to be quickly whittled down by the electoral environment of 1996. The primary and caucus schedule for this year offered an unprecedented number of contests in the period immediately following New Hampshire.

The nomination calendar for 1996 had been front-loaded to the extent that the GOP nomination was now almost certain to be decided by the end of March. Inevitably, the fund-raising imperative became more important to survival than ever, as did the pressure to perform well in the early contests. Phil Gramm, sensing problems for his message and appeal in Iowa and New Hampshire, attempted to circumvent both contests by encouraging other states to challenge the traditions of the first caucus and first primary. In failing to achieve a more favorable opening round of contests, Gramm signed the death warrant for his own campaign. After dismal showings in the early Louisiana and Iowa caucuses, he withdrew from the race. This withdrawal had been preceded by the end of the Wilson and Specter campaigns due to lack of financial support and persistently low poll ratings. The Iowa campaign was notable for the sudden rise in Steve Forbes's media profile and poll numbers. The publisher, who had refused federal matching funds in order to utilize his personal fortune, spent nearly $14 million during the period from December 1995 to January 1996.

The intensity of the barrage worried campaign watchers in New Hampshire since a Forbes victory would be interpreted as a sign that the Granite State had surrendered its retail politicking tradition. The novel appeal of the Forbes campaign rested on his proposal for a 17 percent flat tax to replace existing tax bands. The candidate claimed the new tax would be payable by all citizens, would simplify the tax return process, shrink the size of the Internal Revenue Service bureaucracy and end the debilitating pressures on Washington of special interest lobbyists pressing for tax concessions.[81] The proposal carried the added attraction that the first $36,000 of family income would not be taxed, thus removing the poor from the tax bands altogether. Taxes on savings, dividends or other unearned income would be abolished. The proposal sent shock waves through the Dole camp, which believed it would carry enormous appeal in New Hampshire, a state noted for its antipathy toward taxation. Buchanan derided the notion as another idea dreamed up by "the boys at the yacht club."[82] The Republican party establishment was also concerned at the possibility of a Forbes nomination since the publisher had positioned himself as a Washington outsider and nonpolitician.

The Forbes campaign, anxious to demonstrate that his appeal in New Hampshire did not revolve entirely around the tax question, set up a focus group over the weekend of February 4–5 in which fourteen Granite State supporters discussed the Forbes candidacy while reporters looked on through a two-way mirror. The clear impression, the journalists subsequently reported, was that Forbes's appeal, like that of Buchanan, was rooted in his outsider status. Unfortunately for Forbes, the momentum was lost as rival candidates and the media began to focus on the negativity of his ads attacking other candidates' records. New Hampshire polls recorded a rapid slippage in Forbes's support after Iowa, dropping from 26 percent to a projected 12 percent of the vote. Worse, Forbes's unfavorable ratings in New Hampshire outstripped those of all other candidates.[83] Buchanan, gaining from his strong caucus showing, leapt ten points in New Hampshire, giving him a one-point lead over Dole by February 13.[84] Although Buchanan's negatives were only one point behind his favorable rating in the *Concord Monitor* poll of February 16, an underlying trend pointed to trouble for Senator Dole. Fifty-three percent of Buchanan supporters indicated their firm intention to stick by their candidate; Dole registered only 46 percent in this category.[85] Buchanan's right-wing credentials had attracted a more stable voting bloc to his camp, while doubts over Bob Dole's age and political vision made his support vulnerable to raids from other candidates.

The Buchanan campaign enjoyed the endorsement of the Manchester *Union Leader* but faced an unexpected problem when Larry Pratt, director of Gun Owners of America and a campaign co-chairman, stepped down after allegations linked him to white supremacist groups. Pratt acknowledged that he had spoken at a 1992 antigovernment meeting at Estes Park, Colorado, to defend gun ownership rights in the wake of the killing of the wife and son of white supremacist Randy Weaver by federal agents.[86] He argued that he had merely tried to collect information from people at the meeting who might have been involved in the Weaver incident. The presence at the meeting of Aryan fringe group leaders, however, was enough to taint Pratt with the charge of racism. Buchanan himself believed that the campaign against Pratt was part of a coordinated effort to undermine his campaign message. In 1992 and 1996 the candidate had been dogged by protestors, some dressed in the uniform of Nazi death camp prisoners, alleging his anti-Semitism, racism and homophobia. Though disputing some interpretations placed on his comments on homosexuality, Israel and the Holocaust, Buchanan knew the extremist image alone was sufficient to damage him.

Pervasive doubts about the prospects of unseating Clinton and disillusionment among party moderates with the field of right-wing candidates added to a general air of disillusionment among the electorate in both Iowa and New Hampshire. Commenting on the large number of undecideds in Iowa, Iowa Professor Steffen Schmidt commented to reporters, "It's as though the undecided have turned their backs on the real candidates and are waiting for a guy on a white horse to ride into town and sweep them away."[87] This disillusionment appeared to be enhanced by bitter accusations hurled between the candidates as the race in New Hampshire quickly turned into a demolition derby. National party officials became increasingly concerned as the tone of the primary campaign descended into bitter feuding and the image of a party united against Bill Clinton evaporated before their eyes. Reports of subversive telephone canvassers, phoning voters on the pretense of soliciting their support for a candidate while falsifying the records and policies of that candidate to make them appear unattractive and alarming, surfaced in both early states. Accusations of racism, hypocrisy, underhanded tactics and lying produced the most divisive New Hampshire Republican primary since 1964. The *Boston Sunday Globe* reported, "Instead of serving as the scene for a coronation, New Hampshire has become the setting for a Republican tong war."[88]

The February 15 debate at the Manchester studios of WMUR did little to improve matters. Steve Forbes attacked Alexander for an ad portraying him as a Wall Street insider, while Buchanan accused Dole of distorting his writings on nuclear weapons and of setting up a subversive phone canvassing bank to spread the view to voters that Buchanan was too extreme to be electable.[89] The scene degenerated rapidly as Dole, claiming to have been offended at unflattering pictures of himself in Forbes's ads, offered the millionaire some different ones. Forbes's response, that changing the pictures would not alter the political reality of Dole's record, drew a sharp retort from the majority leader, "Yeah, yeah, I know your problem. You've got a lot of money. You're trying to buy this election."[90] Despite adverse press reactions to the tone of the debate, a *USA Today*/CNN tracking poll of 416 Republicans gave a clear indication of the final primary result to come, with Buchanan defeating Dole and Alexander taking third place from Forbes.[91]

The primary had become a three-horse race, with New Hampshire polls indicating a possible surprise victory for Lamar Alexander. The Tennessean hoped an angry electorate might reject both Dole as too old and Buchanan as too radical, leaving him as the only politically experienced alternative. This was termed by his state campaign chairman, Tom Rath, "the classic breakthrough strategy."[92] An endorsement from William Bennett, former federal drug czar under George Bush, strengthened Alexander's viability but was overshadowed in New Hampshire by Phil Gramm's withdrawal on the same day. Alexander was hampered throughout the campaign by dwindling financial resources and repeated questions concerning his personal financial transactions in the period between stepping down as governor and taking up an appointment as president of the University of Tennessee. An embarrassing incident, in the best New Hampshire tradition, occurred in Milford when a reporter asked Alexander the current price of a gallon of milk and a dozen eggs. The candidate, who had made a high-publicity walk across the state in 1995 to stress his close links to grass-roots voters, was unable to reply but sent an aide for the information. A delighted Dole manager, Scott Reed, commented, "Next time he's walking across New Hampshire, he might want to stop at a supermarket."[93] The incident, occurring only five days before the primary, was widely reported and slowed the pace of Alexander's rise in the polls.

The Dole camp continued the search for political endorsements from key figures. Three days before the primary, the senator arrived, in the passenger seat of a white flatbed plow truck, at the Salem home of former governor Sununu. Refusing a direct endorsement, the former White House chief of staff indicated his inclination toward a Dole victory. Far more political capital was gained for the senator on February 18, the final Sunday of the campaign, when Phil Gramm arrived at a packed press conference in Manchester to announce his support for Dole. Gramm shared many conservative views with Pat Buchanan but vehemently opposed the Buchanan's protectionist trade policies. Rumors that racist literature, circulating during the Louisiana caucus and attacking Gramm's foreign-born wife, originated from the Buchanan camp also helped push the Texan toward Dole.[94] Gramm's endorsement did not bring with it a large and loyal voter bloc, but the by-now desperate Dole camp calculated that it would reinforce the image of a two-man (Dole–Buchanan) race and swing some moderates away from Alexander.

During the final days of the race, tracking polls indicated a statistical dead-heat for first place among the three leading Republican contenders. Governor Merrill revealed the tension of the Dole camp on primary eve, remarking, "If he wins by one vote, I'm going to declare it a landslide."[95] Buchanan continued to mix the three main themes of his campaign—appeals to antigovernment sentiment, protectionist trade policies and the call for a return to Christian moral values—but was angered by the new "revelations" appearing thick and fast in the last hours of the primary. An accusation first leveled in 1992 reappeared in press reports that, as a staffer in the Nixon White House, Buchanan had written a memo suggesting a gay group should be encouraged to make a donation to the campaign of Nixon's 1972 primary opponent, Pete McCloskey. This donation would then be leaked to the *Union Leader*. Buchanan dismissed the charge but had a harder time refuting an article he had written in 1983, claiming that women were psychologically weaker than men and therefore less suited to high-power careers. His sister and campaign manager, Bay Buchanan, blamed the Dole camp but lamely admitted, "He used words that I don't think were the wisest choices of words."[96] Buchanan launched a final assault on his fellow Republicans via last-minute radio ads accusing Dole of smear tactics.

Lamar Alexander also lamented the negative slant of Dole's final ads, although he had himself been the first to use them in broadsides against Pete Wilson in 1995. The former governor continued to attack Buchanan as too radical and Dole as a Washington insider, playing to the middle-ground and middle-class constituencies in New Hampshire and utilizing populist symbols such as his trademark red-and-black plaid shirt. The *Concord Monitor* cynically noted, "His main message, that people should ask less from Washington and more from themselves, is broad enough to defy characterization, and that's just how Alexander likes it. If the Republican party has splintered into various camps, Alexander wants to have a foot in each."[97]

The victory of Pat Buchanan on February 20, 1996 was received with mixed emotions by participants and observers of New Hampshire's most bitterly fought Republican contest. Journalist Charles Brereton had predicted trouble for the state's first-in-the-nation tradition if Buchanan won, arguing that such an outcome would convince the national parties that the primary was more trouble than it was worth. In the event, Buchanan's win was quickly overshadowed by Forbes's victory in Arizona and Dole's nine-state sweep in the Junior Tuesday New England regionals, but the Granite State had lived up to its national reputation for giving all candidates a detailed hearing and a vigorous shakedown.

CONCLUSION

Examining the most notable New Hampshire primaries since 1952 offers some indication of the importance of this contentious tradition to presidential candidates but does little to provide a firm basis for predicting future outcomes. Campaign themes, tactics and results have varied dramatically from campaign to campaign, from election to election since the Eisenhower–Kefauver sweeps, and few consistent response patterns are discernible in state voting tendencies. Some preliminary observations, however, may be useful.

Incumbent presidents, like incumbent front-runners, are often vulnerable in the Granite State since the primary is the first real opportunity for any electorate to register its satisfaction or discontent with the administration's record, congressional midterms notwithstanding. Yet the roll of presidents successfully traversing the New Hampshire rapids is long: Dwight Eisenhower, Lyndon Johnson, Richard Nixon, Gerald Ford, Jimmy Carter, Ronald Reagan, George Bush and Bill Clinton all secured endorsements for a further term in office from the primary voters of their respective parties. Eisenhower, Nixon, Reagan and Clinton did so with margins of landslide proportions. Incumbent casualties are usually only indirect—Ford undoubtedly suffered for Reagan's strong showing in 1976.

Only one incumbent president can be considered a direct casualty of the Granite State—Harry Truman. Truman remains the only incumbent to have lost in over forty years of presidential preference voting, and his defeat can be linked more to his nationwide unpopularity and misjudgment of the primary's importance than to a tantrum by the primary electorate. Two other presidents have been seriously weakened by New Hampshire, Lyndon Johnson and George Bush. Both *won* their respective contests but press interpretation handed moral victories to their opponents.

Candidates entering the contest as media-annointed front-runners have not fared as well. Bob Dole, Walter Mondale, Adlai Stevenson and Edmund Muskie all fell badly at the first primary hurdle, but overconfidence or poor strategy accounted, in almost every case, for their defeats. Stevenson did not bother to campaign in 1956, while Mondale, Muskie and Dole pursued, to varying degrees, above-the-fray strategies that antagonized reporters and challengers and bored the electorate. Interestingly, despite the blame laid at New Hampshire's door, Dole, Mondale and Stevenson all went on to capture the nomination. Of equal importance, all the notorious front-runner stumbles occurred in years when the opposing party had a virtually unchallenged incumbent in the White House. Out-of-power parties seeking to depose unchallenged presidents display an habitual tendency to create their own president-in-waiting by annointing one senior party figure as front-runner. This is always done early in the race in the hope of fostering unity for the battle ahead but usually too early for party and independent voters who, denied a real choice on one side, often decide to provoke a fight on the other. Both Stevenson and Muskie expected a stately progress toward the convention en route to confronting Presidents Eisenhower and Nixon, neither of whom faced serious opposition within their party. Mondale and Dole were more aggressive in campaigning, but both encouraged the view of reporters that their nomination was inevitable. Both faced unchallenged presidents—Reagan and Clinton. In years when incumbent presidents face significant challenges in their own party, the opposition tends not to coalesce around one candidate quite so rapidly. In 1976, 1980 and 1992, with Ford, Carter and Bush fighting hard for nomination, their eventual opponents emerged from far more difficult primary contests.

The history of the primary provides no evidence of consistent voter preference for candidates on the right, left or center of the political spectrum. Barry Goldwater performed badly in a state that might have been considered fertile ground for his campaign themes. John Ashbrook was soundly defeated in 1972, as were Reagan, more narrowly, in 1976, Pete DuPont in 1988 and Patrick Buchanan four years later. Such results call into question the stereotypical view of New Hampshire as a haven for right-wing candidacies. Also undermined is the notion that a Democratic primary electorate skewed to the left favors liberal contenders. The candidacies of Eugene McCarthy and George McGovern were helped by New Hampshire's Democratic and Independent voters, yet both failed to win a majority of the votes. Michael Dukakis and Paul Tsongas professed generally conservative fiscal policies tempered with qualified social liberalism. Both faced challengers who were more clearly liberal in outlook, yet both won their primaries.

Bill Clinton, styling himself a New Democrat, proved particularly hard to classify. Nonetheless, the comeback of a candidate who had confessed to marital problems, pot-smoking and a dubious draft record is perhaps indicative of a distinct lack of insularity among New Hampshire voters.

These results suggest that far from skewing primary results in favor of candidates of one ideological background or campaign style, New Hampshire endorsements tend to cover a broad political range, encompassing the left, right and center of both major parties. The triumph or failure of incumbent presidents and right or left-leaning insurgents can often be regarded as a reflection of national mood swings or as the consequence of the strengths, weaknesses, tactics and mis-judgments of other candidates in the field. Results since 1952 do indicate, however, a greater degree of predictive accuracy by Republican primary voters than by Democratic ones. Of the twelve contests held by both major parties between 1952 and 1996, Republican voters have failed only twice to choose the party's eventual nominee—in 1964 and 1996. Democratic voters, on the other hand, have a 50 percent failure rate.

Between 1952 and 1992, New Hampshire voters successfully indicated the eventual winner of the race to the White House in every primary season. In twenty-four successive party contests since 1952, the state's party voters have failed only eight times to provide a sendoff for the eventual nominee. Such records, though far from perfect, have added to the allure of the first-in-the-nation primary for the news media and have converted it into a must-win contest for candidates. Yet, the preceding observations apart, the primary's history offers few guarantees for success or failure to any one particular strategy. There is no easy way to conquer the Granite State, no foolproof strategy for victory. Yet candidates who succeed are usually those who pay close attention to local issues, spend time with voters and develop strong local organizations. Such tactics pay dividends but are inevitably affected by external factors such as economic indicators, the presence of incumbents and the strength and financing of campaign machinery. Candidates most likely to fail are those who appear to regard themselves as nominees-in-waiting. Such candidates, lulled into a false sense of security by advisers, tend to neglect the vital aspects of "retail campaigning" and thus open the way for challengers to undermine their Granite State support. New Hampshire primaries continue to confound pundits in the age of sophisticated media and computer targeting precisely because its electorate, accustomed to high levels of exposure and information-soaking, makes its decisions on a campaign-by-campaign basis rather than conforming to predetermined trends generated by reporters and spin doctors on the campaign trail. Candidates may learn from the mistakes of their predecessors, but the primary's history demonstrates that they remain hostages to circumstance in this earliest and most unpredictable of primaries, when voter intentions are fluid, reporters fresh and inquisitive, candidate fields crowded and issue agendas unstructured. New Hampshire results may not always be decisive to the outcome of presidential races, but the campaign landscape can be irrevocably altered by the outcome of the first-in-the-nation primary.

NOTES

1. James Wright, *The Progressive Yankees: Republican Reformers in New Hampshire, 1906–16* (Hanover, NH: University Press of New England, 1987), pp. 94–95.

2. John Gfroerer, "Interview with Richard F. Upton," *Historical New Hampshire,* vol. 42, no. 3 (Fall 1987): 201.

3. Ibid.

4. William M. Gardner, *The New Hampshire Primary: Legislative Background.* Courtesy of William Gardner, State Department, Concord, NH, 1987.

5. Richard F. Upton, Address at the New Hampshire Historical Society on the Opening of the Exhibition, "New Hampshire's Road to the White House: Franklin Pierce to the Presidential Primary," *Historical New Hampshire,* vol. 42, no. 3 (Fall 1987): 200.

6. Charles Brereton, *First Step to the White House: The New Hampshire Primary, 1952–1980* (Hampton, NH: Wheelabrator Foundation, 1979), p. 2.

7. Charles Brereton, *First in the Nation: New Hampshire and the Premier Presidential Primary* (Portsmouth, NH: Peter E. Randall Publishers, 1987), p. 5.

8. William Manchester, *The Glory and the Dream: A Narrative History of America, 1932–1972* (New York: Bantam Books, 1975), pp. 608–9.

9. Herbert S. Parmet, *Eisenhower and the American Crusades* (New York: Macmillan, 1972), p. 51.

10. Stephen E. Ambrose, *Eisenhower: Soldier, General of the Army, President-Elect, 1890–1952* (New York: Simon & Schuster, 1983), p. 522.

11. Parmet, *Eisenhower and the American Crusades,* p. 51.

12. Sherman Adams, *First-Hand Report: The Inside Story of the Eisenhower Administration* (London: Hutchinson & Co., 1962), p. 25.

13. Brereton, *First in the Nation,* pp. 14–15.

14. Robert J. Donovan, *Tumultuous Years: The Presidency of Harry S. Truman, 1949–1953* (New York: W. W. Norton, 1982), p. 396.

15. Ibid.

16. Brereton, *First in the Nation,* pp. 25–26.

17. Roy Jenkins, *Truman* (London: William Collins Sons & Co., 1986), pp. 192–95, and Manchester, *The Glory and the Dream,* pp. 610–11.

18. Kevin Cash, *Who the Hell Is William Loeb?* (Manchester, NH: Amoskeag Press, 1975), p. 19.

19. Brereton, *First in the Nation,* p. 82.

20. Theodore White, *The Making of the President 1964* (New York: Atheneum, 1965), p. 5.

21. Ibid., p. 102.

22. Ibid., p. 128.

23. Ibid., p.110.

24. Ibid.

25. Brereton, *First in the Nation,* p. 83.

26. Ibid., p. 88.

27. Ibid., p. 90.

28. White, *The Making of the President 1964,* p. 110.

29. *Presidential Elections Since 1789,* 4th ed. (Washington, DC: Congressional Quarterly Books, 1987), p. 41.

30. White, *The Making of the President 1964,* p. 108.

31. Brereton, *First in the Nation,* p. 95.

32. Richard Stout, *People* (New York: Harper and Row, 1970), p. 50.

33. *The Gallup Poll: Public Opinion, 1935–1971,* Vol. 2 (New York: Random House, 1972), Survey 754K. Question No. 14C, p. 2093.

34. Ben Stavis, *We Were the Campaign: New Hampshire to Chicago for McCarthy* (Boston: Beacon Press, 1969), p. 4.

35. Ibid., pp. 8–10.

36. Brereton, *First in the Nation,* p. 121.

37. Lewis Chester, Godfrey Hodgson, and Bruce Page, *An American Melodrama: The Presidential Campaign of 1968* (New York: Andre Deutsch, 1969), p. 114.

38. Stout, *People,* p. 169.

39. "Countercharges Exchanged," *New York Times,* March 12, 1968, p. 20.

40. Stout, *People,* p. 157.

41. Chester et al., *An American Melodrama,* p. 98.

42. Brereton, *First Step to the White House,* p. 11.

43. Gary Hart, *Right from the Start: A Chronicle of the McGovern Campaign* (New York: Quadrangle Books, 1973), p. 22.

44. Ibid.

45. Brereton, *First in the Nation,* p. 152.

46. Theodore White, *The Making of the President 1972* (New York: Atheneum, 1973), p. 103.

47. Hart, *Right from the Start,* p. 152.

48. Author Interview, Fred Emery, BBC Lime Grove Studios, London, July 10, 1985. See also James M. Perry, *Us and Them: How the Press Covered the 1972 Election* (New York: Clarkson & Potter, 1973), pp. 85–86.

49. Perry, *Us and Them*, p. 85.

50. Ibid.

51. Author Interview, J. Joseph Grandmaison, Manchester, NH, September 6, 1986.

52.The *Union Leader* ran the subsequent headline, "Senator Muskie Insults Franco-Americans." Perry, *Us and Them*, p. 93.

53. Ibid., p. 95.

54. Ernest May and Janet Fraser, *Campaign '72: The Managers Speak* (Cambridge, MA: Harvard University Press, 1973), pp. 114–15.

55. *Presidential Elections Since 1789*, p. 200.

56. Hart, *Right from the Start*, p. 29.

57. Martin Schram, *Running for President 1976: The Carter Campaign* (New York: Stein & Day, 1977), p. 55.

58. Jonathan Moore and Janet Fraser, eds., *Campaign for President: The Managers Look at '76* (Cambridge, MA: Harvard University Press, 1977), p. 84.

59. Jules Witcover, *Marathon: The Pursuit of the Presidency 1972–1976* (New York: Viking Press, 1977), pp. 228–31.

60. Moore and Fraser, *Campaign for President*, p. 113.

61. Interview with William Gardner, conducted and edited by Stephen Cox, *Historical New Hampshire*, vol. 42, no. 3 (1987): 308.

62. Moore and Fraser, *Campaign for President*, p. 91.

63. Brereton, *First in the Nation*, p. 181.

64. Ibid.

65. "Can Anyone Stop Mondale?" *Newsweek* cover title, January 9, 1984.

66. "Liftoff for Campaign 1984," *Newsweek*, October 3, 1983, pp. 32–33.

67. Brereton, *First in the Nation*, p. 231.

68. Gary R. Orren and Nelson W. Polsby, *Media and Momentum: The New Hampshire Primary and Nomination Politics* (Chatham, NJ: Chatham House, 1987), p. 22.

69. Susan B. Casey, *Hart and Soul: Gary Hart's New Hampshire Odyssey and Beyond* (Concord, NH: NHI Press, 1986), p. 123.

70. Ibid., p. 203.

71. Brereton, *First in the Nation*, p. 234.

72. Robert J. Donovan and Ray Scherer, *Unsilent Revolution: Television News and American Public Life* (Cambridge: Cambridge University Press, 1992), p. 240.

73. Peter Goldman and Tom Mathews, *The Quest for the Presidency: The 1988 Campaign* (New York: Simon & Schuster, 1989), p. 259.

74. Tom Rosenstiel, *Strange Bedfellows: How Television and the Presidential Candidates Changed American Politics* (New York: Hyperion, 1993), p. 84.

75. Ibid., p. 88.

76. *Boston Herald*, February 19, 1992, p. 2.

77. "Read *Our* Lips," *Union Leader*, February 19, 1992, p. A1.

78. Anthony Corrado, "The Changing Environment of Presidential Campaign Finance," in William G. Mayer, ed., *In Pursuit of the White House: How We Choose Our Presidential Nominees* (Chatham, NJ: Chatham House, 1996), Table 7.3, p. 230.

79. Emmett H. Buell, Jr., "The Invisible Primary," in Mayer, ed., *In Pursuit of the White House,* p. 23.

80. Rosenstiel, *Strange Bedfellows*, p. 56.

81. "Want a 17% Tax Rate?" *The Independent*, February 2, 1996, p. 17.

82. Ibid.

83. "Polls Show a Three-Way Race," *Concord Monitor*, February 16, 1996, p. A2.

84. Ibid., p. A1.

85. Ibid., p. A2.

86. "Buchanan Answers Bigotry Charges," *Concord Monitor*, February 16, 1996. p. A2.

87. "Dole Rises on the Back of Voter Apathy," *The Sunday Times*, February 11, 1996, p. 17.

88. "For Stunned GOP, 'It's an Ugly Time'," *Boston Sunday Globe*, February 18, 1996, p. 33.

89. "GOP Pitches for NH Votes," *USA Today*, February 16–18, 1996, p. 1A.

90. "His Smile Did Not Last Long," *Concord Monitor*, February 16, 1996, p. A8.

91. "GOP Pitches for NH Votes," p. 1A.

92. "Alexander Camp Gains Confidence in Stretch Drive," *Boston Globe*, February 19, 1996, p. 9.

93. "'What Price Milk, Eggs?' Alexander Asks Aide," *Union Leader*, February 15, 1996, p. A24.

94. "Dole Collects Endorsement of Former Candidate Gramm," *Boston Globe*, February 19, 1996, p. 8.

95. "Bob Dole: A Resume Not Rhetoric," *Concord Monitor*, February 20, 1996, p. A6.

96. "Radio Ad Responds to Dole Attack," *Concord Monitor*, February 20, 1996, p. A6.

97. "Walk Ends in a Crowd," *Concord Monitor*, February 20, 1996, p. A6.

2

New Hampshire in Profile

Somebody ought to say a good word about New Hampshire. It's very difficult to do . . . (laughter).
— Martin F. Nolan in J. Foley, D. A. Britton and E. B. Everett, Jr., eds., *Nominating a President: The Process and the Press.* New York: Praeger, 1980, p. 18

This is the real world up here.
— Patrick Buchanan, *Boston Globe*, February 11, 1992, p. 12

SOCIAL AND POLITICAL CULTURE

New Hampshire lies in the northeastern United States, wedged "like an inconsequential piece of pie" between Massachusetts and the Canadian border, with Vermont to the west and Maine and the Atlantic to the east.[1] With a population of 1,125,000 it ranks forty-first of the fifty states.[2] The state is 8,993 square miles in size, with half of its population located in rural areas. Whites account for 98 percent of the state population; Hispanics, Asians and blacks make up one percent, 0.8 percent and 0.6 percent, respectively.[3] The emerging image of a WASP state *par excellence* is diluted by the fact that the state's population has been expanding rapidly since the 1960s, bringing new social and cultural trends in its wake. From 1960 to 1975 the population increased by 33 percent and between 1970 and 1990, by 50 percent.[4] This made New Hampshire the fastest growing state in terms of resident population east of the Mississippi with the exception of Florida.

The much-remarked absence of a substantial black community does not preclude ethnic diversity. The state has New England's highest concentration of non-Anglo-Saxon inhabitants, with many of Greek, Italian and Polish extraction whose ancestors arrived during the great immigration waves of the nineteenth century. Neal Peirce notes that by 1920 around 50 percent of the state population was either foreign-born or of first-generation descent from the original immigrants. In 1987, 50 percent of state residents, for a variety of reasons including migration from other states, had not been born in New Hampshire.[5]

The largest ethnic community, the French-Canadians, or Franco-Americans, constitute one-quarter of the population, a fact that has had important repercussions for the economic and political character of New Hampshire since the nineteenth century. Duane Lockard's seminal study of state politics during the 1950s describes French-Canadians as "clannish" and "less given to assimilation into the community" than other ethnic groups.[6] The original French-speaking settlers left French-speaking Quebec harboring mistrust and resentment of the taxes levied on their comparatively poor incomes by the English-speaking majority. Consequently, settlers in New Hampshire developed a deeply conservative and independent-minded parish culture which has made a virtue of opposing both the principle of taxation and efforts to raise taxation levels or centralize administration by state or national governments. The prejudice is deep-seated. New Hampshire's is the only state constitution that includes an express right to revolution among its articles.[7] The highest concentrations of French-Canadians are to be found mostly in the industrial centers and mill towns of Manchester and Nashua, as well as Berlin to the north and Dover and Rochester to the east.

New Hampshire has not been isolated from mainstream national and international economic development. The poor quality of its soil prevented large-scale agricultural enterprises in the eighteenth and nineteenth centuries. Rapid industrialization therefore became a necessity. Utilizing fast-flowing rivers such as the Merrimack to generate power, Manchester became the Queen City and the world's largest textile manufacturing center by the early 1900s. By the late 1930s a combination of Depression, poor management and strong competition from the South had forced many mills into closure, compelling a second industrial transformation. By the 1970s, the state had become a competitive producer of plastics, footwear, electrical components, industrial tools and communications equipment. In the early 1980s, the southern tier cities of Manchester, Nashua and Salem formed a Golden Triangle that constituted one of the foremost industrial growth areas of the Northeast. Gross state product leapt from $1.6 billion in 1960 to $7.8 billion by 1979. This has had a lasting effect on average personal per capita income, which stood at $23,234 in 1993, the eighth highest average for the United States.[8] Outside investors and corporations were attracted to the Granite State by the lack of a large unionized workforce, the absence of a statewide sales and income tax and the interstate highway system bisecting New Hampshire and facilitating large-scale goods transportation. Massachusetts-based companies in particular found it more convenient and profitable to center their expanding operations across the border in New Hampshire. The effect has been to alter, to some extent, the social and cultural nature of the southern region of the state, across the counties of Rockingham, Strafford and Hillsborough.

Just as New Hampshire mirrored the resurgent economic confidence of the United States during the Reagan era, so it became a casualty of the deep recession of the late 1980s and early 1990s. In November 1988 its unemployment total had stood at 2.3 percent, one of the lowest in the nation. By November 1991 it had reached a peak above the national average of 7 percent, falling back to 4.6 percent by mid-1995.[9] Bankruptcies in this period rose by 324 percent as the demand for expensive high-tech goods slumped. New Hampshire's business failure rate during this period was second only to California's, and in fiscal 1991 an estimated 2,700 corporations were dissolved for failure to pay franchise fees or file annual returns.[10] Real estate values declined more sharply than at any period since the Depression of the 1930s. The number of families claiming welfare assistance rose from 5,594 in 1988 to 14,917 by 1991. These deteriorating economic conditions were to play a key role in the 1992 presidential primaries, harming the reelection campaign of

George Bush in much the same way that the positive indicators of 1984 had benefited the incumbent President Reagan. In both instances, New Hampshire voters' verdicts, dictated by its economic condition, were to duplicate those of the national electorate later in the year.

Similarly, the tentative economic recovery by the mid-1990s found New Hampshire's unemployment rate falling to 3.2 percent by December 1995 and its production growth levels running ahead of regional and national trends.[11] The recouped job losses, however, were mostly in new low-paid positions and jobs in the service sector. Jobs paying over $35,000 a year fell by 3 percent in the 1991–94 period.[12] Business bankruptcy rates fell off, though remaining uncomfortably high. Overall, as the 1995 economic report by *Business NH Magazine* claimed, "Like a steam engine on a grade, New Hampshire's economy has slowed but is still gaining elevation."[13]

Other statistics convey the image of a state ahead of national averages in some areas, notably financial and economic, while falling in step with the rest of the United States in others. The New Hampshire poverty rate, assessed in 1990 at 8.5 percent, is almost four percentage points lower than the national level. In terms of income distribution, New Hampshire tends to exceed the U.S. total in the $5,000–$15,000 bracket but has lower proportions of its population above and below these lines. Fifty-two percent of the state workforce is classified as white-collar and 35 percent as blue-collar compared to 53 percent and 31 percent, respectively, for the nation as a whole.[14] Crime and poverty levels are considerably beneath national levels. The proportion of students achieving college degrees and postgraduate qualifications is once again above the national average. Students in New Hampshire score consistently high ratings on the SAT, with the state's score topping the league more than ten times in the past two decades. In 1990 the state ranked seventh in the nation for the proportion of citizens possessing a bachelor's degree or higher educational qualification.[15] Finally, and curiously in the light of its public Puritan image, 44.2 percent of the state population belong to a Christian church organization, five points *below* the national average.

New Hampshire's political culture and economic substructure cannot easily be defined as typical of mainstream U.S. politics. Its mainly conservative and avocational political system is unusual. Its taxation and expenditure practices are likewise atypical and unpopular with neighboring states. Both contribute to the outsider's perspective of an outmoded, Jeffersonian political system, a state out-of-touch with contemporary socioeconomic problems issues and almost mercenary in its approach to revenue-collecting.

The state House and Senate, collectively styled the General Court, is the third largest representative body of its kind in the Western world after the U.S. Congress and the United Kingdom's Parliament. It comprised 424 members in 1995, almost twice the size of the next largest assembly in Pennsylvania.[16] The twenty-four state Senate districts contain an average population of 46,219, while each of the 400 House districts average an unusually low 2,773.[17] Peirce has argued that the size of the legislature has served as an encumbrance to effective decision making and makes a wry comment on the advanced age of many of its members: "A moment of silence is observed for each recently-deceased member when the legislature assembles every two years; so long is the roll that the ceremony lasts for an almost macabre length of time."[18]

Both Peirce and Lockard ascribe fragmentation on many issues in the legislature to weak party cohesion as the result of long periods of Republican dominance of the state government and General Court. Both the fragmentation and the GOP hegemony have contributed to an inability or unwillingness to enact fundamental changes in fiscal or social policy. This inertia is, critics claim, fueled by the voluntary character of political service in New Hampshire. For many participants in the process, politics is more of a sideline than a career. Citizens drop in and out of active service, further hampering the development of strong party machines. Politics is small-scale, with an estimated 8,000 workers employed in state government in 1994.[19] Financial remuneration is rarely an incentive. In 1995 Republican governor Stephen Merrill operated with a staff of twenty-three, received a salary of $82,325 but refused a pay rise and annually returns 10 percent to state coffers.[20] State senators and representatives receive an annual salary of only $100. This nominal sum is the lowest of any state, fully $1,100 lower than the next lowest amount, paid by the government of South Dakota. Members must pay their own telephone bills and receive no state assistance with expenses. In addition, no provision is made in state law for the public funding of candidate campaigns in state elections through taxation. Professor Richard Winters of Dartmouth College claims that the long-term side-effects of this amateurism are a dearth of office-seekers with serious political ambitions and a reduction in opportunities to train competent staff for the future.[21] Interestingly, this apparently old-fashioned system does not prevent women from accounting for around 33 percent of General Court membership, the fifth highest total in the nation.[22]

These unusual phenomena embody attitudes toward government and taxation rooted in the eighteenth century. New Hampshire was the only colony to be ruled directly from England, and its prerevolutionary governments were not noted for their probity. This, combined with the fierce independence of the French-Canadians, produced widespread and deep suspicion of any manifestation of centralized authority. Winters explains this as mistrust based not merely on contempt but on "knowing cynicism of a parochial kind based on the knowledge of past promises broken."[23] Former senator George McGovern echoed this view, regarding such traits as a positive advantage. Fourteen years after his strong showing in New Hampshire propelled him toward the Democratic party nomination, he remained convinced that the state's voters were among the most independent-minded people in the nation.[24]

State politics in the 1990s, as during most of the twentieth century, has been dominated by the Republican party. New Hampshire maintains the highest proportion of elected Republicans, at all tiers of government, in the nation. This dominance, sometimes sustained by a sizable independent electorate, is strengthened by a pervasive libertarian streak in state politics and voters which distrusts state activism in all its manifestations. Gun-related crime is low, in common with the crime index generally, but New Hampshire has the highest per capita National Rifle Association membership of any state except Alaska, and gun-control measures, along with taxation and seat-belt laws, are regarded mainly as infringments on personal liberty. To the surprise of some observers, the aggressive conservatism of the 1990s' New Right has not struck a chord with the state's electorate. Voters appear deeply suspicious of the Christian Coalition and the Gingrich agenda precisely because both phenomena are active-interventionist in style and substance. The moral imperatives of Ralph Reed in particular leave New Hampshire voters uneasy over the state's power to regulate personal conduct, and his Coalition has largely failed to develop a strong base in the Granite State. It is this more old-fashioned conservatism, permeated with libertarian ideals, which doomed Barry Goldwater to defeat in the 1964 Republican presidential primary. Political commentators suggested the 1996 Buchanan victory was a sign of a rightward shift in the state electorate, but polling data suggested primary voters tended to ignore the candidate's social views and focused on his trade policies and promises of greater job security. Given the slant of Buchanan's fiscal platform, the result may also be interpreted as a warning shot across the bows of moderate Republicans suspected by conservative primary voters of contemplating further tax increases.

These Democratic gains aside, state Democrats tend to make only periodic inroads into GOP hegemony, most often in periods of regional or national economic difficulty. In the 1990 elections, with recession biting, Democrat Dick Swett defeated Republican Chuck Douglas in the Second Congressional District, a safe GOP haven since 1915. Swett was unseated, however, in the Republican takeover of the U.S. House in November 1994 and was subsequently defeated by Republican Bob Smith in 1996. After the 1990 state elections, the GOP had a wafer-thin majority of two seats in the state Senate.[25] Since 1960, Democrats have won the governorship in only six of the eighteen biennial elections. The death of Democratic governor Hugh Gallen (1979–82) in 1982, soon after his defeat for reelection, ushered in a long period of GOP rule under John Sununu (1983–89) Judd Gregg (1989–93) and Steve Merrill (1993–97). This gubernatorial drought was finally broken in November 1996 by the victory of Jeanne Shaheen over Republican Ovide Lamontagne. Shaheen became New Hampshire's first female governor and the first Democrat to occupy the office in fourteen years. Despite the state's reputation for supporting liberal Democrats in presidential primaries (McCarthy in 1968, McGovern in 1972), state Democrats are forced to adopt largely moderate, fiscally conservative policies and wait for the opposition to miscalculate. The state party itself is rarely able to dictate the political agenda.

Party registration figures show a steady improvement for Democrats from the late 1960s, when the Republicans held a 42 percent to 26 percent edge. In 1988 the GOP had slipped to 39 percent while the Democrats had risen to 30 percent.[26] By the early 1990s there were an estimated 664,991 registered voters; Republicans claimed 252,199 and the Democrats 210,865. Most notably, however, almost one-third of voters, 198,627, were registered as independent, an unpredictable bloc that is pivotal to an understanding of at least some of the unexpected primary outcomes in the state.[27]

Craig and Winters found the Democratic party to be fundamentally divided between a broadly conservative Manchester wing and a more liberal-leaning area across the southern tier and in some northern areas such as Lebanon. Its weak structural organization compounds the problems facing Democratic candidates. Joe Grandmaison, organizer of the 1972 McGovern and 1984 Glenn campaigns and later state party chairman, believes that Democratic success in New Hampshire is largely predicated on Republican failure. "If their candidate is too far to the right . . . then our candidate can pull in undeclared voters and liberal Republicans."[28]

Opinion surveys since the 1970s suggest that, despite the Republican monopoly and New Hampshire's conservative reputation, voter attitudes remain surprisingly flexible. In a survey of voter opinion during the early 1980s, at a time when criticism of the Granite State primary was reaching new peaks, Richard Winters employed responses to questions from a CBS/*New York Times* poll to frame a profile of political attitudes. The data contradicted some longstanding stereotypes of the state electorate.[29]

The Winters survey revealed that New Hampshire Democrats, when questioned, supported the Equal Rights Amendment more strongly than Democrats in New York or California. They also outpolled other states in opposition to the construction of nuclear power facilities. State Republicans were, on the whole, as or more conservative than their national counterparts of the early 1980s, but the differences were only marginal. Percentages favoring construction of nuclear plants in New Hampshire equaled those in Illinois, New Jersey and Wisconsin and surpassed those of liberal Massachusetts by only 3 percent. Both California and Ohio Republican voters proved more conservative on this issue. Fewer Granite State Republicans opposed ERA than Republicans in Florida or Illinois; in fact, New Hampshire registered the highest GOP total *in favor* of the amendment.[30] If, as William Mayer has claimed, the issue of the representativeness of a state electorate rests with comparisons between state and national party rather than general electorates, such surveys reveal few major discrepancies and, again, differences are far narrower than traditional assessments of New Hampshire's political culture might suggest.[31]

Mayer's own analysis of the characteristics of state partisans, published toward the end of the 1980s, provides useful material for a more balanced assessment. His survey, constructed from state and national market research data, confirms the reasonably close correlation between state and national Republicans (in categories such as religious affiliation, ethnic grouping, income and education levels) but detects a greater disparity between New Hampshire's Democrats and national party voters. The heterogeneous, factional nature of the national party was not duplicated at the state level. Although only a tiny minority in the Granite State, black voters did not support the state Democrats as strongly as those at the national level. New Hampshire Democrats had over twice the national proportion of college graduates

(39 percent to 17 percent) among its supporters.[32] Such differences, while not serious, create the potential for pitfalls when campaigns oriented toward the national party electorate enter the New Hampshire arena. The differences may also go some way to explaining why, in twelve Democratic presidential primaries since 1952, state Democratic voters have failed six times to correctly forecast their party's eventual nominee. In summary, although reliance on polling data is equally as hazardous as reliance on outdated stereotypes, it can be argued that New Hampshire's partisan electorate is not significantly out of step with the electorate of other states on a broad range of policy issues.

General shifts in the national ideological outlook of both major parties have usually been mirrored in the state's primary electorate. The leftward drift of the Democratic party between the late 1960s and mid-1970s found an echo in support for the McCarthy and McGovern candidacies. The anti-Washington themes of Ronald Reagan were already firmly entrenched in New Hampshire politics. The taxation and bureaucracy-cutting philosophy of the Republicans in the 1980s and 1990s made it appear that the national party was moving toward the stance of the state party rather than the other way around. Similarly, the centrist candidacies of Dukakis, Tsongas and Clinton demonstrated that the national Democrats' bid to recapture the center reflected the political reality facing New Hampshire Democrats for years. After fruitless searches on the left of the ideological spectrum, state Democrats have followed President Clinton back to the political center ground, reaping at least some rewards in terms of electability. Although the GOP remains firmly in control, the Democrats' new centrism has the potential to blur the partisan divide. In 1996, frustrated at the right-skewed Republican field, GOP state senator Susan McLane publicly advised primary voters to abandon party loyalities and endorse the president, announcing the formation of a bipartisan coalition, New Hampshire Women for Clinton. McLane confessed disaffection with the education, environment and abortion stances of the GOP candidates and suggested women write in Clinton's name on the Republican ballot.[33] Political commentators have, in past years, judged New Hampshire's Democrats and Republicans to stand to the left and right, respectively, of their national counterparts, but shifts in the national mood and in party ideology now mean that, as Joe Grandmaison observed, "party electorates that used to be unrepresentative of their national brethren now really aren't."[34]

FISCAL NEW HAMPSHIRE AND THE PLEDGE

A significant moment in the battle for the 1988 Republican nomination occurred in the closing week of the New Hampshire campaign during a televised candidate forum from St. Anselm's College, Goffstown. Delaware governor Pete DuPont, who had based his faltering candidacy on cuts in federal government spending, produced a sheet of paper from his top pocket, announced it to be a pledge that the eventual nominee would not raise taxes after winning the presidential election and proferred it to Senator minority leader Robert Dole with the challenge, "Sign it, Senator." Dole appeared momentarily confused, took the paper without even looking it over and muttered, "Give it to George, I have to read it first."[35]

Although the scene bordered on farce, the message was clear. Candidates understood that, in the political environment of the late Reagan years, taxation was an incendiary topic. George Bush would eventually, and disastrously, recognize this during his acceptance speech to the New Orleans Convention. For candidates in a New Hampshire primary, the issue is fundamental. Political definitions in the Granite State tend to revolve around positions on taxation more than any other single topic and a refusal to "Take the Pledge," thereby promising not to raise taxes, carries lethal electoral consequences.

Even in the late 1950s, Duane Lockard described the state as "obssessed" with the tax question, observing that New Hampshire's politicians tended to "convert *all* policy to questions of economy in government."[36] Critics suggest that New Hampshire's entire fiscal system is built on a determined effort to avoid statewide sales or income taxes (the state currently has neither) by persuading its citizens of the virtue of minimal state services while taking out-of-state customers for every dollar they can lay their hands on. The "jerry-built" tax structure of the state is frequently criticized for its lack of provision for schools, mental healthcare and other services. Peirce claims that the financial burden of this system on the poorest citizen, in proportion to income, is double that for wealthier residents.[37]

State authorities work to keep demands on government revenue low in order to alleviate the inevitable problems arising from the absence of broad-based taxes. This is achieved, more or less, through a series of lesser taxes such as those on the state lottery, the first modern state lottery in the nation, which was established in 1963 and based on the sweepstakes at Rockingham Park. There are additional taxes on hotel and restaurant meals, accommodations and cigarettes. These are often referred to locally as the "beer, beds, bets, bellies and butts" taxes, or "sin taxes."

Tourism provides a substantial boost to state coffers, aside from the massive influx of visitors and cash accompanying the quadrennial presidential primary. In fiscal 1994, tourists and businessmen spent over $2.5 billion in New Hampshire, helping to finance an estimated 56,000 jobs. With ten cents on the dollar allocated to state government and three cents to city and town government, the state collectively picked up $260 million over the fiscal year.[38] The presidential primary serves as a useful, but not critical, shot in the arm for the state economy. Shortly after the 1984 primary, *New England Monthly* assessed the material gains of the Granite State. "Every four years they rev up the rusty state machinery, plug in the old primary power source and *generate*. Tourist dollars, political jobs, federal contracts, circus souvenirs—all are to be had in the marketplace of retail politics."[39] The financial benefits are felt particularly in hotel and restaurant takings and can be gauged through revenue from the Rooms and Meals Tax. In early 1995, a review of the 1988 and 1992 primaries by the state Revenue Administration revealed takings of between $2.2 and $2.5 million. According to the state director of travel and tourism development, Chris Jennings, this places gross meals and accommodation spending per primary at between $27 and $32 million.[40] Though significant, this boost to state coffers nonetheless represents, according to the Office of Vacation Travel, only 1 percent of total tourist outlays in any given year.[41]

A further substantial source of income derives from the state's high property tax rates. A survey of selected U.S. cities in 1992 ranked Manchester fourth highest in property tax levels at an effective rate of $2.75 per $100. Of the major cities included in the survey, only Detroit, Milwaukee and Newark ranked higher.[42] These high rates tend to create controversy, with defenders of the state's fiscal system indicating that, as a proportion of total personal income, New Hampshire's 8.18 percent tax deduction rate is far below that of any other New England state. If property taxes are added, however, the figure rises sharply to 14.49 percent, within 1.7 percent of the Rhode Island totals and within 3.4 percent of neighboring "Taxachusetts." An additional, innovative source of state income is provided by a ring of state-run discount liquor stores, conveniently sited along the state boundaries in order to entice residents from Vermont, Massachusetts and Maine. Maine has proved to be the source of a considerable amount of bitterness from New Hampshire's neighbors, who complain that "the grab-it state" has developed the extraction of cash from visitors into an art form.

The taxation question does not divide neatly along party lines, but more support, predictably, is to be found for the state's unorthodox revenue-raising techniques within the Republican party, particularly in its conservative wing. Many, though not all, Democrats express their concern for the long-term future of the state if either a statewide sales or income tax is not introduced, but most shy away from open calls for any wholesale revision of the tax structure. Candidates seek to avoid, at all costs, being branded as "tax raisers," a tag described by Goldman and Mathews as "a sin just short of child molestation or cannibalism in the canons of New Hampshire politics."[43] Democratic governor Hugh Gallen refused to rule out the possibility of tax hikes in 1982 as a solution to the growing state deficit problem and subsequently lost his reelection bid to John Sununu. The crusades of the Manchester *Union Leader* and the efforts of nonpartisan groups ensure that the tax question is kept near the top of the state agenda.

During the early 1990s, recession appeared to be forcing a change in public sentiment, with a 1991 University of New Hampshire poll indicating a majority supporting either a sales or an income tax. Neither was forthcoming. Democrats remain convinced that the long-term imperative for serious fiscal reform is undeniable, particularly as the state government continues to register a heavy annual deficit, but are skeptical of the short-term prospects for change.

During the 1976 Republican presidential primary, Ronald Reagan learned the harsh reality of fiscal politics in New Hampshire after advocating return of control of federally funded programs to the states. The candidate claimed that around $90 billion could be saved and state governments could decide themselves whether to continue with the programs or terminate them. President Ford's managers seized on the implications of this proposal. Since New Hampshire relied on federal funds for 50 percent of its spending, how would it be able to meet the new costs without introducing a broad-based tax?[44] Reagan was unable to answer this question effectively, and it dogged him throughout the campaign. One Ford staffer recalled: "I don't think Ford could have won without that issue. It killed Reagan and threw him completely off guard."[45]

A majority of New Hampshirites support the status quo, particularly transplanted Massachusetts residents who, despite relatively liberal social values, often move across the state line to take advantage of the state's fiscal conservatism. Conservatives regard their unique approach as the mainstay of New Hampshire's political culture and argue that charitable institutions and other private provisions make up for any shortfall in services by channeling money to local authorities rather than into central state coffers. The Community Services Council, the Society for the Protection of New Hampshire Forests, the New Hampshire Charitable Fund, Project Second Start and other organizations form a substantial volunteer network in a small state where demands on the welfare structure are, in any case, lower than the national average. Assessments of the adequacy of such a system are inevitably subjective. New Hampshire's political prominence every four years produces a useful bonus in the form of federal funding, state dependence on which, according to some estimates, ranges from 40 to 50 percent of the annual budget. Presidents facing tough reelection battles are often tempted to roll out barrels of pork to shore up their support in New Hampshire. In 1975 Gerald Ford promised increased government funding for road development and a plum federal position for the former New Hampshire attorney-general, Warren Rudman.

Having survived the recession of the early 1990s, it appears unlikely that New Hampshire will choose to alter its tax structure in the near future. In 1991, amid declining revenues and rising unemployment, Secretary of State Gardner accurately forecast that budget cuts, not tax hikes, would be the state government's approach. In response to criticism of the state's fiscal practices, Gardner claimed that while state per capita spending might be among the nation's lowest, local funding levels are among the highest, particularly in areas such as education.[46] The prevailing consensus dictates that decentralized government and localized funding practices will continue to protect the state from the evils of income and sales tax and, consequently, from the irritants of an ever-expanding bureaucracy. It is a view increasingly echoed in the corridors of Washington.

THE REPRESENTATION DEBATE

New Hampshire is clearly a more complex, multifaceted state than critics have traditionally suggested. In common with other states, it has internal quirks and contradictions, but in terms of social, economic and demographic development it is hardly anachronistic. Deputy Secretary of State Robert Ambrose observed in the early 1990s: "High tech, service industries, tourism, leisure time. . . . New Hampshire is what America is now."[47]

As one of the most highly industrialized states, it is also one of the least urbanized. Only 59.4 percent of state residents live in a metropolitan area, compared to a national figure close to 80 percent.[48] It has limited ethnic problems but hardly on the scale of New York or Detroit. It is comprised mainly of small towns, has no state-funded transport system and only one statewide newspaper, the Manchester *Union Leader*. Yet its southern population is markedly more cosmopolitan and more closely bound to Massachusetts than is generally perceived. There are hustlers on the streets of Manchester, and problems of AIDS, drug abuse, crime, abortion, education and the environment receive no less attention from the local media than in other states of comparable size. Traditional views of New Hampshire are sorely in need of revision, but this imperative has yet to significantly alter the view of critics that the state is out of touch with the rest of the nation and fundamentally unrepresentative of the national electorate.

Assessments of the state's character run the gamut from the bemused to the hostile. Neal Peirce's nationally syndicated *Washington Post* column once denounced New Hampshire's "appallingly smug and uncreative atmosphere," and described it as "the prototype among the fifty states of the unresponsive and irresponsible society."[49] *Time* magazine has characterized state voters as "quirkily independent and cantankerous," while the BBC's Fred Emery referred to them as "a cussed lot!"[50] *Newsweek*'s Howard Fineman noted that the state's voters appeared to find satisfaction in overturning whatever the day's political wisdom happened to be.[51]

These observations, combined with the stereotypical, somewhat outdated, view of the state mean that in defending its primary New Hampshire has often been compelled to defend *itself*. Attacks on the influence it wields within the nomination process are habitually tied to negative perceptions of the state as a cultural, economic and political entity. Jules Witcover described the state as "too small, too remote, too atypical to be seriously regarded as a national political barometer."[52] Writing in the *Boston Globe* during the late 1970s, columnist Mike Royko launched a diatribe against the Bay State's notorious neighbor. Acidly commenting that New Hampshire was "not big enough to have an interesting crime problem," the column continued, "New Hampshire isn't a typical cross-section of American voters in any way—not in race, ethnic composition or party preference. . . . It has no football teams or baseball teams or a big city. It's never hit by hurricanes."[53]

Royko proceeded, tongue-in-cheek, to propose the expulsion of the Granite State from the union on the grounds that the damage it inflicted on the political process far outweighed any benefits it had to offer. In a responding editorial, the *Portsmouth Herald* promptly attacked Royko as "a loud-mouthed columnist," denied New Hampshire was in any way "a bucolic backwash" and pointed out that its residents even read the *New York Times*.[54] Furthermore, it argued, "We are smaller than many states, with fewer people so far than New York and fewer kooks than California, but we are getting there. We're not all that divorced from reality that we cannot serve in our small way as a testing ground for American Presidents."[55] Nonetheless, the line has been picked up by politicians of both major parties, including the chairman of the Tennessee Democratic party, Dick Lodge, who complained in 1986 that the population of his state's capital outnumbered the entire New Hampshire electorate.[56]

Clearly, the question of the representative quality of a New Hampshire primary lies at the heart of the continuing controversy over its elevated electoral status. Unexpected, or freak, results will always draw media attention. If these occur at the beginning of the nomination process, when perceived candidate strengths and weaknesses are based almost entirely on informed speculation, the impact of such results will naturally be greater. Should that impact have, as its point of origin, a small New England state believed to be out-of-step with the national sentiment, the argument to terminate that state's influence becomes stronger.

The notion that New Hampshire is an unrepresentative state is a deeply flawed one, not least because consensual definitions of a representative electorate are hard to come by in a nation of fifty, regionally and culturally diverse states. Yet primary critics have been decidedly lax in defining and applying this term to the Granite State. They have also been notably swift in retreating once the concept of representative electorates comes under closer scrutiny.

William Crotty and John Jackson describe primary representativeness as "an evaluation of how well the primaries are capable of living up to their promise."[57] Primary electorates are often inherently biased since both campaigning and turnout are dominated by activists and voters with distinct ideological preferences, or at least with a higher than average interest in political issues. Thus, any primary result may be a distortion not only of *national* sentiment but also of the *party* electorate. Austin Ranney's 1972 study of eleven state primaries largely supports this thesis. Ranney found primary voters in most states to be demographically quite unrepresentative if their actions were compared to declared intentions of nonvoting partisans.[58]

A majority of studies have drawn on the path-breaking work of V. O. Key, Jr., whose analysis of American state politics in the 1950s postulated that primary electorates consisted mainly of people of certain ethnic or religious affiliations, together with those "especially responsive to certain styles of political leadership or shades of ideology."[59] Key noted that such compositions were usually "markedly unrepresentative in one way or another of the party following."[60]

Scott Keeter and Clifford Zukin offer a distinction between representation as either standing for or acting for. The former, they believe, implies that the representative in some way *resembles* the people he represents and thus is capable of signaling their general sentiments, while the latter merely assumes action (casting a primary ballot) *on behalf of* the wider constituency without necessarily representing the views of that constituency in microcosm. They observed that the notion of demographic representation for which party quotas aimed has always been regarded as flawed. "It required that someone arbitrarily determine which of a myriad of politically important social characteristics was relevant and should be the basis for mandatory representation."[61]

The quota system imposed by the McGovern–Fraser Commission (Commission on Party Structure and Delegate Selection) after the 1968 campaign cycle attempted to ensure that the 1972 Democratic Convention would be more broadly representative of the party's electoral base by mandating certain proportions for each state delegation of blacks, women and young people. This inevitably led to preferential ranking, leaving Hispanics and other groups not favored by the quotas with the feeling that the convention remained unrepresentative. Such problems are, of course, only the tip of the iceberg. The question lies unresolved as to whether quotas should be compiled on the basis of registered party membership, or whether actual voter turnout in primary or general elections would prove a more accurate guide.

The obsession with representative democracy is not solely a product of the era of party rules reform; it is deep-rooted in American political culture, although its application has always been decidedly selective. The Democrats' search for a balanced and fair system of candidate selection returned time and again to this key issue. Convention seating, delegate apportionment and even the 1980s phenomenon of front-loading (in which states move their primary or caucus dates closer to the commencement of the nomination process to dull the edge of New Hampshire's impact) all hinge on competing notions of representative ideals. If it is to be accepted that any primary result will not be an accurate reflection of either national or state party sentiment, or of the wider general electorate, then the accusation that New Hampshire must forfeit its first-in-the-nation status because of its unrepresentative nature tends to lose validity. Such a broad variety of socioeconomic, religious and ethnic characteristics are required that no state would be capable of establishing a claim to represent the national mood or to embody national demography and culture. Furthermore, no state could be regarded as a permanent national political barometer since all tend to vary in electoral significance due to economic, social and demographic changes. Few, if any, maintain static political complexions. "As Maine goes, so goes the nation" was a favored maxim in American elections until the state distinguished itself by voting for the Republican presidential ticket of Landon and Knox in 1936. Even New Hampshire, which had selected the winner of every presidential election since 1952, eventually lost its reputation as a weathervane by choosing Paul Tsongas over Bill Clinton in 1992.

Interestingly, the question of why the straitjacket of representativeness should be imposed on New Hampshire and not on other states is seldom raised. It is not applied to the Iowa caucuses, perhaps because these contests are not taken as seriously in forecasting nomination outcomes or, equally possibly, because the state has a less controversial public image than that of the first primary state. Bob Dole's victory in the 1996 South Carolina primary was hailed by reporters as opening the way for a Dole surge through the Junior and Super Tuesday contests toward victory at the San Diego Convention. No commentators questioned the representative makeup of South Carolina's electorate in making such a far-reaching decision. Only in New Hampshire is any primary electorate required to mirror national voter sentiments, for reasons underlined by Silvio Conte in the 1984 hearings of the

House Subcommittee on Elections: "In the final analysis . . . statistics demonstrate that the state is not representative of the national electorate as a whole, yet this primary is considered a must-win contest."[62]

The 1992 campaign cycle saw New Hampshire turnout rise to 40 percent of the voting-age population, the highest of that year's primary season and five percentage points above its nearest competitor, Montana.[63] Weakness of state party organizations can heighten the competitive intensity of electoral races and thereby increase voter turnout. Oregon and Wisconsin have also developed a tradition of fiercely fought primaries and share, with New Hampshire, the tradition of weak party direction in at least one of the two major parties.

The single most important drive behind reforms of presidential selection mechanisms in the 1970s was to open up the electoral process to ordinary voters by circumscribing the influence of party machines and elected officials. Yet, as Crotty and Jackson point out, it is one thing to make opportunities for the public to choose but quite another to ensure the opportunity is taken up.[64] To an extent, the presidential primary as a voting mechanism has emphatically delivered on its initial promise. Voter turnout in nomination contests rose from around 12 million in 1968 (11 percent of the voting-age population) to over 37 million (21 percent) by 1988. Over 90 percent of this increase could be directly attributed to increases in primary voting.[65] Inevitably, primary turnout is a highly variable indicator, governed by the format of the race (caucus or primary), the number and nature of competitors in the field and the social, economic and political circumstances overlaying the election year as a whole. The presence of a sitting president tends to depress turnout in the incumbent's party races, as demonstrated during the 1984 Republican and 1996 Democratic party races when Presidents Reagan and Clinton sought renomination unopposed. Turnout figures increase correspondingly if strong challenges are made to the incumbent (the Buchanan challenge of 1992) or in the event of open competition for the nomination (experienced by the Democrats in 1992 and the GOP in 1996). Research suggests, however, that primary turnout in New Hampshire is consistently high when compared to that of other state contests and that this superiority may exist regardless of the factors outlined above. Wayne records that the turnout percentages for the major parties in 1992's New Hampshire primary were higher in both cases than the cumulative race average, with Republican voters registering 10 percent and Democrats 4 percent over the national mean primary totals.[66] Indeed, the state's 1992 Democratic primary turnout, at 167,819, was well above the average for the entire 1972–88 period.[67] New Hampshire does not consistently record the highest turnout levels (ranking fifteenth nationally with 0.2 percent less than the average Democratic primary vote in 1984), but its performance has been consistently strong throughout the post-1968 period.[68] The accepted explanation for this strength is that the media and candidate attention lavished on the first-in-the-nation primary stimulates voter participation to a degree not experienced by states later in the calendar when the outcome of the battle becomes clearer and media analysis switches from ground reports to broader-brush candidate and policy assessments. Primary supporters use the high turnout levels as a strong argument for maintaining their first-place tradition.

V. O. Key, in common with most political scientists since the 1950s, has suggested that participation in primary elections requires that individual voters have a higher degree of motivation than is normally necessary in general elections. This can often result in a skewed turnout containing disproportionately high numbers from certain class, age, religion or ethnic backgrounds, people sensitive to particular ideological appeals or "other groups markedly unrepresentative in one way or another of the party following."[69] This problem is often used to bolster arguments that New Hampshire, placed at the head of the nomination calendar, is doubly unrepresentative due to its intrinsic character as a state and as a primary. Such accusations have led Michael Hagen to argue that the relationship between turnout and representation is fundamentally misunderstood. He suggests that political scientists consistently confuse notions of demographic and political representation and assume that one must, of necessity, mirror the other for a truly representative selection system to be achieved. Hagen adds that the mere existence of widespread disagreement over which of these two electorates primary voters are intended to represent should itself counsel caution in any assessment of the democratic merits of primaries generally or any one primary in particular.[70]

Arguments that primaries are dominated by the white, affluent, ideologically motivated and college-educated middle classes are regarded as problematic for the system as a whole, not merely for the Granite State. But turnout statistics suggest that New Hampshire primary voters will go to the polls in consistently greater numbers than their counterparts in most other states.

Surveying the data from a 1980 opinion poll conducted by the *New York Times*, E. J. Dionne commented on an apparent disparity between the knowledge displayed by New Hampshire's primary voters and those in other regions of the nation. He continued that New Hampshire citizens "had received a political education from the campaign, displaying far greater knowledge of the issue positions of the candidates."[71]

The controversial and much-employed argument that New Hampshire citizens are better qualified to render judgment on presidential candidates than voters in other states is considered inaccurate and inflammatory by critics, but has at least some statistical foundation. A 1996 voter survey conducted jointly by University of New Hampshire political science professor Carl Hubbard and Notre Dame professor Samuel Best claimed that "New Hampshire primary voters are more politically aware."[72] Hubbard's survey used a nationwide sample group of 632 likely Republican voters, each of whom was asked five key questions, ranging from the identity of the vice-president to party control of the House of Representatives and the requirements for a congressional override of the presidential veto. Granite State respondents to the Hubbard–Best survey outperformed their national counterparts on each question. Seventy percent were aware of the constitutional requirement for a congressional override, compared to 37 percent of the national sample. Eighty-two percent of the New Hampshire contingent were aware that the

Supreme Court ultimately determined the constitutionality of laws, compared to 68 percent of the national group.[73] Such results, while hardly conclusive, point to the possibility that decades of intensive exposure to national politicians, together with national and international media involvement, may have raised levels of political awareness and knowledge across the state.

Opinion polls also tend to undermine the notion of an electorate sealed off from political realities. The parlous state of the American economy dominated the concerns of New Hampshire voters in 1992, closely reflecting the national mood. In 1996 the *Concord Monitor* published the results of a pre-primary poll by the ICR Research Group for the American Association of Retired Persons' AARP/ VOTE program. They revealed that Granite State voters identified, in order of priority, education, the economy, crime, Social Security and drugs as their key concerns. Again, this list could not be regarded as out of step with the concerns of the mainstream national electorate.[74]

The suggestion that New Hampshire may possess an unusually insightful electorate does nothing to placate advocates of reform who regard the claim as another element in the Granite State's very professional public relations exercise. The June 1995 debate between President Clinton and Republican House Speaker Newt Gingrich at the Earl Bourdon Senior Center in Claremont, New Hampshire, drew plaudits from reporters not only for its friendly and cooperative tone but also for the direct questioning from the audience. Most pundits believed that Gingrich, renowned for his attacks on federal benefits and Social Security, had taken a calculated risk in exposing himself to interrogation by New Hampshire's senior citizens. WMUR-TV's political reporter, Carl Cameron, claimed Gingrich later commented that he had never seen local media and voters "as sophisticated, as insightful and as demanding . . . anywhere."[75] Critics find the claim of unique qualities both irritating and misleading. Former presidential candidate Morris Udall complained, "They talk about it as if there's some sort of mystic connection you get when you're talking to a guy at a paper mill in Berlin. . . there's no more mystic connection there than there is if you're talking with a cowboy in southern Arizona."[76]

Udall and others have suggested that senior political figures pay compliments to state voters more from fear than conviction, with would-be candidates offering ritual answers to the ritual question posed by New Hampshire interlocutors in order to butter up state voters. President Clinton demonstrated a new level of expertise at this game during a WMUR interview, taped in the Old Executive Office Building on February 7, 1995.[77]

THE PRESIDENT: You know, I made an awful lot of friends in New Hampshire and I met people from all walks of life. . . . I just . . . I always believed in the New Hampshire process as an observer. But after I went through it, I felt more strongly about it . . .

Q: Our viewers have heard some talk of other states, whether it's Arizona or Delaware, getting involved in that first-in-the-

	nation vote. Yet you sound like you think New Hampshire should very much be preserved.
THE PRESIDENT:	Yes, I think it would be a mistake. I know the arguments . . . but the truth is that the people there are intensely public-minded and know a phenomenal amount about the issues and they're fair-minded.

Cameron disagrees that such statements are politically self-serving and argues that years of intense exposure to presidential campaigning have simply had a cumulative effect on the attitudes of New Hampshire voters, developing their political awareness and active interest beyond the norms experienced in larger states that have been less heavily exposed to presidential politicking.[78] This process has, in the view of the primary's supporters, created an electoral environment that is both representative and challenging, which is no more skewed in its socio-economic origins than other primary electorates and that matches national concerns and patterns in its voting behavior.

Whatever the outcome of this debate, it is apparent that standards of representativeness are imposed more stringently on New Hampshire, as a result of its high profile, than on any other state. Reform advocates, perhaps misguidedly, seek to ensure that its influence will be removed, or at least diluted and utilize the representative factor as a key argument. In terms of turnout, state characteristics and voter education, however, this argument is highly questionable as a basis for ending a seventy-year tradition. Worse, no consensus exists on any replacement formula that could secure the goal of representativeness without terminating altogether the tradition of a staggered primary and caucus contest. A national primary could solve the problem of who goes first, but even this radical solution would not achieve a representative process since primaries are, by their very nature, intrinsically unrepresentative. A regional system would be longer than a national primary, without achieving higher standards, either in turnout or representativeness. Should Congress finally be tempted to slice the Gordian knot and implement a federal solution, it may find itself forced to choose between unrepresentative evils.

THE STATE AND THE PRIMARY

The cumulative effect of decades of first-place primaries has been to accustom New Hampshire voters to a degree of personal contact with candidates unknown in other, larger states. The candidate field is more crowded and hopeful; therefore, the state's electorate will receive more campaign literature, be exposed to a more varied and intensive diet of political ads and have the opportunity to attend more debates and rallies, gaining personal exposure to the candidates, than citizens of any other state with the possible exception of Iowa. The state's diminutive size and the even smaller geographical area covered by the candidates in their search for votes dictates an up close and personal style of campaigning that persists in the age of satellite television and computerized mailing. New Hampshire is as susceptible as any other state in the union to the convenience of wholesale, media-driven politicking, but this campaign technique, which pays dividends in New York or California, is less effective in the Granite State, as the failure of the Forbes media blitz in 1996 demonstrated.

Sensitivity over the issue of first primary status and constant attacks on the myth of retail campaigning from other states and media outlets may be a significant influence here. Voters, state politicians and the local media have come to regard any candidate refusing to acknowledge the retail dimension of first-in-the-nation campaigns as presumptuous. Overt or implied suggestions that New Hampshire is not the ideal place in which to commence the presidential selection process can therefore cause irreparable damage to a candidate's poll ratings. Senator Phil Gramm's abortive attempt to deemphasize both Iowa and New Hampshire by entering preliminary contests in Louisiana, Delaware and Arizona proved fatal to his support in both early states. To some extent, the nomination rules disputes of the 1980s engendered something of a bunker mentality among supporters of the primary; since then, candidates have found themselves obliged to pay public and fulsome tribute to New Hampshire's tradition to avoid a mauling from the *Union Leader* and other state organs. The campaign of Lamar Alexander performed its homage on December 13, 1995, with a press release timed to coincide with the former governor's filing of his candidacy papers at the State House in Concord. In his statement, Alexander promised to shun the Delaware primary and praised New Hampshire's "strong tradition of low taxes, local control of schools and an effective, part-time citizen-legislature." He added, "I believe that New Hampshire *should* be first in the Nation."[79]

Candidates will also pay a heavy price for neglecting the painstaking construction of a grass-roots activists' network to carry their message across the state. As Edmund Muskie and Robert Dole discovered to their cost, endorsements from state politicians are useful but not necessarily conclusive in the first primary. Instead, organization, by state, town and street, and a high degree of public visibility through small-group and individual voter contact are essential. Bob Dole, perpetually ill-at-ease with this style of campaigning, acerbically noted in 1995, "I know how I got beat before and I'm making the corrections. . . . You do it person by person, kitchen by kitchen. It's tedious and it doesn't mean much—unless you want to win."[80] Campaigning tends to be concentrated in the southern tier of the state, around towns such as Nashua, Derry, Manchester, Goffstown, Exeter and Portsmouth. More northerly towns such as Berlin, Lincoln or Conway comprise a smaller percentage of the population but still receive proportionately higher candidate attention per voter than equivalent communities in other states. These geographic factors, combined with state political culture and decades of pampering by candidates, have created a uniform style for primary campaigns, one that does not alone guarantee success but that, if absent, sets a seal on defeat. Visits to high schools, churches, shopping malls, dog-sled races and hardware stores are regarded as political necessities, although the returns in terms of votes on each individual occasion may be small. Since New Hampshire's primary comes first, the candidate's presence is expected on a regular basis for weeks, often months, beforehand, visiting Town Fairs and Meeting Days, holding barbecues or, like Dole, spending summer vacations in the state. Mark Thurston, co-owner of Weir's Marina and a much-courted activist, recalled receiving personal telephone calls from Bob Dole, Phil Gramm and Lamar Alexander within hours of the withdrawal of former Bush defense secretary Richard Cheney from contention. The GOP activist had been one of Cheney's main state operatives and was now considered up for grabs by the remaining candidates.[81]

The scale of primary campaign operations is dictated by the size of the state and its local community orientation. Almost all the campaigns must work each small area intensively, on a retail basis. Curtis Barry, state coordinator of the abortive 1996 bid by Pennsylvania senator Arlen Specter, believes this makes New Hampshire a harder primary to organize. "We are running ten legitimate county races . . . as if we were running Specter for sheriff in each of the counties. We're aggressively pursuing people who have organized county campaigns . . . that is in addition to the paid media and direct mail that any campaign would normally do."[82]

Media campaigns complement, but cannot supersede, this approach. Again, for the underdog candidacies this is vital since they will have no chance to utilize this tactic in larger states such as Michigan or New York. Susan Casey described the approach employed by the fledgling Hart canpaign in 1984.

Greg Lebel had put together a program and materials that we called our "small town strategy." . . . It consisted of the basics of door-to-door and phone canvassing, personalized direct mail, and visibility programs on a miniature scale. Rather than just write off the hundred and fifty smallest towns that were too rural and too remote to be approached successfully from the ten local offices, staff tried to find just one or two people to take on the whole campaign apparatus for each town with less than a hundred Democratic voters.[83]

The process is time-consuming but cumulatively valuable. During the 1996 campaign, Bob Dole could be found smiling bravely in the West High School Cafeteria, Richard Lugar dropped in at Pauli's Pie and Coffee House in Tilton, Lamar Alexander could be tracked down to Steve's Sports Den on Hooksett Road and political-hopeful Morry Taylor visited Roby's Country Store before entering into one of that season's more bizarre events, a pancake bake-and-flip contest in Manchester, also attended by outsider candidates Robert Dornan and Alan Keyes. Echoes of Gary Hart's 1984 axe-throwing performance are ever-present, as are the perceptions that all candidates follow the style established by Jimmy Carter, the primary's godfather of retail politicking. In fact, the tradition in New Hampshire is older than the modern nominating process itself. Photographs of a pained Senator Robert Taft clutching a chicken in leather-gloved hands and Estes Kefauver on a dog sled bear testament to the primary's heritage of personalized campaign techniques. Small-scale and interpersonal events sustain a two-way impression of accessibility—candidates to voters and media to candidates—which has come to be regarded as a distinctive characteristic of the first primary. In later states such events are few, the main strategic emphasis being on advertising blitzes and mass rallies. Media wars are waged with the same ferocity in New Hampshire, but the playing field is crowded and cramped. Advertising and staged television events therefore cannot form the basis of the campaign unless candidates are willing to risk alienation from local media and voters resentful of their unwillingness to play the game by the established rules. Claiming Granite State retail politics is now more image than reality is in a sense irrelevant since the image has now become a political reality in itself.

The imperative for intensive, personal campaigning is augmented by the importance of local and state political activists to presidential hopefuls. Again, the development of a strong organizational base is a sine qua non in any primary state, but New Hampshire's size, its community orientation and small electorate make this exercise a crucial factor and often an incestuous one. The large state legislature and avocational nature of state politics have, over time, spread political experience through towns and villages and through successive generations of part-time legislator famillies, such as the Dunfey, McLane and Bass clans. This diffusion makes it advantageous for candidates to spread their recruiting nets widely in search of activist support since the dividend in terms of in-state political knowledge and contacts can be decisive. Successive campaigns have courted successive generations of supporters to the point where, as Elizabeth Kolbert of the *New York Times* observed in 1995, "Presidential politics is a sort of statewide pastime."[84] Despite the arrival of computerized mailing and teleconferences, much campaign recruitment still takes place via the mechanism of time-honored kaffeeklatches, in which the candidate and one or two staff will be invited to the home of a campaign activist to meet local residents, allowing other, as-yet uncommitted, activists to assess their policies and viability. These meetings commence on a low-key basis soon after the inauguration ceremonies in Washington have brought the previous year's campaign cycle to a close. Activists shop around during the early postinaugural period and are normally committed to a candidate by the summer of the following year. Hence, Tom Rath, a Concord lawyer and veteran of New Hampshire campaigns, believed that the late (spring 1995) start of Pennsylvania senator Arlen Specter and Indiana senator Dick Lugar in courting local activists seriously impaired their chances for 1996.[85]

Again, the process mirrors that followed in other states but is unique in the degree of personal contact activists will have, at least at this stage, with the candidates. Once aboard, activists such as Rath, Thurston, Jeanne Shaheen, a future Democratic governor, and Susan Duprey, wife of the former state GOP chairman, go to work spreading the message by fax, phone, video and kaffeeklatches, often placing their houses and Rolodexes at the candidate's disposal, aiding in the formulation of local media strategies, targeting areas of strength or weakness and working to bring in endorsements from key state politicians or interest groups. The relative organizational frailty of the state Democratic party makes this process of particular importance for would-be Democratic presidents and incumbents. Jimmy Carter chose to rely on in-state activists and his own Peanut Brigade of Georgian volunteers rather than chase state political endorsements. Overconfidence in the ability of state leaders to deliver a winning margin was considered a key factor in President Bush's embarrassingly weak showing against Pat Buchanan in 1992. Confident that the powerful Sununu would keep a tight rein on Republican voters, Bush neglected his loyalists between 1989 and 1991, allowing Buchanan to make inroads in his support. President Clinton, the first Democratic incumbent since Lyndon Johnson to face a clear field in his renomination campaign, determined not to repeat the mistake. The inveterate campaigner took care to woo Granite State Democrats, inviting hundreds to a New Hampshire Day at the White House in 1994 and arranging a series of visits to the state over the 1995–96 period. As the *Boston Globe* reported in early 1995, "it is not unusual for Democratic activists to find Clinton on the telephone when they face family illness or other milestones."[86]

Inevitably, the long march from 1952 has generated a tiered activist structure characteristic of larger states, which separates the foot soldiers, those confining their activities to distributing leaflets, licking envelopes and holding signs outside polling stations, from the higher-profile activists with significant experience in state politics, important social contacts and a track record in presidential campaigns. In the latter group fall names such as Rath, a former state attorney-general, David Carney, a Sununu operative from 1980 and White House political director under George Bush, J. Joseph Grandmaison, architect of George McGovern's 1972 moral victory, currently working within the Clinton administration, William Cahill, a prominent Republican and 1988 Bush supporter and former GOP national committeewoman Victoria Zachos. Candidate competition for these and other elite activists is normally intense and has been gradually widening in scope since the 1980s. On February 19, 1995, 1,400 GOP activists attended a fund-raising dinner in Manchester at which nine potential candidates, including Dole, Gramm and Alexander, laid out their platforms and visions in a series of ten-minute speeches.[87] Such events, and the high degree of media interest they attract, reflect the now well-established traditions of the first primary but could also portend the increasing professionalization of the activist-candidate nexus in New Hampshire. The development of video meetings, in which activists gather not to meet the candidate in person but to watch a personalized video message, is another symbol of the intrusion of wholesale campaign methods. It is perhaps inevitable that, as the primary becomes more entrenched in the life of the state, New Hampshire activists will increasingly shed their avocational, amateur image.

The importance of the activist network becomes paramount during the early and final days of the campaign. In the latter stage, an effective get-out-the-vote effort can prove decisive to the primary outcome. The 1988 Dole campaign was undermined by a final, massive vote-getting effort by Bush operatives. Ron Kaufman, a national director for Bush's political action committee and presidential campaign, recalled that after the minority leader's Iowa victory, "there was a real wave for Dole, but the strength of our organization allowed us to overcome it."[88] The senator himself noted more bluntly, "I remember what they did to me. . . . I woke up in the morning there and I could see nothing but Bush signs all the way down the street."[89] The last-minute operation of providing lifts to polling stations, planting forests of campaign signs and conducting mass call-ups via telephone banks is not a phenomenon unique to New Hampshire, but, as already stressed, it is a pivotal element in a state where grass-roots organization is the building block for victory.

Student activists, political descendants of Eugene McCarthy's Children's Crusade, comprise a more ephemeral part of the activist network, sauntering across the state lines in the pre-primary year and mostly disappearing as quickly as they arrived after the campaign moves on. New Hampshire students, however, may be encouraged by their first experience to remain in state politics. Interviewed by the *Boston Sunday Globe* in 1996, Steve Root, a thirty-one-year-old campaign worker for Lamar Alexander, described his progress from college to the governor's office, a congressional campaign and, finally a presidential race inside four and a half years. Root noted, "If I lived in any other state but New Hampshire, it would take me 10 or 15 years to have that kind of experience."[90] The use of large numbers of student volunteers paid dividends for Estes Kefauver in 1952 and 1956, for the Lodge draft organizers of 1964 and the McCarthy drive, which demonstrated the vulnerability of all candidates, including presidents as powerful within the party as Lyndon Johnson, to a sustained and coordinated grass-roots challenge. The 1976 Carter campaign did not pioneer the technique but perfected it to a new level within the reformed campaign system—using busloads of Georgian students, most of whom slept in the offices or corridors of local campaign headquarters or were farmed out to the homes of state residents. Telephone and door-to-door canvassing, courting of local activists and exploitation by the candidate and his family of every available media outlet, large and small, were techniques employed on an unprecedented scale. Such saturation campaigning is now standard practice. During the final week of the 1992 campaign, Bush strategists executed a blitz of 400 volunteers working door-to-door to solicit support for the president. They estimated that such a ploy would reach up to 20,000 key Republican voters, complementing the Meet George Bush events scheduled for shopping malls in Bedford and Nashua.[91] While these tactics are now commonplace in New Hampshire, they cannot assure success. Victory in the primary relies on a combination of factors—organization, voter sentiment, message, record and media coverage. Deficiencies in the last three factors can, in certain cirucmstances, be overcome; weakness in the first two is almost always fatal.

CONCLUSION

Critics of New Hampshire and its primary are carefully selective in their use of substantiating evidence, tending to rely on outdated images and to overlook the positive side to holding the first primary in a small state. Over the past four decades, the Granite State has developed an acute ability to adapt its contest to the needs and themes of different candidates. Contenders from the left, right and center of both major parties have prospered and fallen in the first primary, but all have made effective use of the indigenous activist network. The small-scale of primary campaigning has been affected by modern technological developments, but these have never substantially changed the character of the contest since the state's geographical boundaries remain fixed. New Hampshire remains a small and manageable state for any presidential aspirant, affording struggling candidates a unique opportunity to organize an effective campaign and distribute their message to all sections of the electorate.

For its part, the state has gained both financially and educationally from the high exposure levels its primary receives. Surveys indicate that voters have become increasingly sophisticated in their reception and analysis of candidate messages. Residents have not been slow to capitalize on their moment in the political limelight, selling everything from primary boardgames to cartoon primary rule books, T-shirts emblazoned with the motto "I Survived the First-in-the-Nation Primary" and tote-bags declaring "Live Free,Vote First or Die." State Democrats appear particularly keen to make financial gains from the process. In 1984 State Democratic party chairman George Bruno was reported to have sold presidential primary certificates of survival to candidates and activists at $13.50 each and to have charged journalists $25 a head to attend a party function days before the primary vote.[92] The 1995 activists' forum in Manchester netted state Republicans an estimated $80–$100,000 with ticket prices set at $100 each.[93] Such shenanigans, while not unusual, add fuel to the resentment of critics.

The unusual socioeconomic and political conditions prevalent in New Hampshire have undoubtedly contributed to the bad press received by its presidential primary over recent years. However, while the state has its fiscal and social problems, it is, in the 1990s, far from the stereotypical portrait offered by its detractors. Economic expansion, new technology, recession and demographic shifts have wrought considerable change since the 1970s. Political attitudes in the state have kept apace of these developments and have moved, in varying degrees, in line with national sentiment. This has not helped the primary gain a more favorable reception. Reformers continue to insist that unusual characteristics of the state's political or media environment make it an unsuitable host for the nation's first delegate selection contest. Not only are such arguments unproven but also the underlying premise of their use is highly questionable. In no other state are voters vetted for suitability. In no other primary is the state political establishment held up to ridicule. In no other state is a high crime rate considered a prerequisite for a fair contest. The argument that New Hampshire should not hold such a privileged position in the nominating system is only *and can only be* based on structural and procedural assessments of the system itself. It cannot be based on negative perceptions of the socioeconomic features of one state in particular. Efforts to engineer the electoral environment are theoretically flawed and thus doomed to failure from the outset. Persistent demands by reform elements for a more representative nominating system target the Granite State as the largest obstacle to progress. The fact that most proposed reforms, and the arguments underlying them, produce alternative unrepresentative scenarios has not daunted reformers' efforts to rid themselves of the first-in-the-nation primary once and for all.

NOTES

1. Leslie Finer, "Granite State Primary," *The Spectator*, February 26, 1976, p. 7.

2. *New Hampshire Manual for the General Court 1995*, No. 54 (Concord, NH: Department of State, 1995), pp. 105–6.

3. *States in Profile: The State Policy Reference Book 1994* (McConnellsburg, PA: US Data on Demand and State Policy Research, 1994), Table A-1.

4. 1960–75 data: *New York Times*, October 8, 1984, p. 9; 1970–90 figure: Telephone Interview with Secretary of State William Gardner, New Hampshire, January 4, 1996.

5. 1987 figures, *Congressional Quarterly Weekly Report*, vol. 45, no. 35 (August 29, 1987): 1998.

6. Duane Lockard, *New England State Politics* (Princeton, NJ: Princeton University Press, 1959), p. 54.

7. Article 10 states: "whenever the ends of government are perverted, and public liberty manifestly endangered, and all other means of redress are ineffectual, the people may, and of right ought to reform the old, or establish a new government. The doctrine of nonresistance against arbitrary power, and oppression, is absurd, slavish and destructive of the good and happiness of mankind." *Constitution of New Hampshire, Part First, Bill of Rights, New Hampshire Manual for the General Court 1995*, No. 54 (Concord, NH: Department of State, 1995), p. 6.

8. *States in Profile*, Table B-1.

9. Ibid., Table B-8. 1995 percentage—*Business NH Magazine: 1995 New Hampshire Economic Report* (Manchester, NH: November 1995), p. 27.

10. *New Hampshire Sunday News*, Manchester, NH, February 2, 1992, p. 3B.

11. Courtesy, files of Secretary of State William Gardner.

12. "State Economy Is Rebounding—Sort Of," *Valley News*, New Hampshire, February 10, 1996, p. 5.

13. *Business NH Magazine*, p. 23.

14. *States in Profile*, Table C-2.

15. *Statistical Abstract of the United States, 1994*, "State Rankings: Educational Attainment. 1990" (Washington, DC: Department of Commerce, U.S. Government Printing Office, 1994), p. XV.

16. *The Book of the States*, vol. 30, 1994–95 (Lexington, MA: Council of State Governments, 1994), p. 113.

17. *The Election Data Book: A Statistical Portrait of Voting in America, 1992* (Lanham, MD: Bernan Press, 1993), Compiled and edited by Kimball W. Brace and the staff of Election Data Services), p. 603.

18. Neal R. Peirce, *The New England States* (New York: W. W. Norton, 1976), p. 324.

19. *Business NH Magazine*, p. 27.

20. *The Book of the States*, p. 53.

21. Richard F. Winters, "Damn Yankees and Others: New Hampshire's Electorate and What It Represents." Paper presented to the Conference on Primary Perspectives. Sponsored by New Hampshire Council for the Humanities (Hanover, NH: 1980), pp. 21a–22a.

22. States in Profile, Table A-12.

23. Richard F. Winters, "New Hampshire," in Alan Rosenthal and Maureen Moakley, eds., *The Political Life of the American States* (New York: Praeger, 1984), p. 277.

24. Author Interview, George S. McGovern, Washington, DC, August 28, 1986.

25. The GOP held the New Hampshire House of Representatives in 1995 by 258 seats to 136 Democrats, 5 independents and one vacancy. The Senate margin, however, was only 13 to 11. *Election Data Book,* p. 603.

26. Rhodes Cook, *Race for the Presidency: Winning the 1988 Nomination* (Washington, DC: Congressional Quarterly, 1987), p. 13.

27. "Fighting to be First," *Boston Globe,* January 15, 1995, p. 19.

28. Interview, J. Joseph Grandmaison, Manchester, NH, September 12, 1986.

29. Winters, "Damn Yankees and Others," pp. 21a–22a.

30. Ibid.

31. William G. Mayer, "The New Hampshire Primary: A Historical Overview," in Gary R. Orren and Nelson W. Polsby, eds., *Media and Momentum: The New Hampshire Primary and Nomination Politics* (Chatham, NJ: Chatham House, 1987), p. 26.

32. Ibid., pp. 26–29.

33. "Women Endorse Clinton," *Concord Monitor,* February 16, 1996, p. A2.

34. Interview, J. Joseph Grandmaison.

35. Tom Goldman and Peter Mathews, *The Quest for the Presidency: The 1988 Campaign* (New York: Simon & Schuster, 1989), pp. 257–58.

36. Lockard, *New England State Politics,* p. 47.

37. Neal Peirce, "How Valid Is New Hampshire's Verdict?" *Washington Post,* January 29, 1976, p. 5.

38. Glenn French, "Tourism Industry Gateway to New Hampshire," *Union Leader,* June 12, 1995, p. C1.

39. Joseph P. Kahn, "Quick, What Created Jobs, Filled Hotels, Sold Drinks and Had Very Little to do with Politics?" *New England Monthly,* April 1984, p. 34.

40. "Primary Can Mean Big Bucks for State," *New Hampshire Sunday News,* February 26, 1995, p. A9.

41. Ibid.

42. *Statistical Abstract of the United States, 1994,* p. 310, Table 481.

43. Goldman and Mathews, *The Quest for the Presidency,* p. 254.

44. Jules Witcover, *Marathon: The Pursuit of the Presidency 1972–1976* (New York: Viking Press, 1977), p. 341.

45. Charles Brereton, *First in the Nation: New Hampshire and the Premier Presidential Primary* (Portsmouth, NH: Peter E. Randall Publishers, 1987), p. 186.

46. Interview, Secretary of State William Gardner, State House, Concord, NH, February 19, 1992.

47. Burt Solomon, "Where America Is At," *National Journal,* September 26, 1987, p. 2405.

48. "New Hampshire and the Nation," *Boston Sunday Globe,* February 18, 1996, p. 33.

49. Peirce, "How Valid Is New Hampshire's Verdict?" p. 14.

50. Interview, Fred Emery, BBC Lime Grove Studios, July 10, 1985.

51. Interview, Howard W. Fineman, *Newsweek,* Washington, DC, August 26, 1986.

52. Witcover, *Marathon,* p. 222.

53. Mike Royko, "Enough! Throw Out N.H. and Its Ego-Trip Primary!" *Boston Globe,* September 20, 1979, p. 17.

54. Editorial: "We're Not So Different," *The Portsmouth Herald,* September 26, 1979, p. 4.

55. Ibid.

56. Charles Brereton, "Yet Another Bad Idea," *The Nashua Telegraph*, March 10, 1986, p. 6.

57. William J. Crotty and John S. Jackson, *Presidential Primaries and Nominations* (Washington, DC: Congressional Quarterly Books, 1985), p. 84.

58. Austin Ranney, Jr., "Turnout and Representation in Presidential Primary Elections," *American Political Science Review*, vol. 66, no. 1 (March 1972): 36.

59. V. O. Key, Jr., *American State Politics: An Introduction* (New York: Knopf, 1956), p. 153.

60. Ibid.

61. Scott Keeter and Clifford Zukin, *Uninformed Choice: The Failure of the New Presidential Nominating System* (New York: Praeger, 1983), pp. 27–28.

62. *Hearings Held Before the Subcommittee on Elections of the Committee on House Administration*, U.S. House of Representatives. Ninety-eighth Congress, Second Session 1984 (Washington, DC: U.S. Government Printing Office, 1984), p. 9.

63. Interview, Secretary of State William Gardner, January 4, 1996.

64. Crotty and Jackson, *Presidential Primaries and Nominations*, p. 84.

65. "Guide to the 1992 Democratic National Convention," *Congressional Quarterly Weekly Report*, Supplement to vol. 50, no.27 (Washington, DC: Congressional Quarterly, 1992), p. 71.

66. Stephen J. Wayne, *The Road to the White House 1992: The Politics of Presidential Elections* (New York: St. Martin's Press, 1992), p. 104.

67. Ibid. Cumulative average figures for 1972–88 were 101,562.

68. 1984 Democratic turnout, *Congressional Quarterly Weekly Report*, vol. 42, no. 27 (July 7, 1984): 169.

69. V. O. Key, Jr., *American State Political Parties and Elections* (New York: Knopf, 1956), p. 47.

70. Michael G. Hagen, "Voter Turnout in Primary Elections" in Peverill Squire, ed., *The Iowa Caucuses and the Presidential Nominating Process* (Boulder, CO: Westview Press, 1989), p. 75.

71. "New Hampshire Poll Backs View of Volatile Mood Among Voters," *New York Times*, March 2, 1980, p. 4.

72. "Poll: NH Voters Most Savvy," *Union Leader*, February 1, 1996, p. A1.

73. Ibid.

74. "Poll: Education Matters," *Concord Monitor*, February 16, 1996, p. A2.

75. Interview, Carl Cameron, WMUR-TV, Manchester, NH, June 23, 1995.

76. Ben Stocking, "Primary: Truisms or False?" *Concord Monitor*, March 9, 1987, p. A5.

77. Internal Transcript, "Interview of the President by WMUR-TV, New Hampshire," Office of the Press Secretary, The White House, Washington, DC, February 7, 1995, p. 1.

78. Interview, Carl Cameron.

79. "Alexander Backs New Hampshire Primary," Press Release, Alexander for President, December 13, 1995.

80. "Dole's Kitchen Magician," *Time*, July 31, 1995, p. 33.

81. "In NH., An 'Invisible' Primary Is Heating Up," *Boston Globe*, February 17, 1995, p. 1.

82. Interview, Curtis Barry, Concord, NH, June 21, 1995.

83. Susan B. Casey, *Hart and Soul: Gary Hart's New Hampshire Odyssey and Beyond* (Concord, NH: NHI Press, 1986), p. 187.

84. "Republicans Pursuing Campaign Foot Soldiers," *New York Times*, July 5, 1995, p. 14.

85. "In NH, An 'Invisible' Primary Is Heating Up," p. 1.

86. "Clinton Plots N.H. Strategy for 1996 Run," *Boston Globe*, January 28, 1995, p. 1/16.

87. "N.H. Attracts Large Field to GOP Kickoff," *Boston Sunday Globe*, February 19, 1995, p. 1/38.

88. "Field Organisation May Tip Scales," *Boston Globe*, February 20, 1996, p. 8.

89. "In NH, An 'Invisible' Primary Is Heating Up," p. 1.

90. "Campaign Workers Go Wherever Action's Hot," *Boston Sunday Globe*, February 18, 1996, p. NH1.

91. *Boston Globe*, February 11, 1992, p. 12.

92. Kahn, "Quick, What Created Jobs," pp. 33–37.

93. "N.H. Attracts Large Field to GOP Kickoff."

3

The Nomination Environment

One ought never to multiply devices uselessly, or employ twenty thousand men to do what a hundred picked men could do much better.
— Jean-Jacques Rousseau, *The Social Contract*

PRESIDENTIAL PRIMARY DEVELOPMENT, 1901–68

The unique contribution of the New Hampshire primary to twentieth-century election politics combines the state's unusual social and political character with a prominent media profile and high degree of accuracy in forecasting outcomes of presidential races. For a clear understanding of its key role in the nomination process, however, New Hampshire must be observed as part of the wider nomination process.

The state's importance to potential presidents has risen since 1916 only because the selection process itself has undergone fundamental change. Primaries have achieved dominance as the most favored method of choosing between candidates. Television has altered the nature of election campaigns and has exerted a profound influence on the strategies of all would-be nominees. Campaign finance reforms have similarly altered the priorities and tactics of candidates. Political parties have undergone revolutions in their structure, their support bases and their leadership selection practices. Some of these alterations took place gradually, almost haphazardly; others came as the result of party-directed reforms. The cumulative effect has been to transform the nomination system from a closed, partisan, elite-driven process to one galvanized by grass-roots activity and media interpretation.

New Hampshire's primary has changed. But the introduction of the presidential preference ballot in 1952 was little more than a response to prevailing trends, while the 1975 first primary law represented a belated recognition of the state's new importance in nomination politics. New Hampshire's rise to political prominence was not self-willed but came as the result of changes to its electoral environment which were beyond its control.

During the late nineteenth and early twentieth centuries, the supremacy of boss politics and the smoke-filled room went virtually unchallenged. Party organizations were tightly constructed and well-marshaled, with political power and patronage vested in party officials from the city machine to the state boss. The selection of presidential nominees during national conventions of the period resembled mass auctions but were driven, usually behind the scenes, by bargains, bribery or threats between competing campaign organizations and the leaders of various state convention delegations. The only serious challenge to this *modus operandi* came from the Progressive movement during the Roosevelt–Wilson era. Progressives regarded traditional partisan politics and electioneering as irretrievably corrupt and unrepresentative. They aimed to effect a redistribution of national wealth and authority by advocating tighter controls on business, greater government regulation of the economy and improvements to the quality of life of the nation's poorest citizens. Progressives disavowed parties as conduits for voter opinion, regarding them as narrowly based and sectional and thus as impediments to democracy. Inevitably, electoral reform and improving the quality of political leadership were seen as essential in realizing the promise of American democracy. Through direct election of senators, nonpartisan elections and statutory regulation of political organizations and campaign financing, the Progressives hoped to "purify the political process and make it more responsive to the people."[1] This goal involved the management of state and city politics, with an emphasis on efficiency rather than on party interest and proposed replacing partisan mayors and accompanying patronage structures with business-like city managers. Voters were to be offered a wider, more direct role in political debate and policy formulation through the introduction of referenda, recalls and initiatives designed to provide direct access to policy-making and to bypass the interpretive, politicizing influence of Republicans and Democrats.

The ramifications of the reform impulse were profound for American politics both in the narrow electoral and wider policy-making spheres. While partisan officeholders may, in certain cases, be corrupt, their prime motivation will normally be the establishment of stable and effective government, even if the underlying intention is merely to strengthen their own patronage-based support. In short, partisan officials are primarily concerned with *ends* and are less scrupulous about the means used to achieve them. As Gerald Pomper and Susan Lederman observe, however, "The participatory advocates certainly hope for good results from democratic government, but their emphasis is at least as much on the means used to accomplish policy ends."[2]

The flawed notion that the quality of political leadership would be improved by the elimination or reduction of backroom dealing prompted reform advocates to press for changes that would broaden both the accountability and electoral legitimacy of political officeholders. The mechanism of the primary election appeared ideally suited to this purpose.

Crotty and Jackson place the first use of a primary election in the 1840s, in Crawford County, Pennsylvania, but the practice assumed more widespread significance in statewide elections during the 1890s.[3] In 1901 Florida became the first state to pass a primary law empowering state parties to elect nominees for any posts up to and including those of national convention delegates. Wisconsin's primary law was passed in 1905 in the aftermath of a disagreement the previous year at the Republican National Convention during which the delegation of Progressive governor Robert LaFollette was challenged and unseated by a caucus-elected delegation from his home state. Triumphantly, LaFollette declared: "No longer will there stand between the voter and the official a political machine with a complicated system of caucuses and conventions by the manipulation of which it thwarts the will of the voter and the rules of official conduct."[4]

The first modern primary law, arranging for delegate selection and provision for expression of voter preference between presidential candidates, was enacted in Oregon in 1910 under the sponsorship of Senator Jonathan Bourne. The law provided for a two-part ballot permitting voters to select between competing candidates as well as competing slates of delegates, each of whom was required to indicate his political loyalty.[5]

The number of presidential primaries grew rapidly during the early twentieth century. New Jersey, California and North Dakota introduced primary legislation in 1911, Maryland and Illinois in 1912. Twelve states had made the adjustment from the party-oriented, elite-directed caucus system to the primary by the end of 1912.[6] Practitioners of the old-style politics expressed concern at the potential disruption to the status quo. Hamiltonian interpretations of American democracy's evolutionary processes warned strongly against the prospect that the presidency should become available to men skilled in "talents for low intrigue and the little arts of popularity."[7] Although political parties had proved themselves more than adept at such arts, producing a string of colorless, figurehead chief executives during the late nineteenth century, they considered Hamilton's counsel a warning against broad public participation in democratic processes and concluded that, as Pomper and Lederman stated, "Since government is a specialized skill, it is madness to entrust it to the general public."[8]

During the early years of the century, and much later during the reform era of the 1960s and 1970s, such arguments were fashionably seen as undemocratic. By the 1980s, however, with the ebbtide of reform flowing strongly, similar arguments were echoed in calls by politicians, journalists and academics for heightened elements of peer review in the nomination process.

Republicans and Democrats received a foretaste of what was to come during the 1912 presidential nomination season, the first in which primaries played a serious role. Attempting to wrest the nomination from his chosen successor, President William Howard Taft, Theodore Roosevelt tried to circumvent Taft's hold on the national Republican convention and state parties by demonstrating his popularity in primary states. He gambled that the public pressure of a series of primary victories would compel the incumbent president to stand aside. Roosevelt won nine of the twelve primaries, but Taft's strength, particularly in southern caucus states, and his control of the Credentials Committee which ruled on questions of contested delegations, assured Taft's ultimate victory.[9]

The use of the primary reached a temporary peak in 1916, by which time Republican primaries numbered twenty and accounted for 58.9 percent of convention delegates.[10] In neither party, however, did primaries play a decisive role in choosing nominees. In 1916 Woodrow Wilson was an unchallenged incumbent, while Republican Charles Evans Hughes entered and won only two primary contests before the GOP convention. In 1920 neither Democrat James Cox nor Republican Warren Harding performed strongly in the preconvention contests. Both men emerged as their party's nominees only after stronger candidates deadlocked in convention. The backroom deal remained the dominant force in American nomination politics. By this time, the primary had lost much of its original appeal. It had not produced candidates with mass popular appeal and had proved time-consuming and often prohibitively expensive. The prospect of unwanted nominees foisted by ignorant voters on reluctant party leaders dimmed its luster still further, while to most party officials the primary represented an open invitation to fratricidal conflict.

Predictably, as the Progressive era gave way to 1920s normalcy, the reform impulse slipped into reverse. In the Democratic party the total percentage of convention delegates selected in primaries dropped from 53.5 percent in 1916 to 35.5 percent by 1924.[11] Presidential nominations remained largely gifts to be bartered and battled for under the podiums and in the backrooms of party conventions. For James Davis, the 1920s and 1930s represented a long retreat from participatory democracy in partisan politics as a nation preoccupied with Depression and world war lost interest in debates concerning the nature and quality of representative democracy.[12] Primaries did not disappear altogether, but eight states had returned to the caucus method by 1935. Other primaries were neutered by laws forbidding the expression of candidate sympathies by potential convention delegates.[13] During this period, presidential primaries served only as isolated indicators of regional voter sentiment. Candidates could utilize the results to make a point to party leaders but no more. Governor Al Smith of New York demonstrated to Democratic leaders in 1928 that a Catholic nominee would not be shunned by the electorate beyond New York. Herbert Hoover used the primary route in the same year to quash the nascent draft-Coolidge movement which threatened to overturn the Commerce secretary's bandwagon.

In 1932 New York governor Franklin D. Roosevelt used the primaries to break free from his erstwhile mentor, Al Smith, defeating him in three of the four contests they fought. These victories were not sufficient, however, to discourage Smith and others from opposing FDR's candidacy at the Democrats' Chicago convention. The nomination was eventually decided through a behind-the-scenes deal with Texan John Garner.[14]

Throughout the New Deal period, the primary system remained relatively insignificant in presidential politics, although in 1944 its negative potential was demonstrated through Wendell Willkie's candidacy in Wisconsin. Four years earlier, Willkie had all but hijacked the Republican nomination despite garnering only 0.7 percent of the primary vote to Thomas Dewey's 49.7 percent. In 1944, with one electoral defeat behind him, Willkie felt constrained to travel the primary route to demonstrate the durability of his appeal. Unwisely, he chose to make a stand in Wisconsin, a state with firm isolationist sentiments where Willkie's internationalism would not gain a sympathetic reception. Douglas MacArthur, not an announced candidate, took 72.6 percent of the state vote to Dewey's 14.9 percent. Willkie came in a distant fourth and his chance of nomination evaporated. This surprise result, with its mortal implications for Willkie, captured media attention and gave added strength to the primary system. A further boost came in 1948 when Harold Stassen, the former boy-governor of Minnesota, performed unexpectedly well against the eventual nominee, Tom Dewey. Viewed as something of an upstart by his political contemporaries, Stassen utilized the primaries as they would be used in later decades—as "the underdog's classic route to power in American politics."[15] The "upstart" planned a string of primary victories that would generate momentum not only in primary states but also, through media publicity, in states where he did not actively campaign. In Wisconsin on April 6, 1948, he upset Dewey, taking 39.4 percent of the vote to the New York governor's 25.2 percent.[16] One week later he triumphed in Nebraska and in Pennsylvania on hurriedly organized write-ins. Stassen failed to win the nomination, damaging his cause by battling Robert Taft in his home state of Ohio and diverting valuable resources from the more important task of beating Dewey in Oregon. Taft took Ohio, whereas Dewey took Oregon and proceeded to capture his party's nomination in Philadelphia on the third ballot.[17]

The point had been made, however. The presidential primary's potential as a vehicle for dark horse contenders had been established, and between 1948 and 1952 states such as Indiana, Montana and Minnesota revived their defunct primaries. Since delegate majorities could not be amassed solely through the primaries in this period, bargaining and compromise at conventions and in state caucuses remained the principal method for securing delegates. This status quo might well have been maintained for decades had the presidential election year of 1952 not witnessed a fortuitous conjunction of man, medium and method in the candidacy of Dwight Eisenhower. In this year, the appearance of television as a viable and effective medium for the transmission of political images coincided with a new stage in the development of presidential primaries and with the rise to political prominence of a personality easily capable of capitalizing on both developments. The year 1952 thus marks a pivotal year in the emergence of the modern campaign process.

The candidacy of General Eisenhower was launched by the New Hampshire primary of March 1952. In this and succeeding primaries, the general's backers demonstrated their candidate's popular appeal to national and state Republican party leaders and to the electorate at large. Eisenhower's victories proved crucial for delegate accumulation and in wresting the nomination from Robert Taft at the convention. The Democrats also experienced the growing primary influence with the victory of Estes Kefauver over President Truman in New Hampshire. By 1956 Adlai Stevenson was campaigning actively in preconvention primaries in open acknowledgment of their influence and despite his status as the front-running contender for the party nomination. While still not decisive, primary votes were now becoming integral to the calculations of candidates seeking to demonstrate their widespread appeal while building up high profiles in the new medium of television. The party machinery remained in overall control of the nomination process, but popular backing was becoming increasingly important. Most state primary ballots during the 1950s contained no presidential preference section, thus still leaving delegates free to move between candidates during the convention. Each state held selection contests under a variety of regulations and provisions, facing presidential aspirants with what Crotty and Jackson describe as "a morass of legislative and administrative requirements," to the point that primaries were still attractive "only to those who had no realistic alternative."[18] The future was clearly written, however. Primaries, with their grass-roots appeal and publicity value, were harder for delegates and bosses to ignore and constricted their freedom to maneuver. The last multi-ballot conventions of both parties took place in 1952.

By the 1960s, the respectability of primaries had risen and stabilized, having become a useful tool of participatory democracy coexisting with elitist political practices within a strongly partisan structure. The new role of television ensured that primaries would have continued to grow steadily in importance, checked always by state variations and elite manipulation. However, sudden and radical changes in presidential campaign politics occurred during the late 1960s. Party-sponsored reforms rapidly accelerated the growth of primaries and altered the dynamics of the entire nomination process. The subsequent rise in the number of primaries was an unintended side-effect of these reforms, but by the mid-1970s, the preeminence of the primary over all other delegate selection contests had been secured. The implications for New Hampshire were to be profound.

OPEN POLITICS: THE SIXTIES AND SEVENTIES

President Lyndon Johnson's embarrassingly narrow victory over Minnesota senator Eugene McCarthy in the New Hampshire primary of March 1968 prepared the way for Johnson's withdrawal from the race and the entry of Vice-President Hubert Humphrey and New York senator Robert Kennedy. While McCarthy and Kennedy engaged in open competition through the primaries, Humphrey chose to amass delegates using the more traditional and predictable mechanism of state caucuses. In these latter competitions, the vice-president could rely more on the help of the still-powerful Johnson and years of contacts and accumulated political IOUs. In 1968 a majority of convention delegates were still selected via this route, with only 40.2 percent chosen in primaries.[19] Humphrey's chances were therefore high while his campaign visibility remained low.[20]

Since Kennedy and McCarthy ran activist-oriented primary campaigns and opposed U.S. policies in Vietnam, both attracted large levels of student volunteer support and grass-roots liberal activists. Both campaigns were ad hoc operations, short on resources and long-term planning. (Kennedy's late entry had already disqualified him from entry in some of the earlier contests of the spring.) Ironically, given the impeccable establishment credentials of their chosen figureheads, the insurgent activists of 1968 abjured traditional partisan politics, regarding its beliefs and practices as outmoded, corrupt and irrelevant to modern societal needs. Like the Progressives before them, though with less ideological coherence, the advocates of the impatient New Politics of 1968 saw their own party leadership as an obstacle to representative democracy in the United States. Less inclined to abandon partisan politics altogether, they still sought to push the political establishment in a new direction, toward a more open and representative system. From the outset, the clash of priorities symbolized what Paul Beck and Frank Sorauf described as the "uneasy relationship" between party regulars and the new democratizers.[21] McCarthy supporters in particular were enraged by arcane regulations and winner-take-all formulas in state primaries and caucuses which frequently left the senator sizable popular vote tallies but few delegates pledged to him. In May 1968 the harassed Democratic party leadership sanctioned the formation of a Commission on the Democratic Selection of Presidential Nominees under the chairmanship of Iowa Governor Harold E. Hughes.

The Hughes Commission's report to the 1968 Chicago Convention was blunt in its attack on existing nomination procedures and in its prescription for reform. Its preamble stated: "This convention is on trial. . . . The crisis of the Democratic party is a genuine crisis for democracy in America and especially for the two-party system."[22]

The report contained calls for the abolition of three of the five existing methods of delegate selection, the implementation of mandatory racial quotas in state convention delegations and abolition of the Unit Rule by which a state could throw its entire delegation behind one particular candidate by simple majority vote. The Rules Commission of the August 1968 convention rejected most of the Hughes recommendations but, as a placatory measure, agreed to the establishment of another commission authorized to review delegate selection procedures. The commission was weighted in favor of the party leadership, whose candidate, Humphrey, had just secured the presidential nomination. It contained, however, representatives from the defunct, disgruntled Kennedy and McCarthy organizations who refused to sign their names to the moderate Majority Report and instead produced a secondary Minority Report, which was also reported out to the convention floor. Convention leaders, busy dealing with the disorders spreading inside and outside the convention hall, paid little attention to the substance of the Minority Report or, as Byron Shafer speculates, may have simply misunderstood its implications and endorsed it as a sop to New Politics contingents. Consequently, it was the Minority Report that was passed on a floor vote at 11.40 P.M. on Tuesday, August 27, 1968. The vote was to have wide-ranging repercussions for electoral politics and the primary system. It was, in Shafer's words, "the 'mandate'—the hunting license really—for the greatest systematic change in presidential nominating procedures in all American history."[23]

On instruction of the Minority Report, a Commission on Party Structure and Delegate Selection was established under the chairmanship of South Dakota senator George McGovern. When McGovern resigned to run for the presidency,

Representative Donald Fraser of Minnesota took the chair. It was to be the first in a long line of reviewing bodies designed to democratize the nomination process. Proposals differed widely in scope and intent, but all reflected a desire to make party elites responsive and accountable to grass-roots cadres. Reformers believed these changes would give the wider electorate greater input into leadership choice and policy formulation and, more importantly, would be more reflective of intrinsic American values, downplaying the importance of peer review and backroom bartering and instilling into nominations a certain mathematical predictability based chiefly on the popular vote. This, of course, suggested a distinctly un-Hamiltonian approach. The Founding Fathers had established the Electoral College in 1787 specifically to avoid a system based entirely on the direct vote of the people. Despite declarations of a return to original intent, reformers were set on devolving the power of selection to groups ill-experienced in wielding it. The New Politics represented a distillation of the old Progressive spirit but proved far more successful since it faced a partisan establishment demoralized by protest and already in the throes of gradual but profound change which, since the 1940s, had weakened the bonds of party allegiance and destabilized its voting base.

The reforms did not cause a new political system to evolve; rather, they re-inforced a trend that was already underway. The power of established party leaders had certainly begun to wane before 1968, particularly when the New Deal reforms of the 1930s undermined the party's traditional social role in urban society. Their central position in the selection system was already being challenged by transient, less strongly partisan groups and by the rise in primary contests. The multi-ballot convention, the characteristic sign of elite bargaining, disappeared a full sixteen years before the McGovern–Fraser Commission began its deliberations. William H. Lucy suggests that another important factor, the restraining influence of opinion polls, primaries and the news media on party officialdom, could be traced as far back as the late 1940s.[24]

The first immediately apparent consequence of commission-inspired reforms was the proliferation of primaries on an unprecedented scale. Arthur Hadley regarded this as the herald of a quiet revolution in American politics, with ramifications stretching far beyond the mere decline of caucus—convention methods of delegate selection.[25] The reform commissions themselves did not make mandatory the transition from caucus to primary contest, and, in all likelihood, the sudden rise in primary numbers would have occurred with or without McGovern–Fraser. The new guidelines accepted the continuing existence of caucus voting as an alternative method but clamped down heavily on other practices. Delegate primaries (by which only individual delegates were selected by state voters) were outlawed, as were Committee selections in which party officials met privately to choose delegates for the convention slate. Caucuses were reformed through abolition of the closed caucus, an event open only to registered Democratic party voters. The commission clearly favored those mechanisms that appeared more open and public in their deliberations—the Candidate Primary (allowing voters to express preference among presidential candidates) and the Participatory Convention (larger meetings open to any interested voters). Lengle and Shafer observed the additional impetus toward a more open and accountable process through new specifications for unseating convention delegations chosen in breach of national party guidelines. Uncertain and more than a little confused by the sudden rush of detailed regulations, many state party officials "responded with what was apparently the surest method of avoiding this threat: they simply threw all aspiring delegates on the ballot."[26]

A further incentive for state leaders to adopt the new rules swiftly were signs that the new activists were proving uncomfortably adept at playing the political games of the old politics. In abandoning their caucus–convention systems and opting for primaries, many state leaders were acting less from a sense of democratic altruism than from a determination to keep the noses of hotheaded activists out of state party business. Since much of that business was conducted at the state conventions in addition to presidential selection, primaries appeared tempting as a way of diverting the attention and energies of grass-roots workers. Nelson Polsby notes, however, that one outcome of this trend was to be a reduction in the ability of state parties to "channel, limit or accommodate group demands."[27] The arrival of the new era was signaled by the expulsion of the Illinois delegation, led by the once all-powerful Chicago mayor Richard Daley, from the 1972 Democratic convention for alleged noncompliance with national selection directives. This was both a moment of sweet revenge for the New Politics activists with bitter memories of 1968 and a portent of the centralization of rules authority to come later in the decade.

A final determining factor in the rising popularity of primaries was their publicity value. The Democratic party's image had been tarnished by association with Vietnam but also by the scenes outside the Chicago Coliseum in August 1968 when demonstrators battled with police, turning Hubert Humphrey's nomination into a bloodbath. Reformers believed that primaries would reduce party divisions by legitimizing the nominee, providing him with a wider and more visible support base, making him more sensitive to the needs of his support coalition and baptizing him with months of free, preconvention publicity. In the political atmosphere of the late 1960s and early 1970s, primaries also carried an explicit rejection of boss politics. Regional hearings of the McGovern–Fraser Commission often ignored the views, sometimes even the presence, of state party officials, relegating them by implication to the role of supervising the bare mechanics of the new voting system. This did not prevent state party leaders from continuing to play important roles in primary campaigns.[28]

A substantial loss of state party influence in the nomination system occured in the 1970s due, in James Ceaser's view, to the new, closely interactive relationship between candidate, media and voter.[29] Crotty and Jackson believe that this development presaged a longer-term, "unintended consequence" by which state leaders and party machines were downgraded to "a position of subservience to the national Democratic Party in regard to presidential nominations."[30] After McGovern–Fraser, the perceived need for a uniform, universally applicable set of nomination rules grew gradually stronger, and the Democratic National Committee (DNC) became increasingly determined to act as overseer and enforcer.

Advocates of the new system were taken aback by the speed and extent of their revolution. Eli Segal, a member of the first reform commission, recalled, "We were always waiting for some people to wake up and say 'Hey, they're stealing our party from us,' and it never happened."[31] Predictably, the crucial shift in emphasis to primary-driven dynamics took place more rapidly and with greater emphasis in the Democratic party than within the GOP since the drive came chiefly from Democratic grass-roots activists. Resultant alterations to state delegate selection laws were normally accepted and adopted by Republicans in states where the GOP did not control the government. The impact of the McGovern–Fraser reforms was therefore widespread and almost immediate. By 1972 a majority of delegates in both parties could be accumulated solely through the primary system.

Tables 3.1 and 3.2 indicate the rapid rise in the number of voters participating in presidential primaries during the height of the reform era and the concomitant increase in proportions of delegates selected in primary contests in the same period.

Table 3.1
Numbers of Voters Participating in Presidential Primaries, 1968–80

Year	Democrats	Republicans
1968	7,535,069	4,473,551
1972	15,993,965	6,188,281
1976	16,052,652	10,341,584
1980	15,143,890	11,139,195

Sources: *Congressional Quarterly Weekly Report.* July 5, 1980, p. 1874; Crotty and Jackson, *Presidential Primaries,* p. 16.

Table 3.2
Rise in Proportions of Delegates Selected by Primary, 1968–80

Year	Democrats	Republicans
1968	1,276 (49%)	601 (45%)
1972	1,977 (66%)	715 (53%)
1976	2,264 (75%)	1,501 (66%)
1980	2,378 (71%)	1,502 (75%)

Source: Adapted from tables in Polsby, *Consequences of Party Reform,* p. 64.

The Mikulski Commission, set up to oversee the new format and recommend further changes for the 1976 cycle, reinforced the dynamics unleashed by McGovern–Fraser with a series of new rules mandating proportionate allocation of delegates among presidential candidates. Shafer notes that the pursuit of mathematical equity had become something of an obsession of the early reform commisions.[32] Both Mikulski and McGovern–Fraser took a dim view of winner-take-all primaries (in which first-placed candidates swept the delegate slates regardless of popular vote margins). Reformers focused on the inequities of delegate distribution between candidates, a problem that dogged both main parties throughout the 1970s. The McCarthy, Reagan and Jackson campaigns complained that the various state formulas had repeatedly shortchanged their campaigns because delegate awards did not match popular vote tallies.

Winner-take-all states, particularly California, were compelled by the DNC to adopt proportionate allocation plans, and the Mikulski report called for the establishment of a 10 percent threshold beyond which all candidates would be entitled to a share of delegates proportionate to their popular vote. Despite objections that such a threshold would rule smaller candidacies out of contention for delegates, thereby constituting a shift away from representative democracy, the move was approved by DNC chairman Robert Strauss. The threshold was eventually raised to 15 percent. In 1980 the Winograd Commission came under pressure, ironically from the Carter White House itself, to raise the threshold again in order to discourage challenges to the incumbent president. Carter wanted the threshold raised to 20 percent in the campaign's second month and to 25 percent thereafter, increasing the likelihood that the front-running candidate would secure early and unstoppable momentum. The Winograd Commission eventually adopted a proposal put forward by South Carolina State party chairman Don Fowler (later to head the post-1984 Fairness Commission) permitting caucus and primary states with at-large delegates (those elected by the entire state rather than by single districts) to set their own thresholds. For districted contests an overall threshold of 25 percent was established. Winner-take-all primaries were banned for the 1980, season but later commissions relaxed the restrictions, permitting states to add extra delegates to the victor's slate on a winner-take-more basis. This rule prevailed in the 1984 and 1988 races, before being banned once again in 1992, with a 15 percent threshold operating once again.[33] The DNC's prevarication over this issue was symptomatic of the vulnerability of successive rules reviews to the whims of powerful candidates such as Carter, Mondale and Jesse Jackson. It also demonstrated the importance that delegate allocation was deemed to have in determining the dynamics of primary momentum. Proportionate allocation, the commission believed, would take the edge off Iowa and New Hampshire by slowing the pace of delegate accumulation and forcing candidates to spread their resources more evenly. The presence of winner-take-all primaries later in the contest was, conversely, seen as essential in persuading candidates not to fold their tents after discouraging early results.

The impact of proportionate delegate allocation proved as important for campaign dynamics as the proliferation of primaries, each change serving to reinforce the other and increase the focus on the Iowa caucus and New Hampshire primary. With delegates to be harvested even from second- or third-place showings, candidates started raising funds, formulating strategy, hiring advisers and making campaign visits at ever earlier dates. Again, such preparations were particularly apparent in early states. Official declarations of candidacy also began to move up. Michael Goldstein detected no fewer than ten candidacies in both Republican and Democratic party races for 1988 whose official announcements preceded June 30, 1987.[34] By the late 1970s, official announcements carried no surprise, being little more than confirmations of the obvious. In advance of the 1988 New Hampshire primary, most Republican and Democratic contenders had fully staffed headquarters in place by mid-1987 and had visited the state at least once. In the 1996 election cycle, active campaigning began still earlier. Emmett Buell records that Lamar Alexander had made five separate visits to Iowa by the end of 1993, the year of President Clinton's inauguration, and another three by June 1994. In New Hampshire, Alexander attended various Town Meetings in November 1993, spoke to students at the University of New Hampshire and returned in 1994 for a meeting of the Durham Board of Education in March, an interview on WMUR-TV in April, swiftly followed by appearances at a Republican Neighborhood Meeting in Bedford and a Lincoln Day dinner in Portsmouth.[35] In the modern era, therefore, active campaigning normally precedes official an-nouncements.

Early starts were not uncommon before the reform era. Although his New Hampshire headquarters were not officially opened until the winter of 1968, Richard Nixon had been campaigning indirectly for the Republican nomination since the 1966 congressional midterms. Similarly, John Kennedy's campaign began intensive planning and preparation soon after the 1958 midterms. What has been noticeable, however, is that pre-reform early starts generally confined themselves to strategy sessions and bridge-building among party officials. Post-1968 candidates must do more spadework because primary proliferation and the news media have effectively widened the size of the constituency any candidate must reach. Longer calendars and proportionate delegate allocations effectively canceled out the possibility that candidates can seize the nomination through a series of planned swoops on selected primaries. Instead, a war of attrition is required, with candidates such as Mondale, Bush or Dukakis adopting "run everywhere" strategies. These require intensive preparation and enormous financial and volunteer resourcing. Potential candidates must begin planning and raising funds immediately after the conclusion of one election cycle if they are to survive beyond the first few contests of the next.

The effect has been to push the window of opportunity for candidates back to the earliest weeks of the nomination contest, giving additional emphasis to the Iowa and New Hampshire battles in particular. Candidates emerging from one or both of these contests, having failed to meet media or self-generated expectations, are unlikely, as a rule, to survive long. Conversely, a strong showing, particularly in New Hampshire, can act as a catalyst for a cycle of rising public recognition and approval, growing volunteer support and increased financial strength. Weaker candidacies, those with low poll ratings and limited funds, are forced to stake everything on these contests—ironically, a final gamble in the opening round of the nomination battle—but strong campaigns must also focus energy and resources on Iowa and the Granite State in order to meet media and self-generated expectations. As the 1984 Mondale and 1996 Dole campaigns discovered, a poor result in these key early battlegrounds disrupts the self-sustaining cycle of publicity and dollars and opens the race to longshot candidates. The prime unintended consequence of reform, therefore, has been the institutionalization of the strategic importance of New Hampshire's primary. Delegate accumulation rules, fund-raising requirements and media benchmarking raised the stakes in the first caucus and first primary to the point at which impressive showings were crucial.

Table 3.3
Candidate Performance in Iowa and New Hampshire Prior to Nomination, 1976–96

Year	Candidate	Iowa	New Hampshire	Nominee
1976	G. R. Ford	1st	1st	Ford
	J. E. Carter	1st	1st	Carter
1980	J. E. Carter	1st	1st	Carter
	R. W. Reagan	2nd	1st	Reagan
1984	R. W. Reagan	1st	1st	Reagan
	W. F. Mondale	1st	2nd	Mondale
1988	G. H. W. Bush	2nd	1st	Bush
	M. S. Dukakis	2nd	1st	Dukakis
1992	G. H. W. Bush	1st	1st	Bush
	W. J. Clinton	2nd	2nd	Clinton
1996	W. J. Clinton	1st	1st	Clinton
	R. J. Dole	1st	2nd	Dole

First- or second-place showing in one or both of the first major tests of voter opinion is now crucial to winning the nomination (Table 3.3). Only Bill Clinton in 1992 succeeded in taking his party's nomination without a first-place showing in either Iowa or New Hampshire (that year's Democratic primary being complicated by the presence on the ballot of Iowa senator Tom Harkin and Massachusetts' former senator Paul Tsongas, both of whom exerted considerable regional pulls on voter loyalties). Clinton aside, no candidates since 1976 have succeeded in taking the nomination without winning one of the two early bird contests.

The reformed system raised New Hampshire's primary to an unprecedented level of influence. Before 1968, when the pace of presidential campaigns was altogether slower and primaries fewer in number, first place held little intrinsic importance. Uncommitted delegates, favorite son candidacies and party leadership influence could all be utilized to filter or divert the trends of popular opinion voiced in the primaries. Once these factors were removed and replaced by television, voters and grass-roots activists, the position of the earliest primary suddenly assumed much greater significance. The rise of New Hampshire now stands, to critics, as a symbol of all that has gone wrong with the brave new primary system.

FIRST IN THE NATION: THE POST-REFORM NEW HAMPSHIRE PRIMARY

The 1952 Eisenhower–Kefauver victories had already marked New Hampshire out as an important campaign arena. As early as 1961, seven years before the McGovern–Fraser Commission began the arduous process of adapting Democratic party nominations to the demands of the television age, Theodore White could remark that the 1960 nomination outcome "hinged on the primaries; and the problem of the primaries focused on the first primary in New Hampshire."[36] Journalist Richard Stout observed of the 1968 Granite State primary: "Of course, the most important fact about New Hampshire politically was that its primary was the first."[37] Its significance, however, was to pale by comparison with the status it claimed after 1968. Before the reforms, the primary had evolved gradually, in response to incremental changes in election politics. After 1968, this pace was forced and quickened.

Post–Mikulski reformers switched the reform focus from the pursuit of mathematical equity to efforts at controlling the unwieldy, momentum-driven system they had created. This switch could be portrayed as a natural second step, pursuing representational fairness through a careful balancing of the timetable. The question of balance, however, carried highly subjective connotations. With the formation of the Winograd Commission in 1976, primary scheduling became a target for candidate organizations seeking to mold the timetable to their political advantage, and post–Mikulski reform bodies soon degenerated into intraparty squabbles between the most influential candidates of the period. Patrick J. Caddell, former pollster to the Carter White House, explained in his testimony before the 1986 House Subcommittee on Elections, "The earlier reform commissions had had to do with opening the process up. . . . In 1978 we crossed the line and they became candidate interest oriented. . . . They all had an agenda for having a process that would nominate someone quickly, someone well-known."[38]

This agenda encouraged the trend toward front-loading, whereby states jumped their primary and caucus dates forward to bring them closer to the media spotlight. Strong candidacies favored the trend as a way of foreclosing the options of dark horse candidacies. State parties saw front-loading as a means of deemphasising

Iowa and New Hampshire. Some denied to any one state the right to head the primary timetable; others simply objected to New Hampshire fulfilling this role. The principal complaint was that saturation media coverage had made the election's early phase decisive, devaluing the perceived importance of later contests. Georgia secretary of state Max Cleland told Congress in 1986, "I think what did concern me was that . . . by the time you got to my section of the country, the battle was either over or you couldn't have a sense of being important."[39]

The result, since 1980, had been a protracted game of timetable leapfrogging. The first southern regional primary, nicknamed Super Tuesday, was held in 1984 on the second Tuesday in March, the early limit set by the Hunt Commission. Five states held primaries on that day, with four others simultaneously initiating caucus–convention procedures. Southern officials believed that candidates more acceptable to southern voters habitually dropped out of the race after New Hampshire, lacking funds and poll support, thus bestowing on the Granite State the job of winnowing the field for the South. By banding together, states such as Alabama and Georgia aimed to offer conservative and moderate Democratic candidates a reason to hang on after a poor New Hampshire showing or even to bypass the Granite State altogether. In 1988 Democratic front-loading increased, with twenty-one states holding delegate selection competitions on the second Tuesday of March.[40] The DNC seemed to encourage this trend, despite serious concern over its potential effect on low-profile, poorly funded candidates. Although no new rules commission was appointed for the 1992 nomination cycle (the first time this had happened since the 1960s), the DNC's Rules and Bylaws Commission moved the delegate selection window from the second to the first Tuesday of March 1992. The effect was to greatly augment the front-loading phenomenon. Thirty-one states held primaries or caucuses before the end of March 1992.[41] The 1996 calendar was even more compressed, creating a regional New England primary through which Bob Dole was able to deliver a mortal blow to the Buchanan challenge in 1996. Dole's campaign was dangerously low on funds, but the speed of the primary process now enabled him to override what might otherwise have been fatal defeats in New Hampshire and Arizona.

The effects of front-loading for New Hampshire and the nomination race as a whole have always been double-edged. Candidates can find their post–Granite State momentum heightened or suffocated by having to move so swiftly to the wider arena. Gary Hart followed his 1984 win with a creditable performance on Super Tuesday, but the superior resources and planning of the Mondale machine enabled the former vice-president to nullify the effect of New Hampshire. In 1988 Michael Dukakis was unable to make his New Hampshire victory decisive and only managed to split the southern bloc more or less equally with rivals Al Gore and Jesse Jackson. New Hampshire did help, however, in establishing the Massachusetts governor's credibility in southern states. Pat Buchanan's first primary triumph in 1996 was countered by losses in the newly relocated primaries of Delaware, South Carolina and Arizona. Conversely, George Bush used New Hampshire to recover from his 1988 shock in Iowa, converting his momentum into decisive victories on Super Tuesday against Bob Dole. Bill Clinton left New Hampshire with three wheels on his wagon in 1992 but moved, drained of funds and supporters, immediately into safer territory in the southern regional contests, while the Harkin, Kerrey and Tsongas campaigns were compelled to fold before or immediately after Super Tuesday. Clearly, Super Tuesday has the potential to nullify, slow or even reverse a New Hampshire-generated trend. Yet it also remains feasible that the primary's "knock-on" influence can be amplified by the close proximity of other states, as Bush and Clinton discovered in 1988 and 1992. Candidate fields vary from election to election. Some will contain candidates particularly well-placed in the South; others will produce candidates with strong constituencies in the Midwest or West. The fate of one candidate is thus inextricably linked to the presence or absence of another. Add to this the continually changing primary calendar, and it becomes clear that nomination dynamics cannot be predicted with any degree of accuracy and that the course of the post–New Hampshire momentum is never a racing certainty.

The dominance of primaries has long been accepted by national and state party officials, although the number of contests has continued to fluctuate. The Democratic party held only twenty-five primaries in 1984, a fall of ten from the previous cycle, but this climbed again to thirty-five in 1992, when two-thirds of Democratic delegates and three-quarters of Republican delegates were selected via primaries.[42] The Democrats' post-1980 Commission on Presidential Nomination (the Hunt Commission) set itself the task of controlling the pace of front-loading and of restoring some lost clout to party officials. Superdelegates were created, comprising national and state party officials automatically admitted to the convention but not formally committed to any candidate. The commission also sought to restore the convention balance between grass-roots activists and elected officials. Representation of the latter group had dropped from 96 percent in 1968 to 44 percent by 1976—the peak of the reform wave. After Hunt, levels rose again, reaching 100 percent by 1988.[43] One in five delegates to the Democrats' 1992 convention in New York were superdelegates.[44] In this way, the commission tried to prevent an early rush of delegates to one candidate by restoring the element of peer review lost during the reform period. It hoped that superdelegates would remain uncommitted through the primaries and act as counterweights to candidate bandwagons at the convention, thus fostering the impression that early successes could not guarantee nomination.

The commission's action finally buried the specter of 1970s amateurism but had no real impact on front-loading. Media fascination with Iowa and New Hampshire could not be overridden by half-measures, and the superdelegate system did nothing to weaken the early states' winnowing powers. Consequently, states wishing to select from a full candidate list had no option but to move their dates closer to New Hampshire's primary. Some sought to bury the Granite State once and for all by going ahead of its primary date, but the Hunt Commission ruled this option out after 1984 by special party exemption. Nevertheless, the lead-up periods to subsequent elections, particularly 1996, became scheduling battlegrounds as each state sought to maximize its own individual or regional influence on the choice of nominee.

The proliferation of primaries encouraged by McGovern–Fraser and Mikulski had left a legacy of discord and instability in the nomination process, threatening the viability of the weak candidacies they were intended to encourage and placing New Hampshire in the spotlight as jealous guardian of a tradition that now appeared unfair and undemocratic. Objections to its status are not, therefore, restricted to complaints about its social, economic and political character but derive mainly from the new significance of first place and the changed nature of the contest that unfolds in its aftermath.

The modern nomination places a premium on early and impressive starts, and political scientists consistently set the preparatory period and early contests apart from the later races. John Kessel defines two distinct stages characterizing the opening rounds of the nomination, covering the period from the congressional midterms to the Iowa and New Hampshire elections. These he labels Early Days and Initial Contests.[45] In emphasizing the distinctive qualities of these phases, Kessel reinforces to some degree Arthur Hadley's Invisible Primary hypothesis. Published shortly before the start of the 1976 election season, Hadley's work identified the activities of the pre-primary stage, from staff-hiring and fund-raising to polling and policy development, as determining factors in the nomination struggle. So important are these preparations, Hadley claimed, that the primaries themselves have become little more than window-dressing. The die is cast before the first polling booth curtain closes. He states emphatically, "Far from being decisive politically, the primaries appear more as a ritual encounter, a symbolic show whose results reinforce a victory already decided."[46]

The invisible primary thesis has come to be regarded as a cornerstone of academic and journalistic interpretation, even if its categorizations and implications have been criticized as oversimplified. Kessel, for example, broadly endorses Hadley but parts company with him over the strategic importance of early contests, pointing out that in closely contested nomination battles, early results and their knock-on effects can be highly unpredictable. Hadley, in fact, does allow for this unpredictability but assigns it a lesser role. Seven tracks are laid down, by which candidate electability can be judged. The fate of presidential candidates depends on their individual progress along each track. The tracks defined are Psychology (of the candidate), Strategy, Staffing, Finance, Media and Constituency. The seventh track is labeled Chance, an eventuality for which Hadley is prepared, albeit reluctantly. "Muskie fell in New Hampshire when he cried. . . . But unless a candidate trips, his arrival at the far bank to receive his ballot-studded crown will be determined by his unnoticed maneuvering to be first in line at the near bank, not by his widely reported leaps from primary to primary."[47]

Hadley was the first to note the importance of long-term preparation for modern candidates, but some inherent assumptions in the theory are open to question. The assertion that the victorious candidate will be the one best prepared in key areas is not a revolutionary notion and could be applied equally to pre-1968 candidates.

The role of chance (in a system where unpredictability was squeezed out of the national conventions, only to reappear in the primary season itself) is also underplayed. It occupies a separate track in Hadley's theory, rather than maintaining integral importance to each of the other six. Muskie's emotional outburst in 1972 may, or may not, have been fatal to his chances of nomination. Similarly, Ronald Reagan's 1976 challenge to President Ford was dogged by strategic errors such as Mel Thomson's outspoken support, the candidate's departure from New Hampshire on the final weekend of campaigning or the decision to name Pennsylvania senator Richard Schweiker as Reagan's potential running-mate. It is difficult to state categorically that one or another, or a combination, of such errors may have cost Reagan victory in Kansas City and harder still to state with certainty that, without them, the Californian would have emerged victorious.

The 1984 Mondale campaign initially appears to support at least part of the theory. Here Mondale's initial preparation, his strong, well-staffed and well-funded organization, withstood the Hart tidal wave that struck after Iowa and New Hampshire. Despite torrents of unfavorable media coverage and mass defections by voters, activists and potential donors, Mondale regained his balance and fought back. Hart's comparatively weak support base fatally undermined his ability to capitalize on New Hampshire. Hadley's theory runs into difficulties thereafter. Mondale's problems may have been solved by a combination of candidate psychology, strategy and heavy financial backing, but it is arguable that perceptions of these elements, and the image of inevitability and complacency they engendered, caused many of the problems in the first place as reporters and voters began casting around for a livelier, more innovative candidate with a better chance of defeating President Reagan in the fall.

The theory might also be faulted for understating the fact that success in the nomination race depends not only on action but also on *reaction*. A front-runner's strength along each track depends to a large extent on the relative weakness of the same track for his challengers and on media responses to these flaws. Had Hart responded effectively to the infamous "Where's the beef?" jibe, Mondale's momentum might not have been so easily regained. Jimmy Carter's 1976 success owed much to strategic errors by Henry Jackson and Morris Udall. Bill Clinton's travails in the early days of 1992 helped Paul Tsongas to win in New Hampshire, but his confrontational approach to the character issue added to Tsongas's limited regional appeal and permitted the Arkansan to reemerge as front-runner. The national media appeared to downplay the significance of the Gennifer Flowers incident, not to mention draft-dodging allegations, an approach that helped spur Clinton's revival but that could not have been foreseen.

In sum, campaign twists and turns can rarely be explained within a single analytical framework without overreliance on retrospective judgment. To assert that the best-prepared candidate will proceed triumphantly toward the nomination, *unless he doesn't*, somewhat dilutes the theory's impact. The Invisible Primary thesis remains strong as a description of the complexity of modern campaigning but unreliable as a guide to ultimate outcomes.[48]

The question remains, what particular set of circumstances combines to confer such apparent significance to the first caucus and primary of election year? Three major causal factors are detectable: (1) the general character of the early nomination campaign; (2) the nature of the dynamics unleashed by the first concrete results of the election year; and (3) the reinforcement and channeling of those dynamics by the news media.

The modern nominating process is characterized by high-intensity planning and campaigning, a wide geographic and demographic focus, a plethora of state and national party regulations and exhaustive media coverage. Voters, should they be inclined to turn out at the polls, must negotiate a path through spot ads and leaflets, through televised debates and media analysis, without the normal guiding reference to party labels. By its very nature, internecine party warfare confuses voters and renders the behavioral tendencies of particular voting groups less predictable in primaries than in general elections. This undoubtedly influences turnout levels in primaries and caucuses, which are always significantly lower than corresponding levels in general elections and produces a voting spectrum that may often be ideologically skewed and unrepresentative of the wider state electorate. As Barbara Norrander indicates, the total average primary turnout for 1988 stood at 24.4 percent, roughly 50 percent of the general election figures.[49] The potentially unrepresentative nature of a primary contest can thus increase the unpredictability of results.

In the first contests, these difficulties multiply in proportion to the number of declared candidates in the field. These, too, have risen substantially in the post-1968 period. James Lengle calculates an average of four presidential contenders in the Democratic party's nomination battles between 1952 and 1968, compared to the twelve candidates active in 1976 and the seven registered in both 1984 and 1988.[50] The Republican candidate field in February 1996, after the withdrawals of Pete Wilson and Arlen Specter and the abortive effort to recruit General Colin Powell, stood at eight.

Crowded candidate fields tend to reduce the ideological gap between contenders except in circumstances in which one candidate clearly stands to the left, right or center of all others. The result is a tendency to overplay differences in policy minutiae, to stress character traits and deficiencies of individual candidates or to develop single-issue themes, such as Richard Gephardt's protectionism in 1988 or Bob Kerrey's national healthcare proposals in 1992. The heavy concentration of conservatives in the 1996 Republican primary led to a welter of differing proposals for reform of the tax system, following the lead of Steve Forbes who built his entire candidacy around the issue. The only significant factor outside this policy discussion were discussions concerning the age of erstwhile front-runner Bob Dole and the alleged extremism and racism of Pat Buchanan and his supporters. In the fluid primary environment, comparatively trivial revelations can assume disproportionate significance. Muskie's crying incident, Ronald Reagan's aggrieved citizen impression, Bill and Hillary Clinton's frank confession of marital problems and the resignation of Buchanan adviser Larry Pratt for alleged membership of a white supremacist organization have all registered in New Hampshire polling data. Since candidate numbers are at their greatest during the period of the first caucus and primary contests, unpredictability at this stage can reach its peak.

The Iowa–New Hampshire period is characterized by a unique set of dynamics, normally grouped together under the umbrella definition of momentum. The search for momentum is the sine qua non of modern nomination politics. All candidates seek to set in motion a series of self-reinforcing advantages that will influence later state races and deliver victory. Since momentum must originate with the first concrete results, it represents one of the keys to the importance of New Hampshire's first-in-the-nation primary.

John Aldrich defines three basic elements of this phenomenon.[51] First, momentum derives strength from theories of probability generated by assessments of the candidate's strengths and weaknesses and the likely impact of each on his chances of success in the nomination race and general election. The failure of Paul Tsongas to capitalize on his 1992 victory in New Hampshire was attributed to the widely perceived weakness of his policy message and comparatively liberal social attitudes beyond his New England base. Media reporting thus confined itself to assessments of voter moods in New Hampshire and did not project Tsongas as a likely nominee. Conversely, the survival of the Clinton campaign can be accredited to general political and media beliefs that the governor would, despite his perceived character flaws, run the strongest campaign against President Bush in the fall, utilizing policies on taxation, crime and deficit reduction which would carry broad geographic appeal. At the earliest stages of the campaign, the news media naturally plays a major role in shaping these criteria since there is very little substantive electoral evidence on hand. Again, as with candidate numbers, probability theories make maximum impact in early contests and magnify their significance to candidates.

Second, momentum will be sustained or lost, according to Aldrich, through the results of caucuses and primaries. Timing becomes a crucial factor here. Henry Jackson's decision to bypass New Hampshire in 1976 was considered a major strategic error that left Carter free to develop momentum from his first two victories. The eventual waning of Hart's 1984 prairie fire was partly accredited to the timetabling of primaries and caucuses directly after New Hampshire in which Mondale could be guaranteed success. These wins helped to cancel out the New Hampshire effect and regain momentum. In the later 1980s and early 1990s, the presence of a large bloc of southern states early in the nomination calendar offered a daunting challenge to some northeastern candidates who might conceivably have grown stronger had the focus switched directly from New Hampshire to other Atlantic or midwestern states. Nomination calendars and candidate fields vary from election to election, making broad generalizations as to the progress of momentum difficult. Nevertheless, a potential bandwagon effect is ever-present, as experienced by Reagan in 1980 and Bush in 1988.

Finally, momentum is created and sustained through the generation of expectations, an activity that again places the news media in a central and powerful position. The electoral successes of Johnson in 1968 and Muskie in 1972 were both translated into defeats through media reports that the second-placed challengers in each New Hampshire contest had outperformed expectations. Predictably, all candidates seek to impose their interpretation of the result on reporters. Bill Clinton, the self-styled "Comeback Kid" of the 1992 New Hampshire Democratic race, largely succeeded in preventing the media from casting him as a two-time loser (in Iowa and New Hampshire), but Pat Buchanan's unwise forecasts in the 1992 Republican race undermined his challenge to President Bush despite Buchanan's strong support. Nomination outcomes are determined by hard delegate counts, but the low delegate yields of Iowa and New Hampshire render moral victories of the McCarthy–McGovern type far more significant in this distinct campaign phase. Inevitable landslides aside, these are the only victories that count in the early days.

The potential effects of post–New Hampshire momentum on the primary–caucus schedule can be gauged from Table 3.4. The results of contests in the spring of 1984 demonstrate the extent to which Gary Hart's campaign, dogged by low funding and poor organization in 1983, was able to capitalize on the senator's unexpected New Hampshire win, while the Mondale campaign, which was initially expected to sweep most of the contests, was reduced to fighting a rearguard action to stem the worst of the damage.

Table 3.4
Democratic Primary and Caucus Results, February–March 1984

Date	State	Contest	Winner
Feb. 20	Iowa	Caucus	Mondale
Feb. 28	New Hampshire	Primary	Hart
Mar. 4	Maine	Caucus	Hart
Mar. 6	Vermont	Primary	Hart
Mar. 10	Wyoming	Caucus	Hart
Mar. 13	Alabama	Primary	Mondale
Mar. 13	Florida	Primary	Hart
Mar. 13	Georgia	Primary	Mondale
Mar. 13	Massachusetts	Primary	Hart
Mar. 13	Rhode Island	Primary	Hart
Mar. 13	Hawaii	Caucus	Mondale
Mar. 13	Nevada	Caucus	Hart
Mar. 13	Oklahoma	Caucus	Hart
Mar. 13	Washington	Caucus	Hart

Source: Congressional Quarterly Weekly Report, vol. 42, no. 17, April 28, 1984, p. 978.

Similar patterns can be detected in the 1976 Democratic and 1980 Republican primaries. After his defeat in New Hampshire and subsequent loss of momentum, one-time front-runner George Bush managed only five more victories (in Massachusetts, Connecticut, Pennsylvania, District of Columbia and Michigan) before succumbing to the inevitability of a Reagan nomination.[52]

Although both Iowa and New Hampshire have the potential to spark powerful bandwagons in support of particular candidates, their effect on later states is by no means predictable. Jimmy Carter's triumphal progress to the 1976 New York Convention was not an uninterrupted string of post–New Hampshire victories. The Georgian captured virtually every contest, primary or first-level caucuses, between New Hampshire on February 24, 1976 and Connecticut's caucuses on May 11. Only the first rounds of caucuses in Wyoming and Hawaii fell to Udall, with Washington's caucuses and the Massachusetts primary falling to Jackson and South Carolina's preliminary caucuses to George Wallace. However, the two-month string of successful results for Carter began to falter in the early summer. Of the ten contests between the Nebraska primary on May 11 and Montana on June 1, Carter was defeated in six states, losing Nebraska, Idaho, Oregon and Montana to Senator Frank Church and Nevada and Maryland to California governor Jerry Brown.[53] Since Carter went on to lose both California and New Jersey before the primary season ended, it appeared that earlier challenges by Church, Brown or another party heavyweight might have called the final convention outcome into question. Other results indicate that victory in Iowa or New Hampshire by no means guarantees nomination—witness Dick Gephardt's and Robert Dole's Iowa successes in 1988 and the wins of Harkin and Tsongas in Iowa and New Hampshire, respectively, in 1992. The claim that either of these contests holds a lock on the nomination is clearly fallacious, but so, too, is the notion that momentum dynamics are irreversible. Momentum is a volatile phenomenon based, as Kessel demonstrates, on interlocking factors. The financial resources of individual campaigns, sudden changes in advertising strategy, staff reorganizations and unexpected setbacks or endorsements all contribute to the success or failure of campaigns, but their impact is race-specific, variable in scope and cannot be set within a stable predictive framework. Aldrich makes the point that, contrary to Hadley's Invisible Primary thesis, momentum can be altered or diverted: "even miniscule variations in early events would have changed the dynamics of most of the recent nomination campaigns. The smallest changes in strategy could have led to very different results. A more efficient get-out-the-vote campaign by Udall's organization in New Hampshire in 1976 . . . might have given him an early win and momentum. It certainly would have slowed, if not stopped, Carter's."[54]

New Hampshire's position at the head of the primary timetable gives it enormous potential to direct the course of the nomination race. Nevertheless, this influence is qualified and limited. As a Granite State campaign can turn Invisible Primary wisdom on its head, so unforeseen events during or after the primary can derail New Hampshire victors. The reforms of the 1970s raised the stakes for the first primary, but their 1980s countereffect, front-loading, may have gone some way to reversing the trend by making it impossible for winners in New Hampshire to capitalize on their newfound momentum.

CAMPAIGN FINANCE REFORM

Since the enactment of the 1971 Federal Election Campaign Act (FECA) and its 1974 amendments, campaign finance reform has reinforced the imperative for candidates to begin early preparations and perform well in early contests. David Price notes that although rising campaign costs and revelations of corruption in fund-raising and allocation were catalysts for the reforms of the 1970s, concern had been voiced for decades over funding and spending practices.[55] Partly in response to abuse of government funds and property during the ill-fated Harding administration, Congress in 1925 passed the Federal Corrupt Practices Act, while, in 1962, President Kennedy sanctioned the establishment of a Commission on Campaign Costs to investigate campaign financing practices and iniquities.[56]

The pressure for serious reform grew in the 1950s as campaign retinues swelled with media advisers, accountants, advertising executives and strategists plotting paths through the primary thicket. Some feared that prohibitive costs, penalizing small candidacies and favoring wealthy, established political figures, could undermine the democratic basis of the electoral system. Massive fund-raising drives by the Nixon reelection campaign and growing concern at the influence of fat-cat donors making large contributions in return for federal favors prompted passage of the Federal Election Campaign Act, which imposed a ceiling on the media expenditures of congressional and presidential campaigns, mandating detailed reports from both on funding and spending activities. Under threat from the Nixon veto, the laws did not take effect until after the 1972 elections and were amended in the aftermath of Watergate to include tougher measures for enforcing limits and a system of public financing available to all candidates reaching a specified fund level. The matching funds were made available for both primary and general elections.

The constitutional validity of these changes was challenged in the Supreme Court by New York senator James Buckley and former Democratic senator Eugene McCarthy. In the 1976 *Buckley v. Valeo* decision, the Burger Court upheld the law requiring public disclosure of candidate income sources and limits on campaign contributions.[57] It struck down, however, spending limits imposed by the 1974 FECA amendments and ruled the Federal Election Commission (FEC) unconstitutional as a body that violated the doctrine of the separation of powers. Critics were skeptical of the Court ruling and unhappy with the distinction made between spending limits (ruled unconstitutional) and contributing limits (deemed constitutional) and accused the Court of inconsistency in ruling spending limits but not contributing limits to constitute a violation of First Amendment protection of free speech.[58] Chief Justice Warren Burger's separate opinion dissented in part from the Court line and criticized the public financing provisions of FECA as "an impermissible intrusion by the Government into the traditionally private political process."[59]

Nonetheless, for candidates accepting matching funds, the expenditure limits remained operative, as did specifications as to how, and in what amounts, money could be raised in individual states. For the New Hampshire primary, this latter provision was to prove significant. Campaign contributions from individual donors were restricted to $1,000 and contributions from Political Action Committees (PACs) to $5,000. Matching funds were available to candidates able to raise a total of $100,000 or more from different contributors, provided that at least $5,000 came from twenty or more states and consisted of individual sums no greater that $250. The evident intention of these provisos was to encourage candidacies to develop a broad electoral appeal rather than those drawing support from one geographical region or narrow demographic base. PAC contributions and party donations would therefore not be matched.[60] Finally, the FECA set expenditure ceilings for each state, to permit smaller, less well-funded candidates a realistic opportunity to compete on equal terms, at least in early primaries and caucuses, with better resourced campaigns. The formula for each state's ceiling is calculated by multiplying the state voting age population by sixteen cents or is set at $200,000, whichever is the higher figure. In either case, the final total is allowed to rise in line with inflation. The 1996 New Hampshire limit was set at $601,200. California's total was $10.9 million.[61]

The indirect effect of the FECA reforms was to increase concentration on early contests in the nomination race, although fund-raising and expenditure guidelines in no way matched the importance attached to each delegate vote by presidential campaigns. Crotty and Jackson indicate that the expansion of the primary system and introduction of proportionate delegate allocation required campaigns to reach larger numbers of voters, over a longer period, using more expensive technology, thus making an early, impressive showing essential.[62] This process was reinforced by the FECA guidelines since the manner and amounts in which money could be raised became subject to strict guidelines. Active fund-raising needed to begin as early as possible in the Invisible Primary period since all donations received after January 1 of the preelection year qualify for matching federal payouts. Anthony Corrado suggests that this imperative carries potential benefits for both small and well-known campaigns. The first matching-fund allocations come in the last weeks before New Hampshire, providing a much-needed boost for longshot contenders aiming to establish their credibility in the first caucus and primary of the nomination race. More established campaigns also benefit since they can "capitalize on their established bases of support and preexisting name recognition to gain a substantial financial advantage over their opponents."[63] The focus on the early contests is thus intensified as the donation–recognition–media–poll rating cycle tightens to squeeze all but the two or three most viable contenders from the race.

An early victory, particularly if accompanied by media reassessments of the victor as a newly discovered potential president, may have, in certain circumstances, dramatic financial implications. Gary Hart's 1984 campaign experienced a surge of financial momentum in the four weeks following his upset New Hampshire win, with individual contributions to his campaign jumping from $342,000 in February 1984 to $3 million in March.[64] Patrick Buchanan's insurgent

1992 campaign garnered an extra $1 million in donations between his strong New Hampshire showing and the Georgia primary two weeks later.[65]

Uniform spending limits have not proved effective in regulating candidate spending. The notion of an equal playing field for all contenders in the early states is largely fictitious in a financial sense as overspending in New Hampshire and Iowa has become a regular occurrence. Established names such as George Bush, Bob Dole or Bill Clinton often spend up to or over the limit in New Hampshire but do not need to do so simply to gain name recognition. Neither the overspending nor the resultant FEC fines threaten impoverishment of their campaigns, as backup resources are easily available. Smaller candidacies, however, require greater expenditure boosts when going for broke in the early states since their recognition and support levels are proportionately lower. Even this high-risk strategy may not provide the vital breakthrough in poll ratings. Theoretically, therefore, the FECA limits may harm small candidacies more than they help. Candidate budgets have long been designed to accommodate major outlays in early races. Many campaigns ritually break through expenditure ceilings in New Hampshire but try to evade FEC censure and fines by entering Granite State expenses onto the campaign budgets of neighboring states. Stephen Wayne describes how campaign workers in the 1980s "commute to Iowa and New Hampshire from neighboring states, eating, sleeping and renting cars from outside these states whenever possible."[66]

Just prior to the 1992 campaign cycle, the FEC relaxed some regulations relating to state expenditures, having become frustrated at the constant need to monitor the creative accounting techniques of campaign financial advisers. Boston television stations reach audiences not only in the Bay State but also into homes across New Hampshire's southern tier. The FEC therefore permits 85 percent of paid media on those stations to be charged against the Massachusetts limit, enabling campaigns to transmit a large number of New Hampshire primary ads into the Granite State without counting them against New Hampshire spending ceilings.[67] This loophole can also be used for radio ads, out-of-state telephone banks, polling operations and state office overhead. In 1996 such provisions were invaluable since the Junior Tuesday regional New England primary followed close on New Hampshire's heels, giving candidates added value for money. A careful calculation must be made, however, in deciding which television stations to target. WBZ (Channel 4), a CBS affiliate, serves mainly Boston but also reaches into southern New Hampshire. It must be considered in any Granite State ad blitz since candidates can reach New Hampshire *and* regional voters while dodging New Hampshire spending limits.[68] At the same time, WMUR, Channel 9, targets solely New Hampshire voters. Serious candidates cannot afford to neglect it, but its costs count against the state limit.[69] Relaxation of FEC rules allowed candidates in 1996 to count campaign salaries, travel costs, and candidate accommodation against the national rather than the state spending limits.

Some candidates have also turned increasingly to Political Action Committees to help them offset heavy spending in early races, enabling them to capitalize on their early financial advantage despite FECA limits. The *Buckley* decision opened the doors for an escalation of PAC activity from the late 1970s, confirming widespread fears that spending limits would ultimately prove too difficult to enforce. Independent campaign expenditure leapt by over $1.5 million between 1976 and 1980, bringing Hadley's financial track further into question since candidate performance could now be significantly influenced by outside expenditure and advertising not credited to and theoretically independent of the official campaign. Alexander reported that the Fund for a Conservative Majority rescued the Reagan 1980 campaign in New Hampshire after it prematurely hit the $294,400 spending ceiling by spending $60,000 of its own money. Later contributions, particularly in Texas, the adopted home state of Reagan's closest rival George Bush, pushed the Fund's total contribution to $600,000 by the opening day of the Detroit Convention.[70] Between 1985 and 1988, PACs made direct contributions of $860,297 to the Bush presidential campaign, and an estimated $10,795,937 could be added in independent expenditure.[71] Corrado suggests, however, that PAC contributions to presidential campaigns are overestimated since many PACs prefer to target congressional races, while the lack of matching funds leads many potential nominees to eschew PAC support altogether as a public gesture of political cleanliness. All 1992 Democratic contenders, with the exceptions of Bob Kerrey and Tom Harkin, refused PAC money.[72]

This rule has not generally applied to the creation of precandidacy PACs— vehicles for raising and spending money well in advance of the moment when a candidate publicly declares his availability for the presidency and triggers the FECA limits. Such organizations have been used since the late 1970s to enable potential candidates to organize voter lists, recruit workers and raise money without the resultant donations being registered against state spending limits. Walter Mondale, John Glenn and Ernest Hollings all used precandidacy PACs as a way of generating, and paying for, campaign activity in the invisible primary phase of the 1984 cycle.[73] In advance of the 1996 cycle, Bob Dole, Phil Gramm and Lamar Alexander had established, respectively, Campaign America, Leadership for America and Republican Fund for the 90s as front-organizations for their embryonic 1996 campaigns. Such PACs can prove vital, as George Bush's Fund for America's Future demonstrated in the run-up to the 1988 New Hampshire primary. The Fund targeted supporters, allocated money and created a comprehensive network of volunteer activists through social fund-raisers in the period 1985–87, giving the vice-president an enormous advantage to add to the already-acquired support of Governor John Sununu's influential state organization. The Fund provided ample speechmaking opportunities for Bush and contributed to some local and congressional races while offsetting the costs of pre-New Hampshire operations such as the 1986 Michigan caucuses.[74] Precandidacy operations can be advantageous in shaping the policy agenda of the nomination cycle, raising funds, collaring activists, increasing candidate name-recognition and cultivating political contacts and IOUs without overexposure of the future candidate himself. By 1988 more than $25 million had been generated and spent by pre-declaration candidate PACs, none of it included in FEC expenditure estimates.[75]

Under such pressures, both established and longshot candidates will stake far more on New Hampshire than on later primaries, but whereas established campaigns can afford to wage simultaneous operations in the Granite State and the upcoming Super Tuesday races, smaller ones must stake everything on the gamble that the Iowa–New Hampshire phase will generate publicity and dollars for later contests. This latter tactic does not often prove effective. Sudden injections of extra income cannot necessarily offset months of painstaking advertising, canvassing and polling carried out by well-funded rivals, particularly when mass-mailing outside the FEC's twenty-eight-day window do not count against state limits. Nor is it likely to provide enough cash to cover the escalating costs of television advertising and computerized mail. An unintended consequence has been to aggravate the effects of front-loading. The disproportionate perceptions of the Iowa–New Hampshire influence were detectable, from the late 1970s onward, not merely in column-inch media coverage but also in the comparative amounts spent by candidates per voter in early and later states. In 1992 the potential ceiling for candidate spending was eighteen times higher in California than in New Hampshire, yet, as Alexander notes, the total amounts of money spent by each candidate in early contests were out of all proportion to the delegate influence of the contests.[76] As early as 1980, Democratic contenders President Jimmy Carter and Senator Edward Kennedy spent 101 percent and 90 percent, respectively, of their Iowa budgets.[77] This averaged out to $13.89 per voter. For New Hampshire the trend was similar, with the Carter camp spending 97 percent and Kennedy 90 percent of the state allocation. Each Granite State voter cost the contenders $8.90. Later contests, however, showed a marked diminution in candidate investment as the pattern for the contest became firmly established. The president spent only 39 percent of his New York budget and a mere 5 percent of his California funds, with Kennedy falling further behind with 16 percent and 8 percent, respectively. California voters cost the candidates only 23 cents a head, even though its total budget per candidate ($3,880,192) outstripped New Hampshire's by $3.5 million.[78] Eight years later, Republican candidates for the 1988 cycle were more or less reproducing these disparities. The Bush campaign spent $481,300 in New Hampshire compared to $254,000 in New York and $30,000 in California.[79] An important caveat to this trend lies in the nature of each individual nomination cycle. When the New Hampshire result is considered more or less conclusive in confirming predetermined trends, later states will find the candidate field diminished and the attentions of the front-runner similarly lessened. If active competition persists beyond the Granite State and Super Tuesday, later states play a larger role and force greater financial outlays. The declining expenditure of the Bush campaign can be attributed to the rapid dissolution of his opponents after Super Tuesday in 1988. California's primary thus represented little more than a final, precoronation display of popularity and cost comparatively little. By contrast, the Democratic race in 1988 was more closely fought, and expenditure figures for the Dukakis and Jackson campaigns show proportionate increases in expenditure in many states after New Hampshire. The Massachusetts governor spent nearly $439,000 in New Hampshire, $937,000 in New York and $489,000 in California. The Jackson totals ranged from $73,000 in New Hampshire to $664,000 in California.[80]

Such imbalances exacerbated the deep resentment felt by late primary states over disproportionate media coverage and eventually started a scheduling stampede-in-reverse. So closely spaced are the primaries and caucuses on the 1990s primary racetrack that the starting gun can easily fire a hole through the finishing tape. The effect, in financial terms, can be double-edged. Well-resourced candidacies may use the opportunity afforded by Iowa and New Hampshire to confirm their front-runner status and deliver knock-out blows to the campaign coffers of their opponents. Conversely, underfinanced operations may find the contests so closely spaced that there is no time to reap the reward of an unexpected early victory. The 1988 cycle saw no fewer than twenty primaries held between February 16 and March 10, but Robert Dole was unable to convert his Iowa victory into a tangible cash reward before being overwhelmed by the Bush juggernaut on Super Tuesday.[81] Front-loading has narrowed the response time for donors, leaving candidates dependent on a post–New Hampshire cash surge less likely to experience one before the next round of contests. As Clyde Wilcox indicates, Richard Gephardt's victory in the 1988 Iowa caucuses prompted him to borrow heavily for New Hampshire but he gained no Hart-style surge in individual donations before Super Tuesday compelled him to suspend his candidacy. Wilcox suggests that the close proximity of the southern bloc to New Hampshire on the 1988 schedules was decisive, while not discounting the possibility that Gephardt's loss in the Granite State to Michael Dukakis was a more important factor.[82] Corrado states that a similar misfortune befell Paul Tsongas in 1992, with South Dakota's primary following too quickly after New Hampshire's to enable him to experience a donation windfall.[83] Again, however, the weakness of Tsongas's appeal beyond his New England base may have rendered this problem largely irrelevant. The potential for an Iowa or a New Hampshire success to confirm front-runners or encourage longshots remains strong enough to reinforce their image as winnowing contests that quickly determine which candidacies will survive and which will be swiftly annihilated. William Mayer notes that, in the 1992 Democratic race, three of five candidates had dropped out within thirty days of the New Hampshire primary and that "by and large, it is money that provides the immediate explanation."[84] If current trends persist, however, this financial winnowing may itself preempt New Hampshire's traditional role.

The 1996 GOP race, with roughly 60 percent of delegates chosen by the end of March, created a brutal financial and political climate in which three major contenders, California governor Pete Wilson, Pennsylvania senator Arlen Specter and Texas senator Phil Gramm, dropped out of the race before the first ballot in Dixville Notch had been cast. All three recognized that escalating costs and a compressed timespan meant that significant poll ratings and financial momentum needed to be in place before rather than as a result of Iowa and New Hampshire. No Carter-style bandwagon was feasible. This harsh reality meant that the 1996 GOP field in New Hampshire had itself already been winnowed. The problems for candidates remaining in the race were no less severe. The Alexander campaign experienced a classic surge of momentum heading out from Iowa but ran into serious financial difficulties in New Hampshire and the contests immediately afterward. The tightened schedule left campaign fund-raisers little time to raise, let alone allocate, the added expenditure needed after the former governor's unexpectedly strong performance in Iowa. The calendar also created problems for the Dole campaign which, after New Hampshire, had already spent roughly $30 million of the $37 million limit. Staff and advertising expenditures in the first contests had been high due to the overconfident Dole campaign's determination to lock the nomination up as swiftly as possible. The self-financed media blitz of Steve Forbes, who did not apply for matching funds and therefore was unconstrained by state or national spending limits, stepped up pressure on the Dole camp, which felt obliged to respond to the Forbes attack ads. The Senate majority leader's narrow win in Iowa and narrow loss in New Hampshire left the campaign starved of momentum and temporarily short of cash with the bulk of primary and caucus battles still ahead.[85] Dole's ultimate victory after the March 1996 regional primaries was probably due less to financial superiority than to the GOP's concern at the prospect of a Buchanan nomination.

CONCLUSION

The nomination and delegate selection reforms undertaken by the Democratic party and, in most instances, imposed on the Republicans during the 1960s and 1970s had been intended to improve the quality of leadership and representation in American national politics. This impulse to deliver the power of candidate selection from party officialdom into the hands of the primary electorate was successful but carried a number of unforeseen and unintended consequences, all of which complicated the nomination environment and many of which contributed to the rapid rise in status and influence of the New Hampshire primary. The weakening of party leadership cliques had the intended effect of opening up the system to activists and voters from all walks of life. Its unintended side-effect was to destabilize the Democratic party by flooding its leadership contests with inexperienced delegates and single-issue or candidate-centered activists. Proportionate delegate allocation rendered contests fairer but simply added to already overwhelming pressures for ever-earlier campaign starts and early primary successes, without which the long haul toward a delegate majority would be impossible to sustain. The reformers achieved their purpose in making presidential primaries the single most widespread and acceptable vehicle for nomination but only at the cost of creating a powerful new dynamic: media-sustained momentum.

Primaries relied far more than the more closed caucus system on journalistic interpretation to spread their message, thereby raising the importance of candidate-oriented media strategies and lowering the ability of the party apparatus to counter the progress of a popular but unelectable nominee. The combined effect was to enhance the role of early nomination contests. The New Hampshire primary, already an established tradition for both parties, mutated under these conditions from a useful test of public sentiment to a crucial battleground. The FECA reforms of 1971 and 1974 were intended to create a more level playing field for candidates and to squeeze out the influence of fat-cat donors. Yet FECA has unintentionally added to the stress now placed on the crucial early stages of the nomination cycle by forcing candidates to begin ever-earlier fund-raising drives and to seek early successes in Iowa or New Hampshire to sustain their campaigns. In its turn, the FECA rules help to create a brutal campaign environment in which increasing numbers of candidates withdraw before New Hampshire, aware that the locked-in dynamics of polling and expenditure make their bid for the White House impractical.

The window of opportunity for presidential hopefuls in the nineteenth and early twentieth century stretched to the convention balloting itself. Candidates such as Blaine and McKinley were able to massage support slowly and surely in the preconvention period. Others, like Harding, could meet with little success in the late spring primaries but emerged triumphant in the convention balloting. The growth of primaries drew this window back as conventions never progressed beyond the first ballot and nominations were decided in the late spring. After the 1970s, the very first contests of the nomination year became crucial and the early spring decisive. The front-loading trend and the financial realities of the compressed calendar now offer the prospect of candidacies dead in the water before the election year has even begun. These conditions make it increasingly difficult for the New Hampshire primary to fulfill its self-proclaimed role as the preserver of underdogs and winnower of the field, and candidates face debilitating problems in deciding on strategy. Low-funded candidates may survive and prosper in the Granite State, but this success drains their operations in other states of much-needed cash and leaves little time for regrouping and reallocation of resources. Neither a third-placed Alexander nor a first-placed Hart can repeat the Carter phenomenon of 1976. The insurgencies are smothered at birth by the punishing schedule. Wealthier campaigns, able to outspend rivals in New Hampshire, may also pay a heavy price. The imperative of early, decisive victory encourages enormous outlays on polling, staffing and advertising, but a narrower-than-anticipated margin of victory will fail to eliminate other contenders and will leave resources depleted heading into Junior and Super Tuesday. The contraction of the window of opportunity has been steady but sure since the 1960s. By the end of the twentieth century, it has created fundamental problems for all candidates. An unstable, iniquitous system eliminates what would once have been viable candidacies, discourages others from entering the race at all and encourages interstate and intraparty squabbling. New Hampshire's primary has been elevated from a useful practice ground to a key indicator and then to a crucial contest, but the systemic factors influencing its rise could also now diminish its importance.

The 1992 elections, when New Hampshire failed to live up to its reputation for choosing presidents, may signify that high-cost campaigning and high-pressure timetables are slowly but surely nullifying the importance of early contests, weakening their winnowing role and reducing their ability to help struggling campaigns. Without fundamental change, which must include concerted action by both national parties to stabilize and spread out primary dates, there is a real possibility that the first-in-the-nation primary as a determinative contest will not survive long into the twenty-first century.

NOTES

1. J. A. Thompson, *Progressivism*, British Association of American Studies Pamphlet Series, no. 2 (Durham: 1979), p. 5.

2. Gerald M. Pomper and Susan S. Lederman, *Elections in America*, 2nd ed. (New York: Longman, 1980), p. 25.

3. William J. Crotty and John S. Jackson, *Presidential Primaries and Nominations* (Washington, DC: Congressional Quarterly Books, 1985), pp. 13–14.

4. Austin Ranney, *Curing the Mischiefs of Faction* (Berkeley: University of California Press, 1975), p. 124.

5. *Presidential Elections Since 1789*, 4th ed. (Washington, DC: Congressional Quarterly, 1987), p. 7.

6. Ibid.

7. Clinton Rossiter, ed., *The Federalist Papers* (New York: New American Library, 1961), p. 414.

8. Pomper and Lederman, *Elections in America*, pp. 15–19.

9. *Presidential Elections Since 1789*, pp. 7–8. TR's success in the 1916 Republican primaries and his subsequent bolt from the GOP convention split the party badly, permitting Woodrow Wilson a second term in the White House and reinforcing the already dim view taken of primaries by national party leaders.

10. Crotty and Jackson, *Presidential Primaries*, p. 16.

11. Ibid.

12. James W. Davis, *Presidential Primaries: The Road to the White House* (Westport, CT: Greenwood Press, 1980), p. 28.

13. *Presidential Elections Since 1789*, p. 9 and James W. Ceaser, *Reforming the Reforms: A Critical Analysis of the Presidential Selection Process* (Cambridge, MA: Ballinger Publishing Co., 1982), p. 24.

14. For a detailed and colorful account of behind-the-scenes maneuvering during the first nomination of Franklin D. Roosevelt, see Richard Oulahan, *The Man Who . . . The Story of the Democratic National Convention of 1932* (New York: Dial Press, 1971).

15. Theodore White, *The Making of the President 1972* (New York: Atheneum, 1973), p. 91.

16. *Presidential Elections Since 1789*, p. 32.

17. Ibid.

18. Crotty and Jackson, *Presidential Primaries*, pp. 17–18.

19. Ibid., p. 16.

20. The most compelling account of the 1968 presidential election cycle is to be found in Lewis Chester, Godfrey Hodgson and Bruce Page, *An American Melodrama: The Presidential Campaign of 1968* (London: Andre Deutsch, 1969).

21. Paul Allen Beck and Frank J. Sorauf, *Party Politics in America* (New York: HarperCollins, 1992), p. 260.

22. Byron Shafer, *Quiet Revolution: The Struggle for the Democratic Party and the Shaping of Post-Reform Politics* (New York: Russell Sage, 1983), p. 25.

23. Ibid., p. 28.

24. William H. Lucy, "Polls, Primaries and Presidential Nominations," *Journal of Politics*, no. 33 (1973): 830–48.

25. Arthur T. Hadley, *The Invisible Primary* (Englewood Cliffs, NJ: Prentice-Hall, 1976), p. 66.

26. James Lengle and Byron Shafer, "Primary Rules, Political Power and Social Change," *American Political Science Review*, no. 70 (March 1976): 25–40.

27. Nelson W. Polsby, *Consequences of Party Reform* (London: Oxford University Press, 1983), p. 139.

28. Ibid., p. 73.

29. Ceaser, *Reforming the Reforms*, p. 8.

30. Crotty and Jackson, *Presidential Primaries*, p. 61.

31. Shafer, *Quiet Revolution*, p. 393.

32. Ibid., p. 127.

33. Beck and Sorauf, *Party Politics*, p. 24.

34. Michael L. Goldstein, *Guide to the 1992 Presidential Election* (Washington, DC: Congressional Quarterly, 1991), Table 2-2, p. 23.

35. Emmett H. Buell, Jr., "The Invisible Primary," in William G. Mayer, ed., *In Pursuit of the White House: How We Choose Our Presidential Nominees* (Chatham, NJ: Chatham House, 1996), pp. 5–6.

36. Theodore White, *The Making of the President 1960* (New York: Atheneum, 1961), p. 36.

37. Richard Stout, *People* (New York: Harper & Row, 1970), p. 57.

38. Testimony of Patrick J. Caddell, *Hearings Held Before the Subcommittee on Elections of the Committee on House Administration*, U.S. House of Representatives, Ninety-ninth Congress, Second Session, March 20, May 8, 1986 (Washington, DC, U.S. Government Printing Office, 1986), p. 108.

39. Testimony of Secretary of State Max Cleland, *1986 Hearings*, p. 66.

40. Beck and Sorauf, *Party Politics*, p. 268.

41. Paul R. Abramson, John H. Aldrich and David W. Rohde, *Change and Continuity in the 1988 Elections* (Washington, DC: Congressional Quarterly Press, 1990), p. 24.

42. Beck and Sorauf, *Party Politics*, p. 258, Table 10.1 "The Use of Presidential Primaries 1968-88" and Abramson, Aldrich and Rohde, *Change and Continuity*, p. 22.

43. Stephen J. Wayne, *The Road to the White House 1992: The Politics of Presidential Elections* (New York: St. Martin's Press, 1992), p. 109.

44. Abramson, Aldrich and Rohde, *Continuity and Change*, p. 23.

45. John H. Kessel, *Presidential Campaign Politics: Coalition Strategies and Citizen Response* (Chicago: Dorsey Press, 1984), pp. 5–7.

46. Hadley, *The Invisible Primary*, p. 2.

47. Ibid., p. 23.

48. Emmett H. Buell offers a detailed and intriguing commentary on the predictive successes and failures of Hadley's Invisible Primary tracks after 1976, referring to the thesis as "erratic, often mistaken but frequently insightful." E. H. Buell in William G. Mayer, ed., *In Pursuit of the White House*, pp. 1–43. Provisional 1996 schedules are listed on pp. 8–10.

49. Barbara Norrander, "The Best-Laid Plans . . .: Super Tuesday in 1988," in Emmett H. Buell, Jr., and Lee Sigelman, eds., *Nominating the President* (Knoxville: University of Tennessee Press, 1991), p. 74.

50. James Lengle, *Representation and Presidential Primaries: The Democratic Party in the Post-Reform Era* (Westport, CT: Greenwood Press, 1981), p. 83.

51. John H. Aldrich, *Before the Convention: Strategies and Choices in Presidential Nomination Politics* (Chicago: University of Chicago Press, 1980).

52. *Congressional Quarterly Weekly Report*, July 5, 1980, pp. 1870–71.

53. *Congressinal Quarterly Weekly Report*, vol. 34, no. 28 (July 10, 1976), pp. 1806-7.

54. Aldrich, *Before the Convention*, p. 117.

55. David Price, *Bringing Back the Parties* (Washington, DC: Congressional Quarterly, 1984), p. 239.

56. Ibid.

57. For an analysis of the *Buckley* decision, see Daniel D. Polsby, "*Buckley v. Valeo*: The Special Nature of Political Speech," *The Supreme Court Review*, 1976 (Chicago: University of Chicago Press, 1977), pp. 1–43.

58. *Congressional Quarterly Weekly Report*, February 7, 1976, pp. 267–69.

59. Ibid.

60. Price, *Bringing Back the Parties*, pp. 241–42.

61. "Spending Limits Are Circumvented," *Concord Monitor*, Concord, NH, December 1, 1995, p. A3.

62. Crotty and Jackson, *Presidential Primaries*, p. 183.

63. Anthony Corrado, "The Changing Environment of Presidential Campaign Finance," in William G. Mayer, ed., *In Pursuit of the White House*, p. 236.

64. Herbert Alexander, "Making Sense About Dollars in the 1980 Presidential Campaigns," in Michael J. Malbin, ed., *Money and Politics in the United States: Financing Elections in the 1980s* (Chatham, NJ: Chatham House, 1984), p. 16.

65. Corrado, in Mayer, ed., *In Pursuit of the White House*, p. 238.

66. Wayne, *Road to the White House*, p. 46.

67. Clyde Wilcox, "Financing the 1988 Prenomination Campaigns," in Buell and Sigelman, eds., *Nominating the President*, p. 101.

68. Corrado, in Mayer, ed., *In Pursuit of the White House*, p. 240.

69. *Concord Monitor*, December 1, 1995, p. 3.

70. Alexander, in Malbin, ed., *Money and Politics in the United States*, p. 15.

71. William G. Mayer, "Forecasting Presidential Nominations," in Mayer, ed., *In Pursuit of the White House*, p. 58.

72. Corrado, in Mayer, ed., *In Pursuit of the White House*, p. 226.

73. Wilcox, in Buell and Sigelman, eds., *Nominating the President*, p. 115.

74. Ibid.

75. Corrado, in Mayer, ed., *In Pursuit of the White House*, p. 241.

76. Alexander, in Malbin, ed., *Money and Politics in the United States*, p. 15.

77. Average estimates taken from *Congressional Quarterly Weekly Report*, vol. 41, no. 49 (December 10, 1983), p. 2607.

78. Federal Election Commission, *Report on Financial Activity 1979–80. Final Report* (Washington, DC: 1981), p. 34.

79. Wilcox, in Buell and Sigelman, eds., *Nominating the President*, p. 110.

80. Ibid., p. 108.

81. Corrado, in Mayer, ed., *In Pursuit of the White House*, pp. 237–38.

82. Wilcox, in Buell and Sigelman, eds., *Nominating the President*, p. 116.

83. Corrado, in Mayer, ed., *In Pursuit of the White House*, p. 238.

84. William G. Mayer, "Forecasting Presidential Nominations," in Mayer, ed., *In Pursuit of the White House*, p. 58.

85. "Campaign Coffers Run Low for Dole," *The Times*, London, February 26, 1996, p. 11.

4

Interpretation Games: The News Media in New Hampshire

Good evening America. Here we are in the Granite State. . . . Don't we look quaint?
— Natham Cobb, "Reporting for Duty," *The Boston Globe*, February 27, 1984, p. 10

PACK JOURNALISM AND THE EXPECTATIONS GAME

The tense coexistence between candidate organizations, elected officials and what can loosely be termed the media establishment has long been an accepted fact of American political life. Modern campaigns for elective office are structured around minutely detailed strategies drawn up by teams of advisers who work ceaselessly to shape public perceptions of their champion, his or her challengers and the relative importance or irrelevance of the issues and arenas in which they fight. At one and the same time, media tacticians seek to impress on reporters the strengths and agendas of their candidate, attempt to feed them favorable news items or to offer carefully staged campaign events, while complaining bitterly of bias and pack journalism when subsequent interpretations do not break their way. As F. Christopher Arterton notes, an "irreconcilable conflict" exists between the worlds of the journalist and the politician.[1]

This conflict, of course, predates the reformed presidential nominating process. President John Adams declared, toward the end of his turbulent eighteenth-century administration, that the question of press regulation was the most difficult and portentous issue confronting the nation, noting that "Mankind cannot now be governed without it, nor at present with it."[2] This jaundiced view of political journalism continued through the era of the muckrakers and the rise of yellow journalism and entered on open conflict during the late 1960s over press reporting of the war in Southeast Asia. By 1970, Vice-President Spiro Agnew was openly attributing a perceived decline in American societal values and behavior to liberal cynicism transmitted through the organs of a mainly liberal media. In Des Moines, Iowa, on November 13, 1970, Agnew lashed out at "the unelected elite" who were gathering "more and more power over public opinion in fewer and fewer hands."[3]

The clash between politicians and journalists is exacerbated by schizophrenic divisions within the media establishment itself as it veers unsteadily between broad policy analysis and the far more appealing allure of trivial campaign events. Presidential elections tend only to intensify this dilemma since they constitute both a referendum on policy and a choice between two personalized images as putative national symbols. During the nineteenth century, the supremacy of party bosses and the strength of urban party machines served to suppress this division since elections could be fought on a more or less regional basis, with messages and policies altered and honed to suit the requirements and priorities of the audience. From the 1930s onward, the gradual diminution in the influence of national parties, combined with the growth of government relief and welfare operations and the rise of television, have served to elevate the importance of the news media as a conduit for the exchange of political views and information at the expense of the party organs that once performed this function. New bureaucracies that flourished during and after the New Deal period contributed to an undermining of traditional quid pro quo relationships between party machines and precinct voters. Television hastened this process by presenting voters with more vivid, more detailed and less partisan information than they had been accustomed to receiving via local newspapers.

The implications of this change in media importance for the opinion-forming process have been dire. The fundamental purpose underlying the national political parties was to construct coalitions and establish a sufficiently broad consensus of public opinion to support an electoral majority. The press has no need to follow such imperatives. Reporters have become increasingly hostile and cynical in their approach to the coverage of politics. Some of this cynicism was transmitted to the electorate through a proliferation of campaign biographies such as Hunter Thompson's *Fear and Loathing on the Campaign Trail* and Jules Witcover's exhaustive, *Marathon*.[4] These fly-on-the-wall accounts, varying in style and focus, further stripped away the facade of electoral politics, revealing, to those who had not already experienced it firsthand, the sometimes subtle, sometimes brutal wars of manipulation, calculation and smear that constituted the modern candidate–reporter relationship. The twin public relations disasters of Vietnam and Watergate, of course, sent this process into overdrive. Revelations of the pathological hatreds simmering in the Nixon White House toward the media in general and certain disloyal reporters in particular provoked a reflex reaction. The damaged but still evident reverence with which many journalists viewed the institution of the presidency evaporated between 1973 and 1974. The Woodward–Bernstein approach to political coverage became increasingly popular. Austin Ranney noted this radical change in attitude, which held that "politicians are suspect; their public images probably false, their public statements disingenuous, their moral pro-nouncements hypocritical and their promises ephemeral. Correspondents thus see their jobs to be to expose politicans by unmasking their disguises, debunking their claims and piercing their rhetoric."[5]

Unsurprisingly, the point in the political system at which this mutual acrimony and suspicion is most acutely developed is during the candidate nomination and election process. Candidate images are more carefully groomed at this time than at any other. Their public statements are minutely calculated and assessed for content, delivery and impact. Public appearances are stage-managed to the point at which spontaneity becomes dangerous, and candidates attempt to reach voters, often over the heads of reporters, to sketch out their vision of the future. The media regards its function in this process as one of reporting but also of contextualization and interpretation. In many instances, this is carried out at the cost of objectivity, but, as Tom Rosenstiel observed, "Few reporters believe in objectivity—the idea that a journalist is neutral. They strive, rather, to be fair . . . by being true to the facts."[6]

The format and dynamics of the modern presidential election process present severe problems for this interpretation of the media's role. Candidates playing for such high stakes are naturally unwilling to leave to reporters the job of assessing who has won or lost an electoral event. The stomach-churning steeplechase that constitutes the post-reform nomination calendar leaves reporters little time for protracted policy analysis. Most inevitably fall back on the more enticing prospect of handicapping candidates' fortunes as each primary and caucus unfolds. Since the 1980s, campaign strategists have turned increasingly to spin control in order either to manipulate or to override major newspaper and network coverage, or to local media outlets and TV chat shows in a brazen attempt to bypass them altogether. Bill Clinton earned memorable national coverage from his 1992 appearance on the "Arsenio Hall" show, saxophone in hand, without having to face the national press corps. Frank Greer, a media consultant on the 1984 Mondale campaign, was one of the first to demonstrate the effectiveness of satellite technology for candidates seeking to blitz the electorate. During the 1986 Georgia Senate race, Greer's candidate,Wyche Fowler, was able to participate in twelve television interviews carried by satellite during a one-hour period without setting foot outside the television studio.[7] The proliferation of new media technology, including mobile satellite trucks, teleconferences and the Internet, has created new potential for the transmission of information but also for candidates and their campaign managers to indulge in intensive television electioneering without the intervening inconvenience of media interpretation.

Journalists often agree that serious problems arise from the general media approach to reporting elections. During the 1980s, news organizations such as NBC made concentrated efforts to avoid trivia-laden stories and to focus on presentation of candidate policy platforms. Inevitably, however, the entertainment imperative tends to override good intent. As David Paletz and Robert Entman note, presidential elections resemble Miss America pageants, the Superbowl or the World Series being, "stuffed with news. Elections overflow with real or contrived drama, contain conflict . . . recur at specified times . . . and have measurable outcomes—voters and victors."[8]

The early stages of this contest are the most fluid and contentious. The position of the first primary is made important by the dynamics of the primary calendar and the pressures of federal election financing laws. New Hampshire's primary occupies a pivotal position and, far more than the preceding Iowa caucuses, heralds the beginning of the active campaigning season. More is at stake during the early contests than at possibly any other stage. Themes and stories developed at this time may come to dominate later interpretations of the unfolding nomination race. With these factors in mind, it is not surprising that the Granite State primary brings out both the best and the worst in the news media.

In sporting competition, a win is regarded as conclusive, a loss is a loss. A close second can be admired but usually carries no fringe benefits beyond a silver medal. In presidential primaries, and in New Hampshire above all, victories can be qualified. A first-place finish can prove insufficient, and a close second can sometimes be represented as a moral victory overshadowing the achievement of the winner. Furthermore, the close proximity of other primaries and caucuses makes the interpretation of the New Hampshire result a matter of crucial significance to contestants.

In an extension of the sporting analogy, the terms employed by journalists and reporters when describing elections are often remarkably similar to those used by sporting commentators. Candidates are collectively referred to as "the field" or "the pack." Reporters "handicap" each contender, speculating which may "fall at the first fence" and which will reach the "home stretch." The talk is of "front-runners" and "dark horses." Sporting terms are perhaps the most appropriate when applied to American presidential elections, in which candidates do not "stand" but instead "run" for office. The grueling marathon that constitutes the nomination process has reached such inordinate length and complexity that candidates often leave the field both financially and physically exhausted. There exists some considerable disagreement within the media establishment as to the precise impact of the form of reporting most often connected with the initial contests—"horse race" journalism. Critics, particularly within the print media, believe that an unhealthy preoccupation exists with the "race" aspects of elections. Reporters can too easily be drawn into discussions of which candidates are ahead, which are behind, which are moving up or falling back, to the detriment of serious, considered reporting of policy debates. Howard Fineman, political correspondent for *Newsweek*, deplored this game theory slant to primary coverage, claiming that "the editors tend not to be interested unless there's some dramatic development in the horse race."[9]

That this view is most often held by the printed press reflects the nature of that medium, with its ability to explore stories in depth and develop at least some thematic continuty in its coverage. Others, notably those in television, view horse race reporting as a reflection and inevitable byproduct of the structure of the post-reform nomination system and suggest that part of the tendency stems from television's original and primary function as an entertainment medium. Also a factor, as indicated by Stephen J. Wayne, is television companies' pursuit of additional advertising revenue by heightening viewer interest in news broadcasts. Horse race coverage provides more entertainment and stimulus than turgid elaborations of issue positions.[10]

Factors such as advertising revenue, audience totals and changing perspectives on the presentation and development of political stories inevitably affect media approaches to election coverage. The late NBC News' senior political commentator, John Chancellor, regretted the horse race aspects but added in the media's defense that it becomes very difficult for editors and television producers to avoid them in the early caucuses and primaries since so many candidates are in the running. "I don't like it. Most of us don't. But we're pretty much strapped."[11]

Pack journalism, a term used to denote reporters' habits of generating and feeding on the impressions and expectations exchanged between themselves during a campaign, is a byproduct of the confusion inherent in the campaign's early days. In a typical New Hampshire primary, at least one party race will be wide open, with five or six serious contenders operating on a full-time basis within the state. In a year during which no incumbent president takes the field, the total number of candidates may climb to around fifteen or sixteen. Media resources will be stretched, even in a state as geographically small or technologically easy to cover as New Hampshire, in an effort to include all candidacies. Reporters covering the primary will stay in the state for anything up to two weeks, a comparatively long assignment by election standards. Many will have previous experience of both state and primary and will congregate at the bars of the Holiday Inn, Concord (or, previously, Concord's famous Highway Hotel), Manchester's Sheraton-Wayfarer, the Merrimack Hilton or the Bedford Inn to swap stories and impressions of the unfolding race. With little substantive information preceding the primary, this discourse can prove crucial to the way impressions of the election are conveyed to the public. Chancellor explained how the media's natural tendency to consult itself in the development of campaign stories had substantive repercussions for the 1984 Iowa Democratic race: "I remember Bob (Robert Healy of the *Boston Globe*) saying at breakfast, "I think something's happening with Hart in this state." A lot of other reporters, he recalled, began to say, "if Healy think's there's something going on maybe I'd better go out with Hart."[12]

Pack reporters will often be substantially influenced by the activities of reporters from WMUR-TV or from the Boston media, both of whom will be more familiar than out-of-state journalists with the probable itineraries of candidates. Channel 9's Carl Cameron explained that "we have an advantage over the visiting media and they know it. What they do is follow *us*."[13] Reporters tend to defer to local media representatives in deciding which candidates to follow and how to gain the best access to them. Cameron adds, "A candidate walks down a street and I know from experience that they will stop at Jean's Coffee Shop. I will forego three blocks of video following this guy and go get a booth in the store. Then 'the pack' comes to us!"[14]

Despite complaints from campaign organizations, pack journalism is not responsible for all instances in which news stories break against particular aspirants. The swirl of speculation during the pre-primary weeks often leads candidates themselves to trigger the meltdown of their candidacies by making comments that raise expectations. Al Gore admitted in the summer of 1987 that New Hampshire had the power to make or break his candidacy, retracting the claim later when it became clear he was making little headway in the state. John Chancellor described a meeting between news reporters and the 1984 Democratic contender John Glenn during which Glenn's open pessimism about his prospects led reporters to conclude unanimously that the Ohio senator was headed nowhere.[15]

Bob Dole was more forthright in February 1995, making an ill-advised assertion during a speech at Manchester's Center of New Hampshire that "If you don't win Iowa and New Hampshire you might as well pack up and go home."[16] With the first caucus and primary still almost one year away and with strong poll leads in both states, Dole felt secure in making the statement, partly as a sop to state residents looking for confirmation of their primary's special status. By February 1996, Dole had slipped in the polls and was looking vulnerable but continued to boost press expectations, declaring on February 14 that "This is the big one. This one is going to be the shot heard 'round the world.'"[17] Campaign staffers tend to feed this habit since they are, in Chancellor's view, keen to trade gossip, seeking to put a particular spin on news interpretation. Bob Beckel happily admitted to some "advance spin control" by trying to persuade David Broder of the *Washington Post* and pollster Lou Cannon over dinner that New Hampshire was not crucial to the strategy of the Mondale campaign.[18] Maria Carrier's ill-chosen comment in 1972 that "If we don't get fifty percent, I'm going to blow my brains out" was later acknowledged as a contributory factor to McGovern's moral victory.[19] Even indirect reference to the crucial importance of New Hampshire can cause problems for candidates. The admission by Dole state vice-chairman Bill Lacy that "Clearly, New Hampshire is the hurdle we have to climb this time in terms of winning the presidency" is, in campaign terms, an invitation to reporters to depict the primary as a must-win contest.[20]

Consequently, it becomes necessary to redefine the phenomenon of pack journalism, at least as it manifests itself in the New Hampshire primary environment. While it cannot always be specifically determined which set of impressions, from reporters, spin doctors, candidates or voters, has made the largest impact on news coverage, it is certain that pack journalism is not purely a media-driven phenomenon. It is the end-product of the haphazard, sometimes impressionistic exchange of views that characterizes candidate–media relations during the New Hampshire campaign and generates strong underlying tensions. The sheer intensity of this tension is unique to the state and derives from its peculiar position as the first in a series of electoral tests but as the last realistic opportunity for most campaigns to make a visible impact. The preceding invisible primary months construct an edifice of media and public expectation built on little more than speculation and the results of various straw polls at state party conventions. Campaign organizations can be assessed for potential but not for performance. The candidates spend their time shadow-boxing while journalists review the form. In Iowa and New Hampshire, reporters' theories and candidates' claims are put to the test for the first time. Swiftly afterward the results of these contests are measured against pre-primary expectations and the end-product randomly imprinted on later races through media coverage and interpretation. The rush of primaries and caucuses thereafter makes it impossible for candidates to exercise any significant influence over media interpretations and makes it difficult to recover ground lost due to serious miscalculations or scandals.

The expectations game is thus the legacy of the Invisible Primary season that is played out in New Hampshire with ferocious energy by both candidates and reporters. It constitutes the central core of the first primary's importance. Candidates cannot afford to lose this game as, for most, it will be their first and last chance to mold the campaign environment. No aspect of the New Hampshire contest is more unique or more critical to campaign hopes. No aspect of the first primary carries higher stakes, and none is more controversial.

The history of the primary affords numerous examples of the tactics employed by campaigns in an effort to win the battle of expectations. During the 1968 primary, supporters of Lyndon Johnson attempted to reduce the status of the McCarthy challenge by talking down the expectations for his final vote tally. Once it became clear that McCarthy would outperform these expectations, Johnson supporters, led by Governor John King, reversed the strategy and raised their stated expectations in the hope that reporters would accept the new inflated levels as realistic benchmarks. Speaking to journalists, one Johnson staffer in New Hampshire allowed that less than 40 percent of the vote would be a disgrace. McCarthy coordinator Curtis Gans advised his staff not to compete in this game, but staffer Ben Stavis discovered that the news media had been busily setting its own benchmarks for the challenger. He was privately informed by an unnamed reporter that a final tally in excess of 30 percent of the popular vote would gain McCarthy serious media attention as a candidate. This situation was reversed in 1980 when candidate George Bush himself accentuated the dimensions and implications of his victory in the Iowa caucuses to such a degree that Ronald Reagan's victory in New Hampshire delivered his candidacy a stunning blow from which it never recovered.

The candidate generally considered to have suffered most from expectation-setting was Edmund Muskie, whose victory over George McGovern became translated by media coverage into a defeat in 1972. Muskie staffers and some media analysts were later to consider the news media principally culpable for this "failure" since press preoccupation with the infamous 50 percent threshold had played a major part in the candidate's loss of momentum. Others, however, have argued that the blame lay mainly with the candidate's poor organization and strategy and the relative softness of his voter support. Brereton records that Gary Gerlach, a volunteer press secretary recruited to the Muskie campaign from Harvard's Kennedy School of Government, had sent an internal memorandum to the senator warning that his press operation was "nosediving towards disaster" due to bad planning and makeshift organization.[21] Joseph Grandmaison, who headed McGovern's 1972 New Hampshire operation, stated his belief that Muskie simply did not understand the demands and pitfalls of the modern nomination campaign. His campaign recruited large numbers of out-of-state workers who were not properly schooled in the culture and characteristics of the Granite State and who were regularly at loggerheads with local staffers. Former senator McGovern disagrees, arguing that Muskie fully understood the implications of the expectations game and simply overplayed their hand. He commented fourteen years later: "I think he set the stage for all that himself. . . . If you're going to run for President you have to understand that the media is going to play with the figures. Ed Muskie was an old pro, he'd been around a long time and he knew the score."[22]

CBS reporter Dick Drayne, former press assistant to Robert and Edward Kennedy, concurred in this view. He believed that the press could not be blamed for the debacle in New Hampshire since the result exposed the fundamental weakness of the entire Muskie campaign, claiming "Muskie lost in New Hampshire for reasons that became apparent later—he was losing everywhere."[23]

Another of the more notorious manifestations of the expectations game occurred during the 1976 Republican primary when Governor Meldrim Thomson, state manager for Ronald Reagan, made vocal and confident predictions that his candidate would defeat President Gerald Ford by at least five percentage points. The Reagan national team, only too aware that the race was tight, had previously been following a strategy designed to play down press expectations in the hope that a win, or even a narrow loss, would pay extra dividends.[24] Subsequently, pollster Richard Wirthlin would attribute the entire near-miss of the Reagan candidacy in Kansas City's Kemper Arena to that single error in the Granite State, claiming that Reagan's inability to claim a moral victory in New Hampshire as a result of Thomson's overenthusiasm "structured all that followed. We played catch-up ball from that time on."[25]

In 1988 Reverend Jesse Jackson attempted to employ the race card as a means of influencing the formation of expectations in both Iowa and New Hampshire. Jackson argued that, given the low levels of black voters in either state, a figure as low as 10 percent should be treated as a victory for his campaign.[26] In the event, the ploy was hardly necessary as it reinforced an already widely held media perception that Jackson's candidacy should not be judged solely on the basis of its performance in mainly WASP New England, an incidence of regional consideration not normally extended to candidates by election commentators.

As late as 1992, the failure of the Buchanan challenge in New Hampshire was put down in part to unnecessarily high expectations generated from within the candidate's own campaign as to his likely final result. The candidate and his staff made what later came to be regarded as a fundamental strategic error in making public their belief, supported by private polling data, that Buchanan could register 40 percent against incumbent President Bush. In the event, the challenger fell three points short of this target, placing him well within the statistical margin of error, but the president, at 57 percent, was two points ahead of his staff's private worst-case benchmark. Buchanan was not awarded the moral victory tag by the news media, and the opportunity for momentum was lost.[27] It was not a mistake the Buchanan camp cared to repeat. In 1996 it played a delicate game in handling media evaluations and profited from the misguided statement by Senator Dole in July 1995 that "if you stumble in New Hampshire, you're dead."[28] In Rosenstiel's view, this is the real New Hampshire primary, "the fragile game in which the media set expectations and then interpreted the vote by watching who succeeds or fails to meet them."[29] Yet the assessment is oversimplified. Candidates themselves play an active role in expectation-setting through public declarations, leaked memos and the pursuit of endorsements. Edmund Muskie, Walter Mondale and Robert Dole each placed great emphasis on accumulating support from leading New Hampshire political figures and newspapers to create the impression of a powerful coalition which, to all intents and purposes, had the state sewn up. While such figures can be of great help (Adams in 1952, Sununu in 1988), they can also be positively harmful (King in 1968, Thomson in 1976) or simply unable to deliver the state to the candidate (Gregg in 1980, Merrill in 1996). Whatever the final outcome, the accumulation of endorsements heightens media expectations and can cause problems for front-runners who set the first hurdle in the race too high for a clean jump. By November 1995, Bob Dole's impressive lineup of state political supporters prompted the Manchester *Union Leader* to suggest that "a 40 percent showing by Dole next February won't be too much to ask, don't you think?"[30] This pro-Buchanan publication had much to gain from raising Dole's credibility barrier, but its statement may nonetheless have helped shape the views of the wider media the following February.

In other states, at other stages of the contest, the need to match expectations is less acutely felt, and strategic errors may sometimes be correctable. In New Hampshire such mistakes more often than not prove fatal as a result of the first primary's ability to generate a media surge of enormous dimensions. Particularly in cases where incumbents or front-runners have been seriously threatened or numerically defeated, a deluge of publicity in the days following New Hampshire can have a highly significant impact on the races immediately following. John Sears, the 1976 national campaign manager for Ronald Reagan, revealed during an election postmortem discussion the following year, how much he believed had been lost through the misguided claims of Governor Thomson and the subsequent loss of the first primary. "A win in New Hampshire was very important to us, given the fact that, limited to $10 million, it was impossible for us to carry on an active campaign in all of the primaries. . . . If we had won in New Hampshire, I think we would have won in Florida . . . and then in Illinois. The week before . . . our polling showed us ahead in Florida; then on the Saturday after the New Hampshire primary the poll showed us eighteen points down."[31]

Such surges, when they did occur, were largely stimulated by saturation coverage in newspapers and on television and were credited with propelling Jimmy Carter toward the Democratic nomination in 1976 and with building Gary Hart's struggling campaign into a serious threat to Walter Mondale in 1984. Clearly, therefore, the expectations game has always remained the central theme of any New Hampshire primary. Candidates themselves never entirely adjust to these harsh realities. George McGovern, beneficiary of media interpretations of his 1972 result, found himself grasping the short end of the stick during the 1984 primary season when his unexpectedly strong showing behind Gary Hart, his erstwhile campaign manager, in the Iowa caucuses elicited no press interest. In an ironic echo of the complaints made by the Muskie camp against McGovern himself twelve years before, the senator ruefully complained about the way in which his strong showing in Iowa had been downplayed by the media in the face of a modest showing from Hart.[32]

PRIMARY COVERAGE

The tangible effects of the expectations game, as candidates emerge from New Hampshire, are often referred to as momentum, a term used to denote a cycle of higher poll ratings, larger financial contributions, more media coverage and volunteer workers, all of which have been stimulated by the positive outcome of the first primary and, on occasion, the first caucus. The cycle is not unbreakable but can prove self-sustaining as it leads to further victories. The news media naturally carry a certain, though hotly disputed, degree of responsibility for stimulating this cycle. Its effects have been measured in two ways—first, by analyzing newspaper column inches or the number of program minutes devoted to New Hampshire results, and second, by examining the knock-on effect of the excessive coverage on campaigns themselves.

In three surveys covering the immediate post–New Hampshire periods in the 1976 and 1984 races, George Washington University professor Michael Robinson uncovered startling trends in media coverage of Granite State election results, revealing the full extent of the television and print media's fascination with the first-in-the-nation primary. Analyzing a total of 616 news stories in both media between November 24, 1975 and February 27, 1976, he found that 250 (41 percent) concerned the New Hampshire primary.[33] Neighboring Massachusetts, with a larger population and larger delegate yields and equally as accessible for correspondents from New York or Washington, held its primary seven days later but was the subject of only seventy-one stories. Further research revealed that ten states held delegate selection procedures of some description before New Hampshire's vote. These accounted for 500 delegates to the two main party conventions. These states, including Iowa's caucuses, were mentioned in only seventy-seven stories. New Hampshire sent only thirty-eight delegates to the Kansas City and New York conventions but attracted three times as much coverage.

Robinson initiated a smaller survey of television coverage alone for the period February 27 to April 9, 1976, the intention being to prevent distortion of results through overconcentration on stories printed or transmitted within what can be termed the New Hampshire window (that period during which the primary is regarded as breaking or current news). Data for this second survey might have been expected to balance the picture somewhat as the primary faded from public memory. Instead, it served to reinforce the established pattern.

New York, with a population forty times that of New Hampshire, received only 30 percent of that state's television coverage during its own primary race. February 28, the day after the New Hampshire primary, saw a total of 2,100 seconds of network news coverage devoted to the story. New York's total on all three major networks was a mere 560 seconds. Robinson commented, "There were more than forty-five times as many Democrats voting in New York as in New Hampshire. Nevertheless, New Hampshire returns received almost quadruple the coverage. [T]hat works out to 170 times as much coverage per vote! No matter how one approaches the data, New Hampshire overwhelms New York and every other state in media coverage."[34]

Touching on the differences between press and television coverage, Robinson noted that television's saturation tendency was more pronounced. Forty-two percent of election news stories in the print media during the February 27–April 9 period were allotted to New Hampshire, but the figure for television stories rose significantly to 60 percent.[35]

These statistics go some way to explaining the media surge for Jimmy Carter in 1976. The crucial factor is the manner in which results are reported and interpreted in the days following the first contests. On the evening of the 1976 Iowa caucus results, for example, the fuse for New Hampshire and later primaries was immediately lit by media interpretation of Carter's less-than-remarkable showing. With the uncommitted vote substantially ahead of him and 23 percent of the total vote going to other candidates, Carter's 29.1 percent came to be interpreted as a major victory. "CBS Evening News" declared, "No amount of bad-mouthing by others can lessen . . . [its] importance. He was the clear winner in this psychologically crucial test. . . . Carter has opened ground between himself and the rest of the so-called 'pack.'"[36]

Television dislikes ambiguity. In presidential races, even before the era of television, issue debates were frequently obscured by discussions of the personality traits and family backgrounds of individual candidates. Primaries enable the visual media to exploit such discussions to the full, while the less publicity-oriented, party-driven caucuses do not. A conclusive win for the uncommitted vote thus tends to leave a dissatisfying impression of conflict unresolved. Under such circumstances, the personality-directed coverage by television led the networks to seize on the highest-placed individual competitor, Carter, and propel him forward. He was well-prepared for this eventuality. Joel McLeary, the Georgian's national finance director, later confessed that the Georgian's campaign had no substantial organizational structures in place beyond the Florida primary, that they had planned only "for the short haul" and that, subsequently, "After Florida it was all NBC, CBS and the *New York Times*."[37]

To reach the safety of Florida, therefore, the Carter campaign was almost entirely reliant on media-based momentum generated from New Hampshire. The strategy was well-conceived. The gap between Carter and the second-placed Morris Udall, just over 4,600 votes, bore no relation to the distance in terms of media coverage between the two candidates in New Hampshire's aftermath. *Time* and *Newsweek* carried pictures of the Georgian on their respective covers, offering in-depth looks at the new front-runner, his family and career. From these and other articles, Carter netted 2,630 lines of coverage; Udall received only 96. Carter's other opponents, whose combined voted total 59,008 to Carter's 23,373, amassed only 300 lines.[38] The bandwagon picked up speed as the candidates moved toward the crucial

Pennsylvania primary on April 9, 1976. In this period, 43 percent of all network news output on the Democratic race was devoted to Carter, together with 46 percent of newspaper coverage and 59 percent of magazine attention.[39] After winning the New York and Massachusetts primaries, Senator Henry Jackson, who had deliberately bypassed New Hampshire, outran Carter in popular vote totals by 1.9 million to 1.6 million. Yet Jackson's media coverage, even when combined with Udall's, represented only 15 percent of newsmagazine column inches and less than 20 percent of combined television and print coverage.[40] Carter's nomination had become an inevitability in the eyes of most media commentators, and the tangible effect of that endorsement, in terms of donations, volunteer support and national name recognition, was to generate an unstoppable momentum cycle.

A similar phenomenon attended the 1984 victory of Gary Hart. The result itself was more impressive than Carter's since the Colorado senator did not face a disproportionately divided ideological field in New Hampshire and succeeded in overturning the momentum of the front-running candidate, Walter Mondale. In another survey, a synopsis of which was presented to the House of Representatives Subcommittee on Elections in May 1986, Professor Robinson warned against overstating the effects that the enormous media surge in Hart's favor may have had on voters.[41] Since it was impossible to fully gauge the impact of televisual or printed election news on public perception, he argued, analysts should allow for other intangible factors. Nonetheless, Robinson suggested a strong causal connection between the rise of Senator Hart and the wave of media interest in him generated by the Iowa–New Hampshire period. He explained, "On February 25 . . . seven percent of the Democrats preferred Hart for the nomination. On March 2 that figure was 34%; on March 6, 38% wanted Hart as the nominee."[42]

According to the survey figures, at this stage an estimated 3 million Democratic voters were switching allegiance to Hart every twenty-four hours, the largest shift ever recorded by pollsters during a nomination campaign. Reviewing this campaign, Howard Fineman claimed that the tumult induced by New Hampshire should be regarded as an inevitable and healthy media reaction to the pre-primary strategy of the vice-president's campaign, in which journalists had been "almost anaesthetized" into believing Mondale had a lock on the nomination.[43] Viewed from this perspective, an unpredictable electorate is far less to blame for the upset result than the very predictable dynamics of the media–candidate relationship. Fineman adds, "the expectations got built up so high that as soon as the first fact comes in that runs counter to it, that sets up an enormous countervailing dynamic."[44]

Fineman regards this as a significant indication of the boundaries to New Hampshire's influence over the nomination process. Rather than dictating the choice of nominee, the state's electorate, as interpreted by the news media, simply selected an alternative candidate from the pack to challenge the front-runner. No amount of press attention or shifts in voter allegiance, however, were sufficient to impose the media's new star on the remaining primary states. The Hart campaign had not thoroughly prepared its messages or its tactics and thus could not convert the media blitz into delegate votes.[45] For Fineman and other reporters, Hart's failure to capitalize on his win demonstrated the weaknesses in the argument that the New Hampshire-induced momentum dictated primary outcomes.

The resurgence of the 1976 Reagan challenge, though ultimately fruitless, further demonstrates that the momentum-cycle can be overcome. By May 14, 1976, Reagan had amassed 432 of the 1,130 delegate votes needed for a first ballot victory, having scored victories across the South and West, while President Ford had gained only 323 votes after his narrow Granite State win. Reagan had effectively reversed the New Hampshire momentum and might have captured the nomination but for his premature, badly miscalculated selection of a running-mate before the convention opened.[46]

The heavy preponderance of New Hampshire-oriented coverage, in comparison to attention paid to other states and other periods of the nomination calendar in 1984, has also been highlighted in Professor Emmett Buell, Jr.'s survey of nomination stories carried in the columns of three major daily newspapers. Reviewing column-inch coverage in the *New York Times, Washington Post* and the *Boston Globe,* Buell makes a comparison between the treatment of New Hampshire and that of other states or periods in the nomination calendar (Table 4.1).

Table 4.1
Comparison of Column-Inch Coverage of the New Hampshire Primary with That of Other Major Events During the 1984 Democratic Presidential Nomination Process

Event	Boston Globe	Washington Post	New York Times	Totals
Iowa	483	1,089	1,031	2,603
Iowa–NH	865	1,072	892	2,829
New Hampshire	2,971	1,412	1,333	5,716
NH–Super Tuesday	2,736	1,960	1,300	5,996
Super Tuesday	1,929	1,794	1,136	4,859
New York	557	334	1,067	1,958
Pennsylvania	203	145	412	760
CA–NJ–WV– SD–New Mexico	1,239	1,100	1,945	4,284

Source: Adapted from statistics in Emmett H. Buell, Jr., "Locals and Cosmopolitans: National, Regional and State Newspaper Coverage of the New Hampshire Primary," in Gary Orren and Nelson Polsby, eds., *Media and Momentum: The New Hampshire Primary and Nomination Politics* (Chatham, NJ: Chatham House, 1987), pp. 62–65.

Table 4.1 offers additional evidence of the dominance of New Hampshire's primary in media perceptions. Its combined total from three newspapers is more than twice that of New York, almost 1,000 column inches in excess of the Super Tuesday total and greater by 672 column inches than combined coverage of the contests in Pennsylvania, California, New Jersey, South Dakota, New Mexico and West Virginia. The results also reveal a substantial bulge in media interest which appears during the New Hampshire primary, peaks rapidly as the results are first reported and then interpreted and then declines precipitously after Super Tuesday as the momentum generated by the Granite State is overtaken by events. Media fascination with the nomination race, building steadily throughout Hadley's invisible primary period and the Iowa caucuses, enters premature overdrive with the first primary, the results of which fuel intense speculation in the following weeks until the Super Tuesday contests put the outcome beyond reasonable doubt. Again, New Hampshire appears to be the focal point of this phenomenon, with ample justification for the stress laid on it by candidates and campaign managers.

David Broder's observation that the New Hampshire primary was "the most heavily promoted media event of our outrageously theatrical nominating system" does not appear to be overstated.[47] Work by Buell and Robinson demonstrates a consistent media bias in favor of the early stage of the nomination race out of all proportion to its delegate worth. Whether this bias exercises any lasting effect on the nomination process remains open to conjecture. In making such assessments, it is impossible to ignore factors unrelated to press and television interpretation, the long-term effects of which are harder to quantify. Such factors include candidate personality, policy development and elucidation, state and national campaign organization, campaign strategy and financial resourcing, regional variations in candidate strength and the format of the nomination calendar itself which, Iowa and New Hampshire excepted, is in a state of almost constant scheduling turmoil. In Hadley's Invisible Primary thesis, such factors can, in varying combinations, determine the ultimate success or failure of a presidential candidacy before the first vote has been cast, media frenzies notwithstanding. Momentum theory is vulnerable to overgeneralization, especially as most claims regarding the inevitability of a nomination are normally made with the benefit of hindsight. It may be misleading to move beyond the fairly limited observation that media attention in the earliest weeks of the nomination process is disproportionate to that of later periods and that New Hampshire primaries are frequently the epicenters of massive shifts in media attention and voter support. This observation, though statistically supportable, does not conclusively demonstrate that such phenomena are decisive in the later nomination race.

A brief review of the post–New Hampshire progress of selected candidates reveals that heavy media attention by no means guarantees success. Carter's 1976 success in the Granite State and its attendant media frenzy did not prevent defeats in Massachusetts and New York. In 1984 Gary Hart failed to emulate Carter's ultimately successful strategy, despite unprecedented voter shifts after New Hampshire and victory in the March 20 Illinois primary. McCarthy's moral victory in 1968 provoked enormous media speculation but did not lead to victory in Chicago. George McGovern, however, was able to convert a second-place showing into nomination. Michael Dukakis's victory in New Hampshire in 1988 was not followed by a clean sweep of Super Tuesday states, which were divided equally between himself, Reverend Jesse Jackson and Senator Al Gore. Ronald Reagan's crucial 1976 defeat in New Hampshire damaged but did not derail his challenge. Instead, the former governor staged a dramatic comeback in the Sunbelt States and by May 1976 led President Gerald Ford in accumulated delegate totals. Paul Tsongas won a hard-earned victory in 1992 but media accolades were consistently qualified by the assertion that the New Hampshire verdict was little more than a regional quirk. Tsongas gained no momentum and did not possess the organizational strength or support to push ahead through the southern primaries. Table 4.2 demonstrates the varying fortunes of Democratic New Hampshire primary winners.

Table 4.2
Actual and Perceived New Hampshire Democratic Primary Victors, Compared to Final Results of Nomination Contests, 1952–96

Year	Actual Winner	Perceived Winner	Nominee
1952	Kefauver	Kefauver	Stevenson
1956	Kefauver	Kefauver	Stevenson
1960	Kennedy	Kennedy	Kennedy
1964	Johnson	Johnson	Johnson
1968	Johnson	McCarthy	Humphrey
1972	Muskie	McGovern	McGovern
1976	Carter	Carter	Carter
1980	Carter	Carter	Carter
1984	Hart	Hart	Mondale
1988	Dukakis	Inconclusive*	Dukakis
1992	Tsongas	Clinton	Clinton
1996	Clinton	Clinton	Clinton

*The general tone of media analysis pointed to New Hampshire as a must-win for Dukakis as a regional candidate. Thus his victory only established him as one among three front-runners.

The results suggest that the news media, while exercising an undeniably high level of influence in the shaping of expectations and interpretation of outcomes, cannot be held entirely responsible for what many consider to be the undue influence of New Hampshire's primary. This is particularly important since the nature and extent of that influence cannot always be accurately gauged. Largely because it occupies a key place in the early weeks of the electoral cycle, New Hampshire campaigns are difficult to report and especially vulnerable to competing interpretations, speculation and the attendant phenomenon of pack journalism. Voter intentions, candidate tactics, media interpretations and policy agendas have yet to crystallize into patterns that will later be judged as characteristic of that particular election cycle. Journalists and commentators, like the candidates themselves, operate in a politically volatile and unformed environment, during which the likelihood of a surprise result is increased in proportion to the number of candidates active in the field. Reacting to this environment, reporters form opinions based on a haphazard mixture of preconception, personal opinion, objective calculation, gossip, statistics and campaign press releases. Until this point the campaign has no clearly defined context, leaving candidates and reporters greater leeway for subjective claims and counterclaims. In later primaries, with the voting pattern clearer and a contextual agenda more or less firmly in place, such fluidity rapidly vanishes. In the preliminary stages, however, the battle of interpretations is the only game in town. As Tom Wicker observed of the 1968 race, "When the contest is complicated, as it has been in New Hampshire, by organized and unorganized write-in campaigns, declared, undeclared, forsaken and minor candidacies, the only certain outcome is an argument."[48]

RETAIL COVERAGE: MEDIA STYLE IN THE GRANITE STATE

White picket fences, wooden churches, Town Meeting Days and Calvin Coolidge clones constitute, for outsiders, the enduring images of a New Hampshire campaign. The state undeniably possesses a character all its own, most of which is genuine, part of which is simply marketed as such, and reporters delight in drawing distinctions between New York's metropolitan chic and the lifestyles and worldviews of the average small-town New Hampshire resident. The byline to a 1968 article in the London *Times*, "In picture postcard villages, a down-to-earth Yankee looks at world issues," epitomizes the media approach to New Hampshire reporting.[49] As the distance between village life and the unappetizing realities of the late-twentieth-century urban existence has grown, the contrast has become both alluring and entertaining, with reporters emphasizing the differences between New Hampshire's problems and those of urban decay, crime, AIDS, drug abuse and homelessness which beset America's larger cities. The importance of this contrast to the continuing appeal of the primary cannot be overstated. Its psychological impact rests largely on the vague hope of a return to the nation's Puritan past, with its echoes of strong religious faith, small close-knit communities, accountable and accessible politicians, small government and low taxation. Jody Powell, press secretary to the Carter White House, confirmed the appeal of the imagery. "I think that pine trees and home towns said something . . . even to people in cities who had never seen a small town because these symbols suggested something that they wanted."[50]

The primary's position at the head of the calendar reinforces this factor. Candidates arrive in New Hampshire generally fresh, reasonably well-funded and keen to announce yet another new beginning for the United States. In later contests, withdrawals, saturation coverage and negative ads tend to blur the picture and reduce the novelty of issues and candidates. Kefauver and Eisenhower called for an end to corruption and cronyism, John Kennedy declared the need to get the nation moving once more, McCarthy and McGovern demanded a new moral basis to American foreign policy and Carter extended this theme to American government as a whole. It was from New Hampshire that Ronald Reagan launched his 1980 crusade to return the United States to traditional values, built on smaller bureaucracies and lower taxes. Patrick Buchanan painted the prospect of a revitalized economy and democracy through trade barriers and the return of power to the states. Gary Hart and Bill Clinton portrayed themselves as the advance guard of a fresh generation of Democrats, untainted by the failures of the Great Society and computer-literate to boot. The consistency of the new beginning theme is a consequence of the primary's first-place status but feeds on, and is reinforced by, the state's cultural environment. For conservatives in particular, this symbolism retains great appeal and goes some way to explaining why most criticism of the state and its primary emanates from Democratic rather than Republican party ranks. Within this collection of images lies the implicit assumption that cynical, simplistic New Englanders are less likely to be impressed by glib campaign promises or ambitious social programs.

The rise of Iowa's caucus as a predeterminative influence after 1976 has not undermined this importance. The media tends to find Iowa neither as distinctive nor as easy to cover as the Granite State. In addition, the caucus rarely provides decisive results. Howard Fineman described the media view of Iowa and New Hampshire as a two-stage process, with Iowa serving as the introductory phase the verdict of which would be confirmed or overturned by New Hampshire in its contest, the final "winnowing" ritual.[51] Reporters tend not to close the book on the nomination after Iowa because of the close proximity of New Hampshire and also because the former state's record in choosing the eventual party nominees has not been impressive.[52] In addition, of course, the caucus format does not lend itself easily to television coverage, a key factor in the adoption of primaries by many states that previously used only the caucus method of delegate selection. Campaigns are generally low-key, and the familiar polling stations are replaced by a series of meetings held across the state at which activists register their delegate and candidate preferences. This process furnishes only limited access or visual stimulus for television cameras. New Hampshire offers higher levels of visual campaign entertainment with its much-vaunted tradition of retail politics. Supporters of the primary maintain that the state is the last bastion of retail politics where elections retain substantial elements of interpersonal campaigning. The size of the state and its community orientation require that candidates campaign in the time-honored fashion, shaking hands door-to-door, canvassing in shops, bars and restaurants, stopping in at voters' homes, becoming acquainted with activists and voters on a personal level, attending kaffeeklatches and town fairs. In short, they deal with voters on a retail rather than a wholesale basis. Congressman and future New Hampshire governor Judd Gregg, testifying before a 1986 House of Representatives Subcommittee on Elections, suggested this as a positive argument in the state's favor, noting it as "a quality to be cherished rather than feared."[53]

Unsurprisingly, critics object that New Hampshire is not the only state in which this happens. Candidates can be filmed meeting and answering questions from Texas ranchers, Ohio farmers, California environmentalists, New York subway patrol officers and Washington State loggers. Certainly, the survival of retail politics at the presidential level, despite its appealing features, appears anachronistic in a modern campaign environment that is almost entirely dependent on mass media and mass marketing. Bob Beckel's view that the Granite State style of electioneering should be viewed as nothing more than a throwback to the days of the Lincoln–Douglas debates is widely shared. The anachronism is quaint but should not be compared to the rest of the race, particularly if a winning candidate in New Hampshire reaches, through retail politicking, only a small percentage of the total voting population.[54]

Despite fervent protests from candidates and pundits, the news media have remained fascinated by the comparative close proximity between candidates and voters afforded by retail politicking. What Carl Cameron describes as a "phenomenal infrastructure of opportunity" for voters also provides equally unique opportunities for journalism, sometimes resulting in a tendency to overplay the human interest element in New Hampshire stories. Cameras and microphones trail candidates from store to store in the hope that the unpredictable citizenry may pillory a hapless candidate on live television. For Cameron, this means that the media moguls and spin doctors are less able to direct the course of debate in New Hampshire than in larger, media-run campaigns. "The most outlandish and confrontational questions that ultimately become the defining moment for a candidate won't come . . . from ABC News or the New York Times. It'll be John Doe, in his dairy field . . . saying to Bob Dole in front of the television cameras, 'You said you were going to get us out of Bosnia and you didn't.'"[55]

Opinions of the relative merits, or even the existence, of retail politics in New Hampshire, vary considerably. Critics, including Beckel and AP bureau chief Walter Mears, believe that the state sustains only the image of retail politicking due to its small size and to reporters' love of human dimension stories. Candidates feel compelled to indulge in small-scale publicity stunts that would not be considered necessary in larger states but that carry enormous weight with the trivia-hungry press pack. Candidates and their staff have long since become wise to this imperative and to its potential pitfalls. Bob Dole's visit to the Top of the Tree bakery in Londonderry in January 1996 was intended to convey symbolic significance as the bakery's sole product was apple pie. A visit to a Derry brewery, however, was quickly canceled when aides realized the Senator would be photographed tasting the brewery's specialty, Old Man Ale. The visit was re-scheduled after protests from Governor Steve Merrill but not before Dole's advisers had scripted a deft reply to anticipated questions from reporters. In this light, similar stories of Gary Hart stopping by to wash dishes in a voter's home, of Al Gore buying porcelain figurines for an activist's collection or of Lamar Alexander taking thirty days to walk the Granite State from end to end appear as gimmicks designed specifically to appeal to reporters rather than voters; gimmicks that become irrelevant later in the presidential race. As Beckel contemptuously notes, "Gary Hart threw an axe into a tree . . . so what?"[56] Retail politicking, he believed, was merely another New Hampshire myth, another wily and cynical Granite State marketing ploy.[57] This view was reinforced by the experience of President Bush during a 1992 campaign tour. Halting his motorcade, the president left his car to stroke a cow named Holiday for waiting photographers. Journalists later discovered that the local farmer holding the animal was in fact the Republican leader of the state House of Representatives to whom Bush was returning a political favor.[58]

Undoubtedly, the media swarm surrounding any candidate during a tour of Portsmouth, Goffstown or Nashua can make it difficult to establish meaningful contact with voters on an individual basis. The nature of media coverage of the primary has also changed since the 1960s, partly because of changes within the news media itself. The major networks have cut back on the number of reporters assigned to the state, and their place has been taken by local media. A distance has thus opened up between candidates and reporters which undermines to some extent the purpose of a retail campaign. Rosenstiel explains, "With shared camera pools and stenographic off-air researchers instead of correspondents, the networks were becoming passive recorders of a campaign driven by local press."[59]

Cameron dismisses this as a fundamental misperception of the dynamics of media coverage. While concurring in the view that the local media now have greater influence, he suggests that reporters generally tend to swarm a candidate only on the first one or two days of his visit until sufficient material for a story has been gained. Touring the state from February 19, 1995, Senate majority leader Bob Dole was unable to conduct a retail campaign during the initial twenty-four hours of his visit, during which time he gave interviews to Channel 9 and several newspapers. On February 20, Cameron claims, the candidate who had been "five deep in camera cables and lights" found the media presence significantly diminished until, by the third day, Dole could walk Main Street, Concord, accompanied by only one or two reporters and a campaign aide.[60] Media deadlines can also serve to facilitate retail politics since cameramen and reporters will disperse in the late afternoon to compile news bulletins or to fax copy. This leaves candidates free to attend Rotary dinners, coffee klatches and other small events relatively free of media interference.

Overall, it does appear that the lengthy campaign, a prerequisite of New Hampshire primaries, combined with the small size of the state and the distribution of its population, does facilitate candidate–voter contact on an unusually intensive level. Only in the campaign's final weeks does retail politicking become something of a hybrid creature—close voter contact being accompanied by vast amounts of sophisticated technological equipment. But the greater amount of retail spadework in the state will already have been done by candidates and their organizers during the uniquely long pre-primary period when media attention and participation are at much lower levels. As a result, the state's citizens are able to quiz more candidates over a longer period. Outsiders are able to remain in the New Hampshire race due to the comparatively low cost of organizing the state and to the low spending thresholds imposed on all candidates at this stage by the Federal Election Commission. These favorable conditions disappear in later contests when, as Frank Luntz notes, polling and media costs, among other expenses, "have all blown campaign expenses out of the water."[61]

Inevitably, the era of retail has given way in New Hampshire, as in other states, to the imperatives and technology of modern campaigning. Candidates still attend large, orchestrated rallies and ride in small motorcades as in any larger state. Candidate debates are often inaccessible to many ordinary voters and dominated by television cameramen. Hollywood stars such as Paul Newman, Dustin Hoffman, Bruce Willis and Arnold Schwarzenegger have all campaigned actively in the Granite State. The arrival of new forms of media, including cable, satellite and computer technology, has broadened the range and scope of programming. Since the 1980s, the primary has become, in the truest sense, a media circus with special election broadcasts on a variety of programs that are at once more entertaining and more sophisticated than the straightforward news reports of previous years. In 1996 the Santa Monica-based organization Rock the Vote, designed to encourage higher turnout among younger voters, worked the state from its MTV-sponsored Choose or Lose bus, offering participants the opportunity to key into an "interactive electoral experience" on MTV sites on America Online and the World Wide Web.[62] The same year saw a special, primary edition of "Donahue" broadcast from Bedford, following the format of a traditional Town Meeting, and Bill Maher's "Politically Incorrect" talk show, live from the Manchester Institute of Arts and Sciences. "Imus in the Morning," one of the more popular radio talk shows of the mid-1990s, transferred operations to New Hampshire on the Tuesday and Wednesday of primary week, enabling C-SPAN, already in the state, to broadcast the show to international audiences.[63] In this way, the primary's role as a defining event has been reinforced and augmented over the past decade by the diversification of the media. Celebrity talk shows, guest appearances, MTV and the Internet have contributed to the conversion of the first primary from a delegate selection contest into a political entertainment ritual of election year.

The retail tradition has not precluded the increasing power and density of television advertizing, which is now more relentless in New Hampshire than in many other primary states. Candidates air regular spot ads on WMUR or WBZ for weeks prior to the first primary. In Iowa and New Hampshire, these are often trial balloons used to test which ad styles evoke the most positive reaction from audiences.

As in any state, access to the main media outlets is essential in the Granite State, and candidate organizations develop careful strategies to utilize media opportunities. In 1988 Lee Atwater ensnared television viewers with a roadblock by purchasing simultaneous half-hour slots on every television station but one serving New Hampshire, leaving the audience to choose between President Bush or "Hee-Haw."[64] Levels of advertising in New Hampshire have escalated dramatically during the 1990s. On Friday, February 6, 1992, a local ABC affiliate station aired no fewer than fourteen political commercials from presidential contenders during one thirty-minute news broadcast.[65] Julie Campasano, program director at WMUR, reported that 1996 commericals were pouring into the station at the rate of ten a day in the campaign's final fortnight—far more than the estimated ten a week in 1992.[66] The barrage reached new heights in 1996 with the Forbes campaign's negative advertising blitz. The publisher–candidate spent an estimated $12 million on television ads in Iowa and New Hampshire, some of which stretched into minidocumentaries.[67] During this period, the average New Hampshire voter was likely to see a Forbes television ad thirty-four times a week. This saturation strategy prompted Larry Sabato, political science professor at the University of Virginia, to declare the retail tradition in both states at an end, arguing that the contests had "become wholesale political events just like all the rest."[68] Forbes's fourth-place finish was therefore noted with some satisfaction by defenders of the primary who claimed this failure as proof that a television-based campaign could make no headway in the state. The candidate had, in fact, stumped the state assiduously in preceding weeks, but the perception that his campaign was wholly negative and based mainly on the media undermined his appeal. The lesson here is the importance of balancing media tactics with retail image in New Hampshire. A disproportionate reliance on the media tends to attract negative coverage from reporters who will accuse the offending campaign of not playing by accepted rules.

Candidates increasingly utilize new technology to supplement retail politicking in a manner that inevitably undermines its original purpose. The Pat Robertson campaign circulated 300,000 audiocassettes to households in Iowa and New Hampshire during 1987–88 explaining the values and goals of the televangelist candidate.[69] In 1988 videoed messages from candidates were increasingly deployed as substitutes for personal appearances. Former Arizona governor Bruce Babbitt mailed 450 videos to a target audience of 450 uncommitted Democratic party activists in New Hampshire, following the examples of Robertson and Jack Kemp. The Dukakis team prepared two different videos aimed at two separate voting constituencies. According to Luntz, "In New Hampshire alone, literally thousands of 'video parties' were held in preparation for their presidential primary."[70] By 1996 videos had become common primary currency, freely available to voters who dropped by local party headquarters. Lamar Alexander used his position as chairman of the Republican Neighborhood Meeting organization to distribute videoed meeting sessions across the state. This form of personalized wholesale campaigning is becoming increasingly popular in electoral politics for its broad range and by lending an aura of intimacy that is offset only by the physical absence of the candidate himself. It enables candidates working New Hampshire to sustain an intensive grass-roots effort at relatively low cost while bypassing not only the media but also critical questioning from activists themselves.

Another change in campaign techniques has come with the rise of the Internet. Candidates increasingly allocate resources to fund web sites offering computer users a wide range of campaign-related information, further reducing the need for personal contact with the candidate. Steve Forbes's 1996 web site offered users a newsletter, issue briefs, copies of recent speeches and a campaign schedule, together with space for interested voters to enter requests for further details and a link to campaign headquarters.[71] Some commentators regard this as a far greater threat to the retail tradition, overlooking the fact that one-to-one campaigning remains the crucial prerequisite for a successful New Hampshire campaign. Videos and computer technology may slowly alter the methods and range of information distribution in the primary but cannot overturn the expectations set by television for personalized politicking. As one GOP operative commented regarding the rising importance of cyberspace, "Even when the World Wide Web is widely used, it will only be a tool. . . . You're only as good as your issues and tactics."[72]

"NOTHING SO POWERFUL": THE *UNION LEADER*, WMUR AND THE PRIMARY

Presidential primaries not only exert a considerable influence on the activities and clout of the national news media but also raise the potential power of the indigenous state media, whose market audiences are naturally the target for intensive campaigning by candidate organizations. For a limited period, therefore, candidates will be as much concerned with local press and television reactions as with established organs with virtually national markets such as the *New York Times* or the major national television networks. Once again, the pole position of the first primary serves to heighten this temporary transfer of power and has brought the state media of New Hampshire under closer scrutiny than possibly that of any other state of similar size. Chapter 2 outlined the major discrepancies existing in the 1990s between the perception and reality of social and political life in the Granite State. These same discrepancies influence outsiders' assessments of state media, many of which remain rooted in the 1960s and 1970s. This period, when the influence of the conservative daily paper, the Manchester *Union Leader*, was at its height, has left a lasting impression on journalists and politicians, despite the fact that its proprietor, William Loeb, died in September 1981. Much of the negative reaction to New Hampshire as a primary state can be ascribed to enduring resentment of Loeb and the opinions he expressed through his paper.

The extent of Loeb's influence in the state between the 1950s and late 1970s is beyond question. The *Union Leader* was, and remains today, the only paper with statewide distribution in New Hampshire, making it central to the strategic calculations of local politicians and presidential contenders. As early as 1960, the organ reputed to be America's worst newspaper came in for a sharp attack from candidate John Kennedy in a speech at the end of his presidential campaign. The future president declared, "I believe there is probably a more irresponsible newspaper in the United States but I can't think of it. (Applause) I believe that there is a publisher who has less regard for the truth than William Loeb but I can't think of his name. (Deafening applause)."[73]

In its heyday, the style of the *Union Leader* was reminiscent of what James Perry describes as nineteenth-century knife-and-kill journalism in which favored candidates and public figures were depicted in laudatory articles as statesmen and patriots while their opponents and others attracting the paper's disapproval were dragged remorselessly through the mud for everything from their public pronouncements to their private lives.[74] The popularity and practice of this venomous style diminished through the twentieth century, particularly as television accustomed the public to less vitriolic and more apparently objective reporting. Bill Loeb kept the flame alive almost single-handedly in New Hampshire. Subjectivity in journalism is not, of itself, grounds for condemnation. Few modern reporters could straightfacedly deny at least some straying from objective criteria. The distinctive contribution of Loeb, critics allege, was the tendency to blur the lines between editorializing and straightforward reporting and to wage unceasing war against some candidates by accusation and innuendo.

The paper remains a subject of contention in the 1990s, although its editorial bite and statewide clout have decreased considerably under the late publisher's wife, Nackey Loeb. But it remains a highly readable, well laid-out paper that is particularly in touch with state affairs and state politics. At least part of the paper's notoriety stems from its archconservatism, a slant guaranteed to antagonize the predominantly moderate-liberal media establishment. Further provocation is provided by the motto printed above the masthead of each edition of the *Union Leader*, reading: "There is nothing so powerful as Truth." The further legend, "Where the Spirit of the Lord is, there is Liberty" follows directly beneath the names of Bill Loeb and his wife. Such comforting quotes have been accompanied, over the years, by some of the most infamous insults in postwar American political history. President Eisenhower was labeled "Dopey Dwight" and "that stinking hypocrite."[75] John F. Kennedy was, in Loeb's view "The Number One Liar in the United States," while Gerald Ford was simply a "jerk."[76] The paper allegedly referred to Henry Kissinger as a "kike," while Nelson Rockefeller's marital problems earned him the sobriquet "wife-swapper."[77] Loeb proudly claimed to have been the recipient of a phone call from jailed Teamsters boss Jimmy Hoffa "twenty minutes after he got out" of prison, thanking Loeb for his help in securing a pardon from President Nixon.[78]

During his career, Loeb attracted at least as much vitriol as he dispensed. A 1974 television documentary narrated by Lyndon Johnson's former press secretary Bill Moyers contained a passage from an anonymous New Hampshire state representative, "William Loeb is a permeating, deadly, sickening, horrible frightening load on the entire state. . . . He's running a daily clip coupon, asking readers to send in names and addresses of the neighbors who they think are cheating on welfare."[79]

Moyers observed that many of the critical sources on Loeb used in the documentary had wished to remain anonymous for fear of a vendetta against them in the paper. He asserted that New Hampshire politics was "littered with the carcasses of reputations fallen victim of the wrath of his hyperbole."[80]

Several surveys during the 1960s and 1970s documented the apparently all-permeating power of the *Union Leader* at a time before the explosion of cable and satellite television brought serious local competition. In a doctoral thesis published in 1975, Eric Veblen claimed that the results of at least four gubernatorial and senatorial primaries between 1960 and 1972 could be directly attributed to Loeb's intervention against or in favor of certain candidates.[81] GOP state legislator William Johnson observed of Loeb's tactics: "He doesn't do it once; he does it fourteen . . . twenty times on page one. In the meantime he kicks your candidate in the fanny ten times by saying what an SOB he is."[82]

According to Kevin Cash, these tactics plumbed subterranean depths in December 1969 over an alleged remark on drugs made by the daughter of Governor Walter Peterson. The alleged but unsubstantiated claim was that fifteen-year-old Meg Peterson had suggested there was nothing wrong in smoking pot. Cash records the feeling of the State House corps that the original UPI-transmitted story had been dissected to emphasize this particular allegation. School officials expressed anger that their statements had been twisted out of context, creating such a furor that Meg Peterson had to be removed from school for the day. At a Goffstown meeting addressed by Loeb, leaflets were distributed asking, "Do you think Governor Peterson is a good parent?"[83]

Loeb's voice, and that of the *Union Leader*, reached its peak of influence during the 1970s governorship of conservative Meldrim Thomson. Cash describes the strong links between the Thomson State House and Loeb's home (ironically, not in New Hampshire but in Pride's Crossing, Massachusetts). He claims that Thomson would phone Loeb up to nine times a day. The governor's actions would invariably be praised in the *Union Leader*, and Thomson would sometimes be allotted space above the masthead for special editorials.[84]

The substantive impact of Loeb's style is difficult to assess. Its importance lay mostly in its perceived influence. Veblen echoes the belief of many New Hampshire politicians that "even if some candidates are not absolutely certain that the apparent Loeb impact is actually real, the safest course is to hedge one's bets and to act as if the paper is powerful with the electorate."[85]

As a result, many candidates thought twice before running for state office, fearful of the effect of Loeb's attacks on their record but more especially on their personality or family. Interestingly, however, Loeb's track record in backing candidates was not a particularly impressive one. Charles Brereton noted that, in state politics, Thomas McIntyre, John Durkin, Hugh Gallen and Norman D'Amours were all elected to the governorship or the U.S. Congress over Loeb's protestations.[86] The paper's support was not sufficient to save Governor Thomson from the Democrat Hugh Gallen in 1978.[87]

The lasting contribution of the *Union Leader* under Bill Loeb was to provide the major motivating force behind the state's existing tax and social welfare structure. According to Brereton, "The state's record of being the only one in the nation never to have imposed a general sales or income tax can be conceded to Loeb's sway."[88]

This power of agenda-setting was, and to a lesser extent remains, the *Union Leader*'s greatest weapon. What the paper has to say on the tax question, and on a broad range of social issues, is a factor that all campaigns, national and state, are compelled to take into account. Since Loeb's death from cancer in 1981, the paper remains a force, exerting a powerful influence not only on statewide debate but also on the memories of reporters and politicians. There exists within New Hampshire considerable resentment that its public image has been principally shaped in the national media by incredulous recountings of Loeb's more harebrained editorials. James Perry wrote in 1973 that "the condition of New Hampshire is testament, in nightmare reality, to the power of the printed word," describing the state as both backward and anachronistic "because Loeb likes it that way."[89] While the accuracy of these generalized insults is highly questionable, the damage done to the state's reputation is not.

The high profile of the *Union Leader* is also a product of its circulation dominance. It remains the only paper in New Hampshire with extended statewide circulation, producing a weekday state and Manchester edition as well as a sister Sunday paper, the *New Hampshire Sunday News*. Its major print competitors, the *Concord Monitor, Nashua Telegraph, Portsmouth Herald, Foster's Daily Democrat of Dover* and *Keene Sentinel*, are smaller in both size and circulation. The paper's strongholds are considered to be in Manchester and its environs, the Bedford–Auburn–Hooksett–Goffstown area. In the counties of Coos, Grafton and Carroll, as well as in large areas of Rockingham and Sullivan, the *Union Leader* is still virtually unchallenged.

Whether the paper reflects or directs political opinion in these areas is debatable but current publisher Nackey Loeb remains adamant that its success lies in involving readers in the vital public issues of the day. Admitting that, to outsiders, the paper is "sort of a pariah," she adds: "Fifty years ago newspapers in this country used to have very strong editorial staffs. They believed what they said and did not hesitate to say it strongly. This has gone out of style now . . . but editorially we still throw brickbats."[90] The publisher vehemently denied, however, that the aeronautical brickbats extended from editorials to news columns, claiming that "we bend over backwards to give, in our news stories, full coverage to the people we oppose."[91]

The *Union Leader*'s ability to influence presidential primary elections, both during and after Loeb's tenure, has not been as great as its notoriety would suggest. Its importance was stressed by the national media, thus reinforcing its weight as a factor in successive campaigns, but Loeb backed a succession of losing contenders from the 1950s onwards—Taft in 1952, Goldwater in 1964, Ashbrook and Yorty in 1972 and Ronald Reagan in 1976. Despite virulent criticism from Loeb, Henry Cabot Lodge and Gerald Ford both triumphed in New Hampshire. Furthermore, the victories of Richard Nixon in 1960, 1968 and 1972 were achieved without any significant input from the paper. After Loeb's death, the *Union Leader* backed Pete DuPont in 1988 and Pat Buchanan in 1992. It achieved its first triumph since the Reagan era with Buchanan's victory in the 1996 primary. This patchy record has not prevented many presidential candidates, before and since 1981, from beating a path to the paper's Manchester offices in the hope that some personal diplomacy might stave off heavy criticism of the sort endured by Representative Philip Crane in 1979, which became so hostile and personal in its tone that the New Hampshire House of Representatives was moved to pass a resolution condemning the *Union Leader* for its "totally unsubstantiated allegations" and the "grossly unfair and vituperative personal attack" on Crane and his wife.[92] Unsurprisingly, therefore, Jody Powell worried over Loeb's potential treatment of Jimmy Carter in 1976 and later admitted to using a local contact, Lucille Kelly, who had good relations with the paper, in an effort to "minimize some of the vitriol and spleen that often comes out of that paper."[93]

In two instances, however, the *Union Leader* has been counted as a major factor in the primary race. The first, and most infamous, occurred in the 1972 Democratic primary and culminated in front-running candidate Edmund Muskie making a dramatic and emotional attack on Bill Loeb while standing on the back of a truck parked by the paper's Manchester offices. Muskie had been a natural target for Loeb's splenetic brand of conservatism and had been variously attacked in the paper as Flip-Flop Muskie, Moscow Muskie or the Vietnam War–Dove–Chicken. Loeb's aim was to siphon off key votes from the Maine senator while building up his own preferred candidate, Los Angeles mayor Sam "Mad Sam" Yorty, a colorful but obscure figure with no real chance of success. For weeks, stories in the *Union Leader* chipped away at the Muskie campaign, quoting a mental health expert who claimed the senator was mentally unsound and denouncing his failure to show up at a Jefferson–Jackson Day dinner as proof that he was taking the state for granted. Muskie finally cracked as the smears turned toward his wife, Jane. The BBC's correspondent, Fred Emery, later expressed surprise at Muskie's reaction to the reprinted *Newsweek* article since "what the *Union Leader* said about his wife was true."[94] Loeb himself claimed to have been startled, telling Bill Moyers that his tactic of pushing Muskie to the brink in the knowledge that he could not take criticism had paid dividends, but "I never . . . in my wildest speculation, ever thought it was going to end up with this dramatic scene of Liza crossing the ice."[95]

Muskie's verbal attack on Loeb drew perilously close to a threat of physical violence, but polls conducted immediately after the incident showed no noticeable change in the fortunes of either the front-runner or George McGovern. In fact, Muskie's totals rose slightly. The scene of the former vice-presidential candidate appearing to choke up in the snow, however, became part of the New Hampshire legend. When he failed to breach the psychologically crucial 50 percent barrier, the disastrous attack on Loeb was held responsible by many commentators. Evidence suggested that the incident did help depress voter turnout for Muskie in Manchester, the paper's backyard, but there is no real indication that without this controversy Muskie would have gone on to a more substantial or impressive showing. Despite some fanciful reinterpretations, the Loeb affair was a symptom, not a cause, of the decline and fall of Ed Muskie.

The 1980 Republican primary, however, offers a different perspective on the paper's influence. In March of that year, presidential contender George Bush received a memorandum from former candidate and Congressman Paul N. "Pete" McCloskey detailing the role played by the *Union Leader* during the recent New Hampshire primary. McCloskey's covering letter listed the Granite State campaigning schedules he had undertaken since 1972. He told Bush: "In all of these campaigns, the Manchester *Union Leader* played an active role, but I have never seen it used in the manner it was on Reagan's behalf and against you last month."[96]

The subsequent report detailed to Bush how Loeb "singled you out as the only real threat to his candidate, Ronald Reagan" and slanted his coverage accordingly.[97] Reagan was the beneficiary, in McCloskey's estimation, of ten favorable editorials and no fewer than seventy-one favorable articles. Bush received twenty-six negative editorials and fifty-four critical articles. Table 4.3 demonstrates the effect McCloskey believed these disparities had on voting patterns in the primary.

Table 4.3
Newspaper Circulation Areas and the 1980 Republican Primary Vote

Area *Union Leader* Sold Daily	Reagan	Bush
City of Manchester	7,361	910
Hillsborough Co. (Manchester excl.)	14,356	6,417
Grafton, Carroll, Coos	13,765	7,710
Sullivan, Rockingham areas covered by *Union Leader*	10,325	4,660
Totals	45,807	19,697

Other newspaper areas	Reagan	Bush
Nashua (*Nashua Telegraph*: pro-Bush)	2,799	1,859
Dover (*Foster's Daily Democrat*: pro-Bush)	1,016	845
Concord (*Monitor*: pro-Anderson)	2,146	1,325
Portsmouth (*Portsmouth Herald*: pro-Bush)	761	816
Lebanon (*Valley News*: pro-Anderson)	382	487
Keene (*Keene Evening Sentinel*: pro-Anderson)	1,287	910
Claremont (*Eagle Times*: No endorsement)	694	383
Laconia (*Laconia Evening Citizen*: no endorsement)	1,369	541
Totals	10,454	7,166

Source: Letter from Paul N. McCloskey, Jr., to George H. W. Bush, March 14, 1980. Courtesy Susan B. McLane.

McCloskey believed that the difference in total votes for each candidate, comparing districts in which the *Union Leader* was the only available newspaper and those in which other papers were sold, could only be accounted for by the vituperative anti-Bush campaign waged by Bill Loeb. An additional study, conducted by David Moore covering the period January 1 to February 25, 1980, produced similar results. In the Moore data (reproduced as Table 4.4), Reagan received 46 percent favorable coverage to only 5 percent for Bush. Meanwhile, 48 percent of Bush's coverage was identifiably negative contrasted with only 2 percent for Reagan.[98]

Table 4.4

Voter Preferences Among Readers and Nonreaders of the Manchester *Union Leader*

	October 1979		February 1980		March 1980	
Read *Union Leader*?	Yes	No	Yes	No	Yes	No
Voter Preference						
George Bush	4%	16%	22%	49%	14%	26%
Ronald Reagan	54%	30%	53%	17%	68%	32%
Others/unsure	42%	54%	15%	34%	18%	42%
Totals (%)	100	100	100	100	100	100

Source: David Moore, "The Manchester Union Leader in the New Hampshire Primary," in Orren and Polsby, eds., *Media and Momentum*, p. 117.

By Moore's calculations, during the crucial last days of the 1980 Republican primary, Bush was 27 points worse off among *Union Leader* readers than among nonreaders. Reagan had correspondingly jumped a hefty 36 points upward in the same grouping.[99]

The support of the *Union Leader* thus appeared to be vital in holding the former California governor's support steady in the face of a Bush surge coming out of his Iowa triumph. Undoubtedly, however, Bush would also have been severely damaged by the Nashua debate incident in February 1980 when he appeared to freeze when confronted on a public platform by a Reagan campaign ploy. Reagan had invited other candidates to the debate, unknown to the Bush camp who had been led to believe the debate would be a one-to-one contest. Bush's steadfast refusal to allow the other candidates, standing sheepishly at the back of the podium, to take part, was widely regarded as peevish and stubborn. Reagan, acting his part to the hilt, had attempted to persuade the debate chairman, Jon Breen of the *Nashua Telegraph*, to permit the candidates to join the proceedings. When a frustrated Breen, realizing what was happening, ordered Reagan's microphone to be switched off, a furious wave of boos and hissing swept the audience, and Reagan stormed, "I am *paying* for this microphone, Mr Green (sic)!"[100] Repeated television reruns of the debacle in all likelihood sealed Bush's fate far faster than any *Union Leader* editorial could have managed.

That the *Union Leader* maintains a wide circulation area and is therefore influential in key areas of the state is beyond doubt. Its backing helped Buchanan sweep the Manchester district in 1996. Its editorial attitudes remain vital to candidates in state primaries and elections, but even here its influence is limited. Nackey Loeb's support for Republican gubernatorial candidate Ovide Lamontagne in 1996 could not prevent the election of the state's first woman governor, Democrat Jeanne Shaheen. Whether the paper actually dictates voter sentiment to an extent that can alter the progress or decline of presidential candidacies remains debatable. Surveys of Bush's 1980 downward spiral may show disproportionate coverage but do not account for the effects of the Nashua debate, a turning point completely beyond Loeb's influence, or the change in strategy by Reagan, who had already drawn nearly level with Bush in New Hampshire polls by the time of the debate. In close elections, the paper's influence over the Manchester area can be important. Crediting the *Union Leader* with the Reagan presidency, however, may be stretching the point.

Out-of-state media have played up the paper's role in past primaries because Loeb's outrageous editorials added spice to primary coverage and because, in the days before satellite and cable television, it represented the single most important media outlet in the state. Loeb's passing and the advent of WMUR-Channel 9 have altered the reality, but the image persists.

Since the mid-1980s, the *Union Leader* has been forced to share the media market with New Hampshire's only major commercial television station, WMUR-TV Channel 9. The ABC-affiliate station began broadcasting in 1954, but its increasing clout only came to be felt in the state when the *Union Leader* was judged to have lost some of its editorial bite and when the steady stream of residents across the Massachusetts border had finally begun to change the political complexion of the state's southern tier. Channel 9, operating from a converted textile mill on the banks of the Merrimack in Manchester, reaches around 250,000 households across New Hampshire and broadcasts nine half-hour segments of news daily.[101] Its potential influence over the transmission and formation of political opinion has come to rival that of the *Union Leader*, its 80,000-strong New Hampshire audience for the nightly six o'clock news being larger than that for all three Boston-based newscasts combined.[102]

The station has attracted some criticism in the past for alleged conservative bias in its news reporting and earned itself the sobriquet W-GOP from state Democrats, some of whom went so far as to unsuccessfully challenge its Federal Communications Commission license on grounds of bias. While the accusation is refuted by station officials, the long predominance of the Republican party in state politics inevitably exerts some influence over the composition of state news. National politicians now tend to court WMUR in much the same way they once paid homage at the door of the *Union Leader*. In 1986–88, Governor John Sununu worked intensively at developing good relations between the nascent Bush campaign and WMUR general manager, David Zamichow, bringing the vice-president along to the station in Manchester in January 1988 for exclusive interviews and posed photographs with Channel 9 staff.[103]

Channel 9's importance to presidential campaigns in New Hampshire was graphically represented in the 1992 Bush–Quayle campaign. By Rosenstiel's account, the White House tried to use Channel 9 as part of a wider strategy of bypassing the national networks by granting a unique private interview with the president at a time when CBS, NBC, ABC and the major newspapers were becoming frustrated at their own lack of access. White House advisers tried, without success, to manipulate the station into airing extensive coverage of the president, promising photo opportunities every hour and an interview with Barbara

Bush, inviting WMUR to send a second camera crew and asking them to postpone their program until the president's return from his trip to Japan. So incessant did the new offers and efforts to set new ground rules become that station manager Jack Heath became exasperated and threatened to pull the plug on the entire project unless two simple and straightforward ten-minute slots with the president and Mrs. Bush were agreed.[104] The eventual broadcast infuriated the White House as it did not provide the laudatory coverage staffers had hoped for. Nonetheless, the new power of local New Hampshire television was established. Major networks were astonished and angered at the privilege accorded Channel 9 but could do no more than bargain for some brief segments of footage from the station's material.[105]

WMUR has become the key player of the modern New Hampshire primary, targeted by all incoming campaigns and placed at the center of every media strategy. Station airtime is a priceless commodity. During the last days of the 1996 primary, forty ads per day were run on behalf of both Steve Forbes and Bob Dole, with Pat Buchanan, Lamar Alexander and Morry Taylor screening around twenty each.[106] The station also receives dozens of last-minute response ads prepared by campaigns for sudden use in a campaign emergency. The *Boston Globe* reported in February 1996, "They are filmed and accumulating in the WMUR storeroom like warheads."[107] Once again, the reality of the New Hampshire media blizzard is somewhat at odds with the down home image of the primary itself. WMUR, in common with other stations close enough to be affected by the first primary, experiences direct and intense exposure to national political personalities as well as national and international news organizations and myriad political interest groups seeking to place their issue agenda under the primary spotlight.

During the 1992 campaign, the National Abortion Rights Action League spent $40,000 producing commercials to air on Channel 9. A similar project was undertaken by the Alliance for Rebirth of an Independent American Spirit, which candidate Bill Clinton subsequently accused of acting as the spearhead for a campaign against him by the Arkansas Department of Veterans Affairs. ACT-UP (Aids Coalition to Unleash Power) had its ads refused by the station in 1992 for containing film footage of homosexual embraces. In an interesting echo, Steve Michael, an AIDS awareness activist running in the 1996 Democratic primary, complained that WMUR had failed to screen his ads in their allotted slots, showing them instead at one o'clock in the morning. A previous Michael ad attacking President Clinton was substituted in the slot by WMUR, and the station had no qualms about screening an ad promoting a phone sex chatline alongside it. These revelations did nothing to reassure Democrats and liberals that WMUR was not operating a sociopolitical agenda of its own.[108] Overall, of 100 political ads aired each day in the 1992 primary season by WMUR, roughly 20 percent were for third parties or independent issue groups. The widespread interest generated by past New Hampshire primaries has resulted in a steady escalation of input from noncandidate groups, aware that candidates are easier to pin down and media attention is easier to attract in the highly charged primary atmosphere. The central role of WMUR, however, raises the same specter that haunted New Hampshire during the reign of

Bill Loeb—that of a single media outlet exercising enormous influence over presidential candidates and campaign issues.

CONCLUSION

Examining media activity and candidate strategy during the first primary reveals a chicken-and-egg dilemma. Do candidates concentrate so much time and effort on New Hampshire because the media compel them to do so, or do reporters focus on the state because the candidates and the structure of the nomination process deem it essential? The most credible explanation is that these two factors are cyclical and self-reinforcing, although less stress should be laid on the media role than on the evolving structure of nomination politics itself. The Granite State has headed the process, after all, since 1920, yet only with the proliferation and rising importance of presidential primaries after 1952 did it become important. New Hampshire was regarded as an important test of early public sentiment in the 1950s and 1960s, but only after the misjudged reforms of the post-1968 period and the new wave of primary legislation these provoked did it become crucial. The news media does carry considerable responsibility for the primary's notoriety and high profile. Its coverage of New Hampshire results is ritually overdone, but this derives only from the primary's role as the winnowing contest, a filter that allows longshot candidacies a chance to compete but that terminates the operations of most of those that fail.

The expectations and interpretation games are not played by journalists alone. They are major weapons in the arsenal of campaign strategists attempting to impose their perceptions of their candidates' prospects on reporters. Complaints concerning media benchmarking almost always arise from campaigns that have played this game and lost. Methods of reporting and interpreting have, on occasion, laid the media open to accusations of bias and blatant agenda-setting. In the last analysis, however, candidate complaints concerning the coverage they receive are unreliable foundations on which to base any proposals for restructuring the early nomination period. It may be significant that much of the criticism of this style of campaigning and the reporting it engenders has come from established, well-financed candidates who have entered reluctantly into an arena in which financial superiority does not naturally translate into an electoral stranglehold and who had the most to lose from a retail environment (Muskie, Mondale, Dole). Two candidates most associated with defeat in New Hampshire, Morris Udall and Bob Dole, were two of the candidates least comfortable with retail campaigning styles.

The stakes in New Hampshire are always high. Consequently, media criticism of candidates and perceived weaknesses in their campaigns is as welcome as the proverbial assertion that the Emperor has no clothes. If election reporting is flawed in content or style during a New Hampshire campaign, these failings are mostly symptomatic of the confusions, expectations and uncertainties that characterize the opening rounds of the nomination cycle and are generated as much by the candidates themselves as by reporters. They are not byproducts of New Hampshire's social or political culture. Indeed, they are likely to occur in any state occupying a similar position. If any broad claim can be made on the state's behalf, it is that its size and demographic composition compel candidates and reporters to approach voters on an individual or small-group basis rather than as an amorphous electoral mass. Rosenstiel records journalists' surprise that questions asked by New Hampshire citizens were so "serious, focused and surprisingly substantive," yet this is a much-observed quality and is a direct consequence of decades of exposure to intensive vote-harvesting by candidates.[109]

In New Hampshire, reporters and candidates alike are exposed to a retail campaigning style that is fraught with danger because it cannot be stage-managed in the manner of a California stadium rally. New technology has impacted on the first primary, but the retail dimension can never be seriously threatened. The up close and personal tradition and logistics of state organization leave little room for maneuver here. If media stories emanating from the Granite State sometimes exaggerate the human interest dimension of the campaign, it is because that dimension *is* unusual and will, in any event, progressively fade from television screens as the primary process moves into high gear later in the spring. Again, as with the broad candidate field and novelty of campaign themes and issues, the New Hampshire arena exhibits unique characteristics that require an approach by observers and participants far different from those that will be required at later stages. For journalists, as much as for longshot candidates and grass-roots voters, the quadrennial Granite State contest affords both opportunities and pitfalls unlike those to be found in any other part of the nomination process.

NOTES

1. F. Christopher Arterton, *Media Politics: The New Strategies of Presidential Campaigns* (Washington, DC: Healt, 1984), p. 186.

2. Richard Harwood, ed., *The Pursuit of the Presidency 1980* (New York: Berkeley Books, 1980), p. 48.

3. William Manchester, *The Glory and the Dream: A Narrative History of America 1932–1972* (London: Bantam Books, 1975), p. 1165.

4. Hunter S. Thompson, *Fear and Loathing on the Campaign Trail* (London: Allison & Busby, 1973); Jules Witcover, *Marathon: The Pursuit of the Presidency 1972–1976* (New York: Viking Press, 1977).

5. Austin Ranney, *Channels of Power: The Impact of Television on American Politics* (New York: Basic Books, 1983), p. 58.

6. Tom Rosenstiel, *Strange Bedfellows: How Television and the Presidential Candidates Changed American Politics* (New York: Hyperion, 1993), p. 49.

7. Frank I. Luntz, *Candidates, Consultants and Campaigns: The Style and Substance of American Electioneering* (New York: Basil Blackwell, 1988), p. 209.

8. David L. Paletz and Robert M. Entman, *Media Power Politics* (New York: Macmillan Co., 1981), p. 29.

9. Interview, Howard S. Fineman, Washington, DC, August 25, 1986.

10. Stephen J. Wayne, *The Road to the White House 1992* (New York: St. Martin's Press, 1992), p. 230.

11. Interview, John W. Chancellor, New York, August 18, 1986.

12. Ibid.

13. Interview, Carl Cameron, Manchester, NH, June 23, 1995.

14. Ibid.

15. Interview, John W. Chancellor.

16. "96 NH Primary Kicks Off," *Union Leader*, February 20, 1995, p. A1.

17. "Two More Governors Endorse Dole Bid," *Union Leader*, February 15, 1996, p. A6.

18. Interview, Robert W. Beckel, Washington, DC, August 24, 1986.

19. Interview, Fred Emery, BBC Lime Grove Studios, London, July 10, 1985.

20. "In NH, an 'invisible primary' is heating up," *Boston Globe*, February 17, 1995, p. 20.

21. Charles Brereton, *First in the Nation: New Hampshire and the Premier Presidential Primary* (Portsmouth, NH: Peter E. Randall Publishers, 1987), p. 36.

22. Interview, George S. McGovern, Washington, DC, August 24, 1986.

23. Interview, Dick Drayne, Washington, DC, August 22, 1986.

24. Witcover, *Marathon*, p. 393.

25. Jonathan Moore and Janet Fraser, eds., *Campaign for President: The Managers Look at '76* (Cambridge, MA: Harvard University Press, 1977), pp. 66–68.

26. Emmett H. Buell, Jr., and James W. Davis, "Win Early and Often: Candidates and the Strategic Environment of 1988," in Emmett H. Buell, Jr., and Lee Sigelman, eds., *Nominating the President* (Knoxville: University of Tennessee Press, 1991), p. 22.

27. Interview, Carl Cameron.

28. "Dole's Kitchen Magician," *Time*, July 21, 1995, p. 33.

29. Rosenstiel, *Strange Bedfellows*, p. 103.

30. "Now, It's the Presidential Expectations Game," *Union Leader*, November 9, 1995, p. A3.

31. Moore and Fraser, *Campaign for President 1976*, pp. 33–34.

32. Interview, George S. McGovern.

33. Michael J. Robinson, "Media Coverage in the Primary Campaign of 1976," in William Crotty, ed., *The Party Symbol: Readings on Political Parties* (San Francisco: W. H. Freeman, 1980), p. 52.

34. Ibid.

35. Ibid.

36. James W. Davis, *Presidential Primaries: The Road to the White House* (Westport, CT: Greenwood Press, 1980), p. 83.

37. Arterton, *Media Politics*, p. 10.

38. Paletz and Entman, *Media Power Politics*, p. 36.

39. Ibid., p. 37.

40. Ibid.

41. *Statement of Professor Michael J. Robinson, Media Analysis Project, George Washington University. Hearings Held Before the Subcommittee on Elections of the Committee on House Administration*, House of Representatives, Ninety-ninth Congress, Second Session, March 20, May 8, 1986 (Washington, DC: U.S. Government Printing Office, 1986), pp. 130–43.

42. Ibid., p. 131.

43. Interview, Howard Fineman.

44. Ibid.

45. For a uniquely detailed examination of the 1984 Hart campaign in New Hampshire, see Susan B. Casey, *Hart and Soul: Gary Hart's New Hampshire Odyssey and Beyond* (Concord, NH: NHI Press, 1986).

46. "Can Ford Stop Reagan?" *U.S. News and World Report*, May 24, 1976, p. 15. Reagan finally opted for Pennsylvania senator Richard Schweiker, thereby offending the party's right wing and propelling many unpledged delegates into the Ford camp.

47. David Broder, *Washington Post*, February 24, 1977, p. 7.

48. Tom Wicker, *New York Times*, March 13, 1968, p. 1.

49. *The Times*, London, March 11, 1968, p. 8.

50. Moore and Fraser, *Campaign for President 1976*, p. 90.

51. Interview, Howard Fineman.

52. Iowa has failed to select the eventual Democratic party nominee three times (1976, 1988 and 1992) since the contest first drew media attention in 1976, and the Republican nomination twice (1980 and 1988). By contrast, New Hampshire Democrats missed their party's mark only twice (1984 and 1992) and Republicans only once (1996).

53. *Statement of the Honorable Judd Gregg, Hearings Held Before the Subcommittee*, 1986, pp. 45–46.

54. Interview, Robert Beckel.

55. Interview, Carl Cameron.

56. Interview, Robert Beckel.

57. Interview, Walter P. Mears, New York, August 18, 1986.

58. Rosenstiel, *Strange Bedfellows*, pp. 94–95.

59. Ibid., p. 99.

60. Ibid.

61. Luntz, *Candidates, Consultants and Campaigns*, p. 216.

62. "Along with the Politicians Comes a Host of Celebrities," *Boston Sunday Globe*, February 18, 1996, p. NH19.

63. Ibid.

64. *Boston Globe*, February 12, 1992, p. 23.

65. "As Late Ads Build, True Power Rests Behind the Scenes," *Boston Globe*, February 19, 1996, p. 10.

66. "Forbes Fortune Leaves Campaign Rivals Trailing," *The Times*, February 7, 1996, p. 12.

67. Ibid.

68. "Will Forbes' Spending Make This the Last for Nation's First?" *Boston Sunday Globe*, February 11, 1996, p. NH6.

69. Peter Goldman and Tom Mathews, *The Quest for the Presidency: The 1988 Campaign* (New York: Simon & Schuster, 1989), p. 247.

70. Luntz, *Candidates, Consultants and Campaigns*, pp. 211–12.

71. "Candidates Set Webs to Snare Candidates," *Boston Sunday Herald*, February 18, 1996, p. 26.

72. Ibid.

73. Theodore C. Sorensen, *Kennedy* (London: Hodder & Stoughton, 1965), p. 210.

74. James M. Perry, *Us and Them: How the Press Covered the 1972 Election* (New York: Clarkson & Potter, 1973), p. 80.

75. Jules Witcover, "William Loeb and the New Hampshire Primary: A Question of Ethics," *Columbia Journalism Review* (May-June 1972), p. 14.

76. David Moore, "The Legacy of William Loeb," *Public Opinion* (December 1982–January 1983), p. 43.

77. On the subject of this particular epithet, Nackey Loeb later explained: "It was actually not an editorial by Bill but by the editor of our Sunday paper . . . the gist of the editorial was that it was crazy that the Jewish people themselves were treating Kissinger as they would treat a person they termed a 'kike', which meant a person who abused his Jewish heritage. When Bill saw it he said, 'Oh boy! We're going to get it for this one!' and he had to say to the editor, 'OK, let's be a little more careful.'" (Source: Interview, Nackey Loeb, Manchester, NH, June 11, 1987.)

78. Aaron Latham, "Can the Pistol-Packing Publisher Win It for the Cowboy Star?" *New York Magazine*, February 2, 1976, p. 41.

79. "The Man Who Made Muskie Cry," Transcript of Educational Broadcasting Corporation production, "Bill Moyers' Journal," March 19, 1974, p. 1. Transcript kindly supplied by New Hampshire senator Susan N. McLane.

80. Ibid.

81. Eric Veblen, *The Manchester Union Leader in New Hampshire Elections* (Hanover, NH: University Press of New England, 1975), p. 154.

82. Ibid., p. 82.

83. Kevin Cash, *Who the Hell Is William Loeb?* (Manchester, NH: Amoskeag Press, 1975). For Cash's full account of the Peterson episode, see pp. 271–79.

84. Ibid., p. 372.

85. Veblen, *The Manchester Union Leader*, p. 170.

86. Charles Brereton, "Loeb's Candidates Seldom Won," *Concord Monitor*, Concord, NH, October 13, 1983, p. 14.

87. Even in its post-1981 era, the paper is still capable of producing vicious epithets to describe the state's political leaders. In 1992 former governor John H. Sununu was ridiculed as "Bush's peripatetic political pimp," and his boss was dismissed as "a political phoney" (*Union Leader*, February 3, 1992, p. 21 and February 2, 1992, p. 2B).

88. Brereton, "Loeb's Candidates Seldom Won."

89. Perry, *Us and Them*, p. 81.

90. Interview, Nackey S. Loeb.

91. Ibid.

92. Brereton, *First in the Nation*, p. 207.

93. Interview, Jody Powell, Jr., Washington, DC, August 26, 1986.

94. Interview, Fred Emery.

95. "Bill Moyers' Journal," pp. 4–5.

96. Letter from Congressman Paul N. McCloskey, Jr., to George H. W. Bush, March 14, 1980, p. 1. Courtesy, Susan B. McLane.

97. Ibid.

98. David Moore, "The Manchester Union Leader in the New Hampshire Primary," in Gary Orren and Nelson Polsby, eds., *Media and Momentum: The New Hampshire Primary and Nomination Politics* (Chatham, NJ: Chatham House, 1987), pp. 112–14.

99. Ibid.

100. Brereton, *First in the Nation*, p. 219.

101. Laurence J. Goodrich, "New Hampshire's Primary Station," *Christian Science Monitor*, April 1995, p. 9.

102. Rosenstiel, *Strange Bedfellows*, p. 84.

103. Goldman and Mathews, *Quest for the Presidency 1988*, p. 265.

104. The full story of the complex negotiations over the program are supplied in Rosenstiel, *Strange Bedfellows*, pp. 86–89.

105. Ibid.

106. "As Late Ads Build," *Boston Globe*, p. 10.
107. Ibid.
108. "WMUR Accused of Censorship," *Concord Monitor*, February 20, 1996, p. A3.
109. Rosenstiel, *Strange Bedfellows*, p. 96.

5

The Importance of Being Earliest

Let's let that little pissant state sit by itself in February and let's all go in April!

— Robert W. Beckel, 1986

BACKGROUND

The successive rules revisions that followed the McGovern–Fraser Commission during the 1970s and 1980s are often regarded as haphazard, bungled efforts by the Democratic party to come to terms both with its increasing heterogeneity and the end of the New Deal ascendancy. In fact, these commissions were primarily a reflexive response to growing pressures for democratization experienced both inside and outside the presidential selection process.

Beginning in the first half of the 1960s, the rise of radical activism on American college campuses presaged changes in established political practice no less radical or disruptive than those accompanying the franchise expansion of the Jacksonian epoch. Deepening hostility within the liberal and conservative wings of both major parties to the burgeoning influence of centralized authority, combined with the appearance of new, mobilizing issues such as civil rights, environmentalism, feminism and consumer rights, presented an incoherent but powerful movement that was fundamentally subversive to the post–Depression political order. The organizers and stewards of this order, party officialdom, found their authority challenged and their monopoly of the levers of power threatened by the rise of television and computer technology, which diversified and diffused political influence and drew hosts of activists into the political arena—activists with transient partisan loyalties and individual policy agendas.

Predictably, the two arenas in which these changes were most deeply felt have been the U.S. Congress and the electoral system, the two arenas most closely dependent on intimate connection with state and national electorates. Both responded to escalating pressures by opening up their procedures to outside scrutiny and diluting elite authority by broadening participation. The Democratic party in particular spent much of the 1970s erecting totems to representation and responsiveness. Attacks on the congressional seniority system and sweeping revisions of procedure were combined with a mania for voting formulas geared to reflect every conceivable variation in social status and public opinion.

The presidential nomination system was perhaps more directly affected by these changes than any other part of the political process. The flood of primary legislation in the states after 1968 created a new, more unpredictable nomination system in which party hierarchies took a back seat to grass-roots voters and activists. With nominations now dependent on, rather than supplemented by, the primary voter, the structure and format of the preconvention calendar acquired powerful political significance. Under these circumstances, New Hampshire's position grew increasingly difficult. In the pre-reform system, its first-place status had been regarded as a quirk, an indicative but far from decisive contest in which public opinion could be registered and noted by party bosses before the serious business of convention bargaining began. Even after 1952, when multi-ballot conventions disappeared, the primary calendar was sufficiently sparse for candidates faring badly in New Hampshire to make up lost ground later.

After 1968, however, the crowded timetable constricted the candidates' maneuvering room. The order of primaries, and the time lapse between each contest, acquired new importance to the long-term calculations of campaign strategists. In this environment, New Hampshire's position as the lead-off contest came under fire from two directions. Reform advocates demanded a system in which either no state would regularly head the calendar or one in which the lead state would be one more representative of the national electorate. Other states, particularly California, began to complain about the disproportionate influence of early contests on candidate selection, demanded an end to special exemptions and started front-loading their contests. The Granite State rapidly acquired an image problem from which it has never properly recovered. Its strenuous efforts to avoid being pushed back into the pack via regional primaries or DNC directives have served merely to increase its unpopularity with senior Democratic party officials, national media commentators and other state parties. The 1975 first primary statute angered the state's numerous critics. The 1995 waiting period dispute rendered them apoplectic.

The clashes between state and national party officials over primary scheduling are instructive. They embody, in microcosm, the divergence of priorities between the old and new political constructs; between conferral of special status and the impulse for electoral fairness; between old-style retail campaigning and the juggernaut of modern, media-based electioneering; between states' rights and a newly assertive, newly centralized party apparatus. New Hampshire's experience in this schizophrenic environment is illustrated in three significant arenas of conflict. The first arises from a dispute between state Democrats, the secretary of state in Concord and the DNC over the timing of the 1984 primary. This problem snowballed from a minor misunderstanding into a threat to unseat the state delegation at the Democrats' San Francisco Convention. This has been, to date, the most serious of the numerous rules disputes involving New Hampshire. More than a decade later, its reverberations continue to affect DNC scheduling policies. The second arena of conflict involves mid-1990s scheduling disputes, during which efforts by Arizona and Delaware to encroach upon New Hampshire's primary window met with stiff opposition from New Hampshire, provoked a bitter interstate dispute and prompted passage of a controversial new addition to the 1975 first primary law. In the third arena, arguments for and against continuation of New Hampshire's special status are framed in congressional committee hearings. In this arena, the case against New Hampshire's primary is put by reformers seeking congressional action to implement a new, regional primary system. In its movement through these three arenas, the sensitive issue of the first primary is dissected in progressively widening perspective: as a party issue, as a state issue and, finally, as an obstacle to the development of a national primary system.

NEW HAMPSHIRE V. THE NATIONAL DEMOCRATIC PARTY

The Winograd Commission established a window for the 1980 Democratic primary season during which all delegate selection primaries and caucuses were to be held. This was partly intended to mollify states complaining that later primaries were deprived of real choice by the winnowing of the candidate field in earlier contests. Rule 10A of the National Democratic Party Delegate Selection Rules for 1984 subsequently stated that no primaries, caucuses or conventions were to be held for the purpose of delegate selection before the second Tuesday in March of the election year or after the second Tuesday in June. A significant rider, however, added that, "The New Hampshire Primary may be held no earlier than seven days before the second Tuesday in March, and the Iowa precinct caucuses may be held no earlier than fifteen days before the second Tuesday in March."[1] The rule proceeded to warn that under no circumstances could a contest scheduled within these dates in the 1980 election cycle move outside the window, in either direction, in 1984.

Gary Wekkin's analysis of national–state party relations posits two circumstances under which state party officials may be induced to actively dispute national party rules: first, if such rules are deemed by the plaintiffs to harm the state's political tradition and, second, if the new rules are perceived to be harmful to both the state party machinery and its political interests.[2] New Hampshire officials have always considered both conditions applicable to their position. Without the first-in-the-nation contest, the state party's leverage at the national level, resulting from high levels of media exposure, would evaporate overnight. Consequently, the state's defense of its first position has traditionally been a bipartisan operation, despite outward appearances. In almost perpetual control of state government, local Republicans have jealously guarded the tradition. This provides a convenient fallback position for state Democrats, most of whom are equally protective of the seventy-five year tradition but whose semipermanent minority status can be useful in tussles with the Democratic National Committee.

RSA 653:9, the New Hampshire statute requiring that its primary must precede all others in each presidential election year, constituted nothing more than recognition of an already established convention. The national Democratic party has little sympathy with this law but has often fought shy of directly confronting New Hampshire, partly through fear of provoking accusations of infringing states' rights and partly through wariness of New Hampshire's increasingly professional defense operation. In a 1983 memo to DNC chairman Charles T. Manatt, party treasurer Paul G. Kirk, Jr., warned, "All citizens of New Hampshire, Republicans as well as Democrats, enjoy, indeed covet, the media attention and notoriety which the state receives from its time-honored tradition."[3]

Attitudes had changed by the early 1980s, when Manatt set himself the difficult task of bringing some order to the party's nomination calendar in an effort to free it from the debilitating rules controversies that ritually surfaced during the 1970s. Disputes over quotas, windows, proportional delegate allocation and front-loading had damaged party unity and presented a public image of disorganization at a time when Republicans, under the chairmanship of Bill Brock and, later, Frank Fahren-kopf, were updating and streamlining the GOP's election machine.

In August 1981 the Hunt Commission set about the task of drafting rules of engagement for the 1984 election cycle. Faced with renewed national and regional opposition within the party to their early contests, Iowa and New Hampshire moved rapidly to shore up their support. Backers of both early front-runners, former Vice-President Walter Mondale and Senator Edward Kennedy, were initially skeptical. Kennedy had been heavily outpolled by President Carter in 1980's New Hampshire contest, and his supporters feared a repeat performance in 1984. Mondale's managers, anxious for a quick kill early in the primary season, were particularly opposed to an early Granite State primary. National Campaign Co-ordinator Bob Beckel later explained that his calculation for a November victory against Ronald Reagan was based on a series of rapid wins in the spring.

That strategy meant winning Iowa, New Hampshire, rolling through the southern primaries and wrapping it all up. In the summer of 1983 we polled New Hampshire extensively . . . we spent $50,000 . . . and we discovered that Mondale had glaring weaknesses. . . . It was a critical state to us and it was the one state we were worried about.[4]

These "glaring weaknesses" included a largely nonunionised labor force and a primary electorate with an apparent taste for insurgent candidacies. Beckel foresaw the danger of Mondale being typecast as an establishment Democrat, a highly unfavorable appellation in the contemporary political climate and often a dangerous one in New Hampshire.

Democratic governor Hugh J. Gallen arrived at the Eastern Regional Hearings of the Hunt Commission on November 6, 1981, accompanied by Representative Norman E. D'Amours of the First Congressional District and New Hampshire Democratic chairman Richard E. Boyer. According to Emmett Buell's analysis of the subsequent debates, seven options lay before the commissioners. The 1980 exemptions could be renewed without change (thereby antagonizing other states who sought to join Iowa and New Hampshire); a regional primary system could be created with an option of four dates from which all states would choose and for which no exemptions would be allowed; Iowa or New Hampshire could be awarded a sole exemption; the nomination window could simply be shortened with no exemptions permitted or lengthened, with a select few allowed to operate outside. Finally, New Hampshire and Iowa could both be exempted, with the stipulation that their contests occur within twenty-one days of the window.[5] The ensuing debate, continuing into 1982, was notable for the joint campaign waged by Iowa and New Hampshire. Iowa staff member Maria Menne recalled that her state "held hands with New Hampshire and ran together" at the hearings, an all-or-nothing gambit against states demanding an end to their favored positions which appeared to pay off.[6] This victory may have been influenced by delegate Edward Campbell, who persuaded Mondale's managers that the vice-president's likely victory in the Iowa caucus would be devalued should the Hawkeye State be pushed back inside the window.[7]

Meanwhile, Bob Beckel and James Johnson, national campaign chairman for Mondale, had hit upon a new and tempting scenario whereby Iowa and New Hampshire might be compelled to pay for their special status by agreeing to go back-to-back in the primary calendar. They conferred secretly with Manatt, Beckel later revealed, and although sympathetic to the chairman's determination to rein in Iowa and New Hampshire, Manatt persuaded Johnson to support a measure that would at least help party unity and quickly decide the nomination. "We said, 'Look, here's a compromise. Why don't you put them back-to-back?', knowing full well that if we'd had New Hampshire the next day, Hart would not have had the eight days of media . . . we probably would have won. It fell through because we couldn't get New Hampshire to buy it."[8] Kennedy's supporters held firm, but with the assured backing of the Mondale camp and the support of Ohio senator John Glenn, another potential candidate, Governor Gallen could count on at least thirteen votes. A further fifteen to seventeen votes would come from labor representatives who were in the process of aligning behind Mondale. Kennedy backers subsequently capitulated, and New Hampshire's March 6 primary seemed safe from further attack.[9]

Within twelve months of the 1982 bargaining, however, New Hampshire found its position tenuous once again. In the rush to cut a deal with the Hunt Commission, insufficient attention had been paid to the question of the Vermont primary, scheduled for the same day as New Hampshire in 1984—March 6. This primary was in fact no more than a beauty contest in which voters expressed a preference between candidates but where no convention delegates were selected. In 1980 it had been held one week after New Hampshire, and Secretary of State Gardner had assumed this would be the pattern for 1984. Vermont could not technically trigger activation of the First Primary law in New Hampshire since delegates were not involved, but in the *Republican* Vermont primary, delegates could have been chosen in 1980 had any candidate gained over 40 percent of the popular vote. This time bomb had gone unnoticed by Governor Gallen and the Democrats, but Secretary Gardner held to the belief that it should be seen as a potential trigger for the First Primary law. This law specifically designated "a similar election" (involving delegate choice) as the reason needed to move New Hampshire's primary date forward. In Gardner's view, Vermont's Republican contest now constituted just such a threat.[10]

State Democrats, grateful for the renewal of their special exemption, were inclined to disregard this new problem. Nonetheless, they recognized that Vermont, along with Maine and Massachusetts which had yet to reschedule their contests to a date after New Hampshire's, could cause considerable trouble.

Former mayor of Concord Martin L. Gross moved quickly to reestablish the First Primary Committee which had been instrumental in the 1982 dogfight. The committee's aim was "to reduce any potential feelings of hostility or suspicion which might reduce our effectiveness in retaining our first primary status."[11] Gross conceded reluctantly that pressure from Vermont could now make it impossible for New Hampshire to stay within the guidelines stipulated by Rule 10A.[12] He revealed that George Bruno, the new Democratic state party chairman, would move to amend 10A at the next meeting of the Rules and Bylaws Committee of the Democratic party on July 15, 1983. His proposal would be to insert into the original clause a more wide-ranging definition to snare Vermont's primary in the same net as other contests. Its proposed amendment would run:

Provided however: The New Hampshire Primary may be held no earlier than seven days in advance of any such delegate selection procedure *or any procedure for determining voter preference.* (Italics added.)[13]

Gross still needed to demonstrate to skeptical national committee members that New Hampshire was not spoiling for a fresh fight. Adopting a wait and see policy, he put out reassuring statements at regular intervals. Chris Spirou, minority Democratic leader in New Hampshire's House of Representatives, made a spirited public attack on Vermont and received a cautionary memo from Gross stressing that 10A did not impose restrictions on beauty contests which did not select delegates.[14] Gross believed they had only to wait upon events. If Maine and Massachusetts placed their contests in violation of 10A, New Hampshire could easily justify as self-defense a move in its primary date. As the former Concord mayor explained, "We could then properly argue that we should be relieved of the limitations of Rule 10A because other states had deprived us of its benefits."[15] Vermont, however, would have to be neutralized by encouraging candidates to stay away from the contest. Here, New Hampshire's influence, built up over decades, would be crucial. Many candidates, afraid of offending the politicians and press of such a pivotal state, were likely to heed the call for a boycott. Even if they did not, New Hampshire had to be seen to move heaven and earth to prevent another showdown with the DNC. The best way to achieve this was to eliminate the image of Vermont as a potential threat. In a letter to George Bruno, Gross stated,

I am specifically asking each member of the . . . committee who represents a presidential campaign to obtain . . . a letter stating unequivocally that the candidate will not permit his name to be entered in the Vermont Primary. . . . It is vitally important that we get such . . . statements, so that we can neutralize whatever legal or political effect the . . . primary might otherwise have.[16]

Buell records that pledges were quickly gained from Mondale, Hart, Glenn, Reuben Askew and Fritz Hollings.[17] At this stage the odds appeared stacked in the Granite State's favor. Nancy Pelosi, chairwoman of the DNC's Compliance Review Commission (CRC), wrote to Edwin Granai, Vermont's party chairman, requesting that the state shift its primary back inside the window, indicating that while Vermont was not in breach of the letter of 10A, it was clearly in intended breach of its spirit.[18] Manatt, though hardly a New Hampshire partisan, lent his support to the boycott campaign.

Secretary Gardner remained convinced that his interpretation of RSA 653:9 had been correct. An underlying reason for what Gross regarded as intransigence by the State House may have been the fear of establishing a precedent. Gardner perceived that the neutralization of Vermont by means other than official party sanction could open the door to future, more serious challenges. Having given way once, New Hampshire might be expected to do so repeatedly. Ultimately, however, Gardner's role would be to interpret and apply Granite State law without reference to the convenience of either political party. His Vermont counterpart would eventually drop the 40 percent threshold but too late to influence the course of events in New Hampshire.[19]

State Democrats were becoming alarmed at the looming confrontation. The question was not merely whether the CRC would be prepared to discipline states that transgressed on the Iowa–New Hampshire timetable but to what extent it would believe that state Democrats had been compelled to act in accordance with state law. Correspondence and later recollections of officials involved cast doubt on whether the DNC properly understood the nature of the state party's problem. Pelosi had also been to visit Bill Gardner, informing him of the DNC's preference that the two contests should be held jointly. How much of this misapprehension was willful is also open to conjecture. Insecure and resentful, the state party was not about to take a fall for the DNC. In a letter to Manatt on March 8, 1983, Richard Boyer claimed that he had warned the Hunt Commission of the pitfalls of beauty contests but "they chose not to address the problem."[20] Boyer, Spirou and others believed that a plethora of such contests could develop ahead of their primary, with the resultant media frenzy preempting New Hampshire's considered verdict and thus negating its special status.[21] Rule 20, Section A of the Democratic party selection rules stipulated that, in the event of a clash between party rules and state laws, the state party was required to take "provable, positive steps" to resolve the difficulty through changes in the state laws.[22]

The First Primary Committee had sent letters requesting changes in interpretation of the 1975 statute to Secretary Gardner and Attorney General Gregory Smith. The Committee would have preferred that Gardner and Smith had not interpreted Vermont's primary as a trigger for the First Primary Law and were prepared to reconcile themselves to going on the same day as Vermont by way of compromise. Gardner and Smith held fast. However, such action could still be nullfied by Section C of Rule 20, which held that, regardless of local activists' efforts, state parties could still be compelled to adopt a new, party-run selection process that did not conflict with national rules.[23] The way lay open for the DNC to end the dispute by mounting a takeover of the Democrats' selection system and setting its own date for a primary. Congressman D'Amours wrote to presidential candidate Alan Cranston, "This matter, clearly, is out of our control."[24]

With the CRC deadline for submission of delegate selection plans fast approaching, Maine announced caucuses for March 4, 1984, in violation of 10A. Iowa promptly set two provisional dates, one within the window and one outside, on February 20, should New Hampshire move up. The New Hampshire date was set for March 6 with an option for February 28 if Secretary Gardner decided the First Primary statute had been triggered. By June 17, 1983, the CRC had rejected all three plans. Resubmissions were set for October 15. The chairmen of the Iowa and Maine Democrats, Dave Nagle and Barry Hobbins, joined Bruno in the search for support from leading presidential candidates. They hoped the CRC would be less inclined to penalize noncompliant states that presented a united front.[25] Secretary Gardner had yet to announce a firm primary date. As his decision would be based on other states' respect for the First Primary statute, New Hampshire's Democrats hoped to be found blameless by the CRC.

On the night of October 15, at Washington's Embassy Row Hotel, the CRC threw out the revised New Hampshire plan with the terse statement: "It is recommended that the New Hampshire plan be held in non-compliance with the 1984 . . . rules until the state party submits a date which is in compliance with Rule 10A."[26]

With their backs firmly to the wall, state Democrats now faced the very real possibility of a convention delegation imposed by the CRC.[27] As Martin Gross commented, "Our number looked like it was up, baby!"[28] The harassed First Primary Committee chairman later threatened drastic measures if the CRC forced his state to abandon first place, telling reporters in spring 1984,

If Manatt pulls any ugly stuff at the convention . . . I'll make him look like far more of a fool than he ever made us seem. I will go out to San Francisco with manure on my boots and tell the press that . . . Mr Manatt happens to be unseating the duly elected representatives of the state of New Hampshire. That ought to play pretty well on T.V.[29]

A twenty-day breathing space was wrung from the CRC after intensive negotiations throughout the night of October 15–16, during which proposals and counterproposals were delivered between different suites of the Embassy Row Hotel. Finally, on November 3, a revised plan was handed to Pelosi. Drafted by Bruno, it contained a three-page memorandum outlining amendments made to the original version in line with CRC demands. These were mostly technical alterations involving unpledged convention delegates and a change in the law on access to the primary ballot. The final point, however, stressed that all efforts to dissuade Gardner, Smith, the General Court, Executive Council or Governor John Sununu from their position had failed.

This appeared to be an admission of defeat but was, in reality, a gauntlet thrown down for the national party.[30] The only way state Democrats could now comply with CRC demands would be to detach their primary from the Republican contest held on the day allotted under state law (February 28, 1984, under Vermont's influence) and hold their ballot on March 6, outside state jurisdiction and thus without police protection or state supervision. There would be no officially printed ballot sheets, no participation by official scrutineers and no official certification of the results. Secretary Gardner had sketched this unpalatable scenario for the Democrats in a document explaining the legal provisions of the primary. Gardner stated that "If the National Democratic Party were to insist that presidential primaries be held within a . . . period which would not include the time provided by New Hampshire RSA 57:1 . . . the New Hampshire Democratic Party would immediately be immersed in a legal problem of major proportions."[31]

The CRC now faced a no-win situation. A separate Democratic primary could indeed proceed but only as a party-operated enterprise, leading to reduced participation, legal complications and considerable political embarrassment. In forcing the state party to comply with its regulations, the CRC would pay a high price. As Gardner's document made clear, it would amount to "a reversal of all the things that Democrats in New Hampshire have worked for for many years."[32]

The New Hampshire primary, both Republican and Democratic contests, took place on February 28, 1984. The Republican ballot was a ritual confirmation for President Reagan, the Democratic an upset victory for Senator Gary Hart, once more boosting the Granite State's notoriety while doing nothing to endear it to the DNC or to the Mondale camp which had tried so hard to prevent it. Yet although both the Iowa and New Hampshire contests took place in contravention of Democratic party rules, neither delegation was unseated at the summer conventions. The CRC eventually backed down less through an inability to enforce its rules than through fear of an embarrassing convention protest that might harm the eventual party nominee, much as Hubert Humphrey and George McGovern had been tainted by the disruptions at Chicago and Miami Beach. Manatt had been determined to achieve his aim of a united party with all states in compliance, but the dispute had subverted this goal by introducing an immovable obstacle—state law.

Gross, Bruno and the New Hampshire Democrats also employed their one remaining ace—a signed statement from most leading presidential candidates arguing the impossibility of changing New Hampshire's primary date. This was the product of the concerted Bruno–Nagle–Hobbins policy to solicit external support for the primary. Attached to Bruno's letter to Pelosi, it increased pressure on the CRC to drop its crusade.

Interpretations vary on the manner in which the signatures were obtained during New Hampshire's October 1983 Democratic convention. Each candidate, upon arrival, was taken to a small room behind the stage, notified of the problem and requested to sign. All except Askew did so. Buell claims that the candidates were not ambushed by this strategy but had been warned in advance of the petition and had already decided on their response.[33] Bruno and the state Democrats were well aware that, with the Mondale campaign juggernaut now rolling, all the other contenders saw the Granite State as their only hope for an upset result and the only important state where they could compete on almost equal terms with limited budgets. The petition constituted a Memorandum of Understanding in every sense of the word. Its import was not lost on Manatt. In 1984 Nagle claimed that he had met Manatt in private shortly after the CRC meeting and the chairman had conceded that a signed petition could clinch New Hampshire's case.[34] Bruno later observed, "At that point we knew we had our insurance policy."[35]

AFTERMATH

Gross sent a copy of the Memorandum of Understanding to Manatt but received no acknowledgment. In his letter of December 5, 1983, he employed a markedly more confident tone in requesting that the DNC provide assurances that New Hampshire delegates would be seated at San Francisco. In his closing comments, Gross offered a barbed olive branch:

I cannot over-emphasize how deeply our presidential primary is ingrained in the political life of this state. To illustrate the point, I am enclosing a complimentary copy of the "New Hampshire Presidential Primary Rule Book" which you may find amusing as well as enlightening. . . . It would be most helpful if you or a member of your staff could acknowledge this letter. I am sure you will agree that communicating via press release is not a very informative or civilized way to proceed.[36]

No reply was received from the DNC.[37] In the period between the CRC meeting and the February 28 primary, a long and detailed private memorandum from Paul Kirk to Manatt may have been influential in persuading the chairman to take no further action. This seventeen-page document, dated December 19, 1983, summarized the political and legal technicalities of the dispute. Since Kirk was about to embark on a dissent from official policy, this memo began with diplomatic praise for Manatt's "laudable and significant achievement" of shortening the nomination calendar by one month.[38] The treasurer summarized the efforts of Bruno, Gross and D'Amours to reach agreement with Attorney-General Smith and pointed out that Smith's replies had been anything but helpful. Kirk described them as "cursory, transmittal letters which would embarrass the number one public lawyers of most states."[39]

Kirk realized that New Hampshire's Democrats had taken "provable, positive steps" as required under 20A. The state party had been well aware from the outset that Secretary Gardner and Attorney-General Smith would not give way in their interpretation of Vermont's statute. Their only course of action could be to loudly and persistently bang their heads against the wall of state law. Kirk drew a reluctant Manatt's attention to this partisan martyrdom, reporting that "the problem we now face was created, unilaterally, by Republicans. . . . I have concluded that the move . . . was strenuously resisted by the New Hampshire Democratic Party to no avail . . . traditional bipartisan cooperation, state laws and national party rules have been ignored."[40]

Kirk described the entire mess as a "Vermont-Iowa-New Hampshire chain" that had been effectively yanked by the Granite State GOP.[41] As the treasurer perceived the situation, nothing short of court action would alter Secretary Gardner's view, and nothing should be done to punish the state party for events beyond its control. Kirk recommended that the DNC accept the situation and allow the primary to go ahead. An unnamed source claims Manatt dismissed Kirk's report due to lack of prior consultation and a suspicion that the treasurer, as a known Kennedy loyalist, wanted to preserve New Hampshire as a way of "screwing Mondale to the wall."[42] In fact, the DNC approach during the entire controversy appeared to consist of a stubborn refusal to confront overwhelming evidence that this was not simply an intraparty disagreement.

Manatt's reluctance to abandon the CRC's position was partly influenced by the growing trend toward firmer enforcement of national party directives. After the chaos of the 1970s, the party in the 1980s was moving rapidly toward greater centralization of resources and a concomitant tightening of organizational links between the national party and state bodies. In this environment, the rules dispute would have been perceived, at the outset, as a test case.[43]

A further aggravating factor for national Democrats was the Granite State's reputation for strongly defending its primary. To officials it may well have seemed that this was simply another aggressive lobbying exercise. In 1984 congressional hearings on nomination reform, Congressman Morris Udall (D-AZ) referred to the zeal with which New Hampshire activists had battled for their primary's status. "They are very good at this; they have been at it for twenty years. . . . They will find out who the national committee people are and they will move in on them [and] you will be told that the country is going to hell in a handbasket and that New Hampshire will go down the drain unless this exemption is preserved."[44]

As the tidal wave of rules reform receded during the 1980s, it became clear that the ideal of a widened, participatory system had been achieved, but that a workable and unambiguous set of guidelines had not. Later commissions had been influenced by presidential candidates such as Carter, Mondale, Kennedy and the Reverend Jesse Jackson, inducing a natural skepticism among observers about their scope and intent.

The 1983-84 clash nonetheless shows the determination of the DNC to tighten its grip on procedural rules and the skill exhibited by state activists in maneuvering between party and state law. James Ceaser noted a "loss of party control" over the nomination process after the first reforms of the 1970s.[45] By the 1980s, however, national staffers, many of whom had once challenged the boss politics of the 1960s, now sought to protect and direct the complicated new nomination process. The disruptive potential of state disobedience was now higher than in the more freewheeling pre-reform days. Inevitably, therefore, the inclination to discipline rebels and recalcitrants became stronger. The nomination may no longer be in the gift of party bosses, but the central core of the party leadership has become, in many ways, more systematic than ever before. Crotty and Jackson believe this condition has effectively brought state Democrats to "a position of subservience to the national Democratic party."[46] However, in a situation in which state and party laws conflict, the national body will normally find itself on the losing end. As Gross commented in 1985, "The plain lesson I drew from this affair was that attempts . . . to control every detail of the delegate selection process ultimately rank in effectiveness with the efforts of the ancient Danish King, Canute, who tried to order the ocean waves to roll back."[47]

George Bruno also came to believe that the dispute had more to do with power-plays than rules disputes. He felt that certain members of the DNC had exhibited "a death wish. . . . They certainly weren't cooperating. We knew it would ultimately be a question of power politics at some point. As we went on it became a question of who would blink first."[48]

Although New Hampshire's "victory" did nothing to improve its image with the national Democratic party, the ultimate effect of its victory was the confirmation of its special status. National Democrats had no stomach for a repeat of this debacle and found it far easier to wave through the Iowa and New Hampshire exemptions in later discussions for the 1988, 1992 and 1996 election cycles. Resentment persists, however, at the national level over what many consider to be the state's high-handed attitude and its determination to control the primary dates of any state coming within its late winter orbit. Republicans, on the other hand, exhibit far less hostility to the first-in-the-nation tradition. State and national GOP bodies, having been less preoccupied with reform over the last quarter-century, were generally more receptive to the appeal of a small, conservative state. This relaxed attitude served New Hampshire well, on the Republican side, until the 1990s when the lack of any specific provision protecting the first primary created a problem equally as serious as the Democrats' dilemma.

Overall, the 1983-84 clash served to fuel speculation that a move to standardized, regional primaries was now inevitable. After Manatt "broke his pick" on New Hampshire, the pressure to avoid future embarrassments grew stronger.[49]

1995-96: THE ARIZONA–DELAWARE CHALLENGES

In 1992 the state of Arizona had abandoned its caucus system in favor of a presidential primary, but state legislation passed soon after mandated that its contest be held on the second Tuesday in March or on the date of the earliest primary election in any state. In response to queries concerning its likely clash with New Hampshire's tentative date, February 20, Arizona officials indicated a willingness to go one or two days after the Granite State vote. The main sponsor of the Arizona law, Republican state senator Bev Hermon, claimed that voters in the West needed the opportunity to express opinions on the candidates before the field was whittled away by voters in the East.[50] Arizona's Republican governor Fife Symington argued that New Hampshire's feeling of proprietorship over first place should not be permitted to stand in the way of the rising economic and political importance of the West.[51]

The apparent flexibility of the Arizona date masked a more serious problem for New Hampshire. Until this point, it had been able to defend itself using the 1975 statute which ruled that it could not be chronologically preempted or matched by any "similar election." This rule was the source of the earlier dispute with the DNC and was by now considered more or less watertight. Arizona's offer to follow one or two days after New Hampshire, however, created a problem. Under Secretary Gardner's interpretation of the 1975 law, his state required a full seven-day pause between its primary and that of any other state in order that the Granite State verdict could be properly assimilated by candidates and pundits.[52] An Arizona primary on Wednesday, February 21, therefore, would still be unacceptable, not least to the DNC, whose 1984 Rule 10A banned any primary state except New Hampshire from operating outside the agreed window. New Hampshire's Republicans had no such window but still moved quickly to help block the Arizona bid.

Using tactics reminiscent of the 1983 dispute, state party chairman Steve Duprey asked prospective candidates to sign a pledge supporting the Granite State's right to stay one week ahead of any other primary contest. At a state party meeting in January 1995, Duprey warned candidates refusing to support New Hampshire not to bother campaigning there during 1996.[53] Governor Merrill promised publicly to do "whatever is necessary" to protect New Hampshire's status.[54] This included approval of a draft letter to Bob Dole, Lamar Alexander and other candidates. Stopping short of requesting a full-scale candidate boycott of Arizona, the letter asked all potential contenders for the GOP nomination to show their hands, concluding, "On behalf of New Hampshire, we ask you to demonstrate your support for New Hampshire's primary by signing the enclosed letter and returning it to Merrill."[55] Sensing the danger to their chances in the early campaign phase, both Dole and Alexander indicated immediate and strong support. Dole advised Arizona in a telephone interview to "leave it like it is," and Alexander publicly urged Symington to abandon the challenge, arguing that Arizona voters would suffer from a primary held in the shadow of New Hampshire since the news media would ignore their verdict.[56]

Senator Phil Gramm faced a greater dilemma. Rumors persisted that Symington had pushed Arizona forward in a deliberate effort to boost Gramm's White House bid. The Texan had built a strong organization in the Pine Tree State but consistently denied any role in Symington's strategy until the governor himself remarked, on January 15 in an interview with the *Boston Globe,* that such a move could benefit Gramm.[57] It did not escape the notice of New Hampshire officials that both Symington and Arizona senator John McCain were Gramm backers. Gramm promised Merrill that he would try to persuade Symington to back off and disingenuously suggested an accommodation whereby New Hampshire could precede Arizona by "at least a day or two."[58] Undoubtedly, Gramm regarded the first primary as an impediment to his prospects for developing momentum and would have preferred a start in a state bordering his own. He found the seven-day waiting period unacceptable because it appeared to further strengthen New Hampshire's ability to unfairly dictate the dates of other state contests. His supporters in Arizona considered the DNC's window ruling inapplicable to Republican primaries and questioned whether the seven-day wait was a statutory requirement or simply an inventive interpretation of the law by Secretary Gardner since the 1975 statute did not specifically mandate such a pause.

Symington eventually bowed to candidate pressure and to the realization that Arizona would need to file its primary date with the Justice Department in Washington under the terms of the 1965 Voting Rights Act, leaving New Hampshire more than enough time to shift its own contest one week further forward. The governor confessed: "I was surprised at the vehemence of New Hampshire, and frankly if it weren't for Phil Gramm's intercession, I suspect we would still be pushing hard."[59] Gramm began a slow process of rebuilding bridges inside the first primary state, claiming credit for persuading Symington to withdraw Arizona's legislation and permit a seven-day gap. The governor salvaged what he could from the debacle, vowing that Arizona's newly acquired second-in-the-nation status would not be challenged by any other state. The *Union Leader* of February 2, 1995 displayed a cartoon depicting the Arizona primary as the corpse of a western gunslinger over which towered Gramm, complete with white stetson and gloves. The caption read, "Nice Shooting Senator."[60] Gramm's campaign was to be further undermined, however, when it became entangled with a second, far more serious challenge to the 1996 schedule, this time from Delaware.

Delaware's 1992 law introduced a presidential primary in order to allow state Democrats to divest themselves of a complicated caucus-based delegate process. It permitted the contest to be held on the first Saturday after the New Hampshire primary, a favored day for elections in Delaware since voter participation could be maximized and schools, used as polling stations, are already shut for the weekend.[61] This legislation infringed both New Hampshire's seven-day waiting period and the 1984 DNC ruling that had been overlooked by the bill's Democratic sponsors.[62] To make matters worse, it would also now be seen as a challenge to Arizona's determination to go second, seven days clear of New Hampshire. Governor Merrill defiantly called on Republican candidates to boycott the state GOP convention in Delaware, scheduled for the weekend of May 5–6, 1995.[63] Lamar Alexander and Patrick Buchanan immediately withdrew from the convention, much to the disgust of the Wilmington *News Journal*, which berated "the gnomes of Concord" and explained to its readers why "the granite heads are insisting that Higher Law forbids any incursion on their week."[64] Bob Dole and Pennsylvania senator Arlen Specter also dropped out. California Governor Pete Wilson announced in early May that he, too, would be absent from the convention. Phil Gramm decided to attend the convention but, in an effort to protect his crumbling popularity in New Hampshire sought to pacify state voters by promising to use the occasion to argue their case.[65] The *News Journal* argued that Saturday was as treasured a tradition for Delaware elections as Tuesday was for New Hampshire and, in a February 1995 editorial, carrying the byline, "New Hampshire must be made to eat dirt in this primary battle," poured scorn on the first primary state:

This far and no further. . . . Have your presidential primary first, New Hampshire. Garner international publicity from the presidential aspirants and a cast of thousands trudging through your snowdrifts every fourth winter. Fill your coffers with profits from overpriced rooms, mediocre meals and watered-down libations. Have your day in the pale winter sun. But not a whole week.[66]

The importance of this dispute lay not in a challenge to New Hampshire's first position tradition but in the threat to the more recent policy of preventing other states from tailgating its primary. Calendar debates during the 1980s and early 1990s had demonstrated that states wishing to dilute or share New Hampshire's prerogative could utilize several lines of attack. One option, clearly unattainable without federal intervention, would be to end the first-place tradition altogether. Another would be to front-load primaries into March, forcing candidates to abandon New Hampshire through lack of time. A third option, moving all state contests to the later part of the calendar, thereby rendering the Granite State verdict irrelevant, is not generally favored. Delaware had selected a fourth option—to place its contest close to New Hampshire's, to siphon off some media and candidate attention or even nullify New Hampshire's impact by producing a contradictory verdict only days later. Aware of the popularity of this option with some states, New Hampshire Republicans and many Democrats had been moving for some time to the conclusion that a statutory gap after its primary was as important as the one currently in force between New Hampshire and Iowa. Unfortunately, the wording of the 1975 first primary law was, to many outside observers, less than specific in its claim to a seven-day waiting period. The law simply stated that New Hampshire's primary would be held on the second Tuesday in March, or on the Tuesday immediately preceding the date on which any other state held a similar election.[67] To these observers, the Granite State, having nailed down the day of its own contest and the weeks preceding it, was now attempting to claim the period immediately after in order to vacuum-seal the primary at both ends. Secretary Gardner insisted that the law had always been understood to include the waiting period, but, by way of reinforcing the point, the General Court's House Constitutional and Statutory Revision Committee rapidly waved through HB 333, a bill specifically guaranteeing the seven-day gap. The House passed the new bill, 259 votes to 86, to the Senate on a voice vote.[68] It was rapidly approved and signed into law by Governor Merrill. The bill's sponsor was Democratic representative Jim Splaine of Portsmouth, the author of the 1975 act, who claimed the new law "follows the intent of my legislation in 1975. . . . We're not taking anything away from any other state."[69] Splaine's revision inserted the words, "at least seven days" into the sentence concerning any Tuesday following a "similar election."[70]

Delaware's Republican chairman, Basil Battaglia, lashed out at Merrill, attacking his tactics and those of state Republicans as "cheap political extortion."[71] In reply to a letter from Pete Wilson in which the California governor urged acceptance of New Hampshire's tradition, Battaglia argued that this role had not been challenged and that New Hampshire was, in effect, moving the scheduling goalposts. He added, "In my view, New Hampshire is being completely unreasonable. They are making threats to Delaware and using political blackmail to keep candidates out of our state."[72] Senator Gramm again damaged his standing in New Hampshire's press by endorsing the state's right to keep first place but pointedly refusing to specify the need for a seven-day pause. His speech fell short of Merrill's requirements since only the seven-day pause was at issue. Returning to New Hampshire, Gramm felt obliged to go further. Reporters in Nashua in May 1995 were informed that he would, upon entering the White House, ensure that the Republican National Committee set up "an orderly system . . . that will preserve New Hampshire as being first, and first by seven days."[73] This effort to play both sides of the political and regional fence did nothing to salvage Gramm's campaign chances.

The DNC was understandably fearful of potential scheduling chaos if Delaware persisted in its efforts and stood by New Hampshire's Democrats, forcing the Delaware party to withdraw its delegate selection plan at a DNC Rules Committee meeting in Washington on June 30. The New Hampshire State Democratic chairman, Joe Keefe, immediately issued a press release claiming partial victory but warning that "Delaware may be back" with a new plan to topple New Hampshire in its revised delegate selection process.[74] Boston Globe columnist David Shribman was amused at the battle of two states which he referred to as "more colorful than consequential," but he reminded Delaware's protagonists that New Hampshire's ability to print all its primary ballots in three days meant it could easily delay the announcement of the primary date until the last possible moment.[75] From a media and candidate perspective, a Saturday primary in Delaware was not thought likely to jeopardize the first primary's clout. Allowing for post–New Hampshire press conferences and a recovery period, candidates left standing after New Hampshire would be likely to arrive in Delaware with only two full campaigning days before the Saturday poll. WMUR-TV's Carl Cameron predicted that this short campaign period would mean "ultimately, most candidates will choose to skip Delaware anyway."[76]

As Keefe and Edward Shumaker, co-chairman of the New Hampshire Clinton-Gore reelection campaign, had predicted, however, the Delaware Democratic party resubmitted its original plan to the DNC. Meeting in Chicago on September 16, 1995, the Rules Committee, headed by Massachusetts Democrat James Roosevelt, again found Delaware in noncompliance with Rule 10A and applied formal sanctions of the kind New Hampshire Democrats had themselves desperately sought to avoid in 1983. Delaware was stripped of some, but not all, of its delegates and superdelegates to the forthcoming Chicago Convention. Keefe, in a letter to

Secretary Gardner one month later, requested that the secretary of state take no action to move New Hampshire's own February 20 primary since Delaware's legislation still linked its primary date to that of New Hampshire. He argued the effectiveness of a two-pronged strategy where the DNC had "essentially shut down the Delaware primary" and where all Republicans bar Gramm and Forbes were inactive.[77] Gardner saw no reason at this stage to regard the Delaware contest as a similar election and move up New Hampshire's date.[78]

In November 1995, the situation began to cloud over once more. Several leading Republicans had requested information and applications for the Delaware primary, although Bob Dole remained aloof, hoping to attract an endorsement from Steve Merrill. As Delaware's December 15 filing deadline approached, Secretary Gardner and state GOP chairman John Stabile waited to see if the GOP field would grow. The entry, on the Democratic ballot, of Lyndon LaRouche prompted fears that President Clinton would be compelled to enter the Delaware race to prevent an uncontested LaRouche delegation from being seated in Chicago. Joe Keefe thought Gardner should still hold to February 20 since "Moving the New Hampshire primary forward to January in response to a non-event between a non-campaigning President and a convicted felon, strikes me as a bit much."[79] Delaware elections commissioner, Thomas J. Cook remained adamant that any attempt by Gardner to detach New Hampshire from Delaware would be to no avail, Delaware would move in a mirror-image of any New Hampshire maneuver, maintaining a distance of four days. By now, Gardner was dropping dark hints of his "trick"—a plan for jumping the New Hampshire primary date forward at three days' notice, permissible under state law and feasible given the speed with which the state government was able to reprint and distribute ballots. The secretary was reluctant to undertake this unprecedented move but believed that he would be obliged to do so in order to comply with the 1975 statute.[80] However, the danger inherent in such a move would be as great as the peril posed by Delaware. The DNC window would be effectively shattered, Iowa's position usurped, the candidates and media hugely disrupted and the New Hampshire verdict potentially devalued. It is conceivable that the secretary never seriously intended to follow such a drastic course but that his publicly expressed willingness to do so was, by itself, the secret weapon designed to frighten candidates and party officials into abandoning Delaware. However the hints may have been taken, Gardner remained firm that "Our law says what it says and we will abide by our law."[81] In private, the secretary voiced concern at the Delaware challenge as a precedent. "If we accept Delaware on Saturday, we would have to take other states on Friday or Thursday. The dam would burst. California is three hours behind us, so do we have to let them go three hours after? Where does it end?"[82] The Clinton–Gore campaign, in a timely gesture of solidarity with the Granite State, decided not to file candidacy papers for the president in the Delaware contest.

In mid-January 1996, Delaware suddenly raised the stakes. Wilmington Democratic senator Robert I. Marshall introduced S.R. 274 into the General Assembly, permitting the state's election commissioner to place on the ballot the names of all contenders who qualified for federal matching funds or collected signatures from 500 registered voters. Thus names would be offered to the Delaware electorate regardless of the wishes of the candidates concerned. The law, explained the Wilmington *News Journal*, had become necessary after New Hampshire had "bullied almost all the presidential candidates into staying away."[83] In order to achieve this change, the recently expired filing period for candidates in Delaware was declared null and void. The bill was immediately signed into law by Governor Thomas R. Carper. A furious Gardner released an uncharacteristically savage press release from the State House in Concord, berating Delaware's "depraved version of a kangaroo straw poll" and declaring, "This shameful disdain for fair elections defames and defrauds the glory of this great nation and the politicians of Delaware won't succeed in robbing the New Hampshire tradition."[84]

It now appeared that Delaware had succeeded where other states had long failed, in outmaneuvering the Granite State primary and encroaching on the seven-day waiting period. Democratic State Senate majority leader Thomas R. Sharpe triumphantly told the Wilmington *News Journal*: "I don't think we can allow New Hampshire to dictate what we in Delaware do. . . . Maybe we'll send a good, strong message to our sister state."[85]

Against the expectations and demands of some New Hampshire officials, neither Governor Merrill nor Secretary Gardner moved to punish Delaware. Gardner argued that a Democratic race in which the president did not campaign and a Republican race in which all names except those of Forbes and Gramm had been forced onto the ballot did not constitute a similar election. New Hampshire's primary date remained unchanged. In the event, Delaware paid a heavy price for its provocation. With little time between New Hampshire primary night and the morning of the Delaware contest, both candidates and media ignored the latter contest almost completely. On the night of his victory in New Hampshire, Pat Buchanan left his victory party at the Courtyard Restaurant in Manchester and flew straight to North Dakota. Steve Forbes, the only candidate still in the race to actively campaign in Delaware, registered an empty victory on February 24 while journalists focused on the upcoming showdown in Arizona.

Delaware's challenge, and the vicious infighting accompanying it, can be viewed from two perspectives. If New Hampshire was acting in the manner long derided by its critics, then the 1995–96 battle represented yet another manifestation of the state's political egotism, a battle in which Derrick Z. Jackson of the *Boston Globe* contended, "New Hampshire . . . made the people vying for the single most powerful political position in the world kiss their feet."[86] From this perspective, the passage of Splaine's revised law was a calculated move by an overconfident state accustomed to facing down its opponents, Delaware, Arizona, the DNC, with one legal *fait accompli* after another. In addition, the tactics employed by Merrill, Gardner and others could be interpreted as little more than irresponsible brinkmanship. An alternative angle places blame firmly on the state's antagonists. Battaglia's exasperated comments in February 1995, "Get me to the bottom line here. Why is coming after New Hampshire a problem for anybody?" carry more than a touch of disingenuity. The state GOP chair and the bill's co-sponsoring Democrats were well aware of the problem their new law posed for state Democrats and the DNC. The decision to place its new primary inside that window was provocative not only to New Hampshire but also to other states with longer primary traditions. Particularly instructive in this area was Battaglia's reaction when reporters asked him how he felt about placing Delaware directly ahead of Arizona, which was now claiming second place for itself. With an ironic disregard for the very principle he was allegedly defending, the chairman commented dismissively, "That's Arizona's problem."[87] Both sides in the dispute enacted key pieces of rushed legislation, HB 333 and SR 274, which, to neutral observers, undermined the credibility of their cause. Each side insisted that the other had contravened accepted practices of nomination scheduling, although, in New Hampshire's case, the Splaine revision represented a codification of assumptions inherent in the 1975 law and the Democrats' Rule 10A. By way of confirmation, the DNC lost no time in ruling Delaware's primary noncompliant.

The Delaware problem arose mainly because the Republican National Committee (RNC), which was habitually more lax in its administration of the nomination calendar, had no mechanism to deal with such quarrels, despite its vigorous defense of the first-in-the-nation principle. State Republicans controlled the legislature that had passed both the 1975 and 1995 laws; it now seemed likely that the party would be forced to act in concert with New Hampshire Democrats to prevent further confrontations in the future. The possibility of joint action had been frequently discussed as the state party chairs and the Department of State dodged and feinted with Arizona and Delaware. In a letter to Bill Gardner, Terry Shumaker, New Hampshire's representative on the DNC, noted the concern of leaders from both state parties over the question of encroachment resulting from front-loading. Shumaker added, "I have also discussed the matter with Republican leaders, including Chairman Stabile and Tom Rath (former attorney general) who agree that a Republican National Committee rule like the DNC's would be of assistance."[88] Rath had urged publicly that the eventual GOP nominee press for this change himself at the San Diego Convention in August 1996, an unlikely scenario given the sensitivities of other state delegations on the scheduling issue. Joe Keefe expressed similar views in a letter to Jim Splaine that December, voicing concern that the Democrats would have a difficult time preserving Rule 10A, the basis of New Hampshire's exemption from the window, if the GOP could not be persuaded to emulate the rule themselves. Failure to carry the GOP with them, he warned, would only lead to further encroachment. Keefe concluded wryly, "Governor Merrill seems to grasp this but I am not certain about the others."[89] Keefe was referring to Merrill's recent promise to ask then-RNC chairman Haley Barbour to champion an RNC equivalent of Rule 10A.[90] Phil Gramm had also promised to approach Barbour on the question, a move for which Merrill had nothing but scorn since Gramm had been at the center of the Arizona and Delaware disputes and was also a prime mover in Louisiana's successful attempt to jump ahead of the Iowa caucuses in February 1996. From November 1995, the winds of change began to blow more strongly. In an interview with the *Union Leader*, Haley Barbour admitted that the RNC would, for the first time, give serious consideration to new rules that could ultimately set an official seal on New Hampshire's first-place position. Such rules would be in place in time for the 2000 election. Barbour explained that

Historically, our party has taken the express position that we do not . . . try to control the timetable. We're organized differently from the Democrats. We are a federation of states party, a bottom up party while the Democrats are organized from the top down.[91]

The main impetus behind the challenges of Arizona and Delaware lay in front-loading, which had accelerated dramatically in the 1992–96 period. States with large delegate yields, notably California, Ohio and New York, chose not to directly challenge New Hampshire but instead moved their own competition dates closer to the first contests in order to tap off some media attention and prevent Iowa and New Hampshire from winnowing the candidate field. During the immediate pre-1996 period, the proximity of large bunches of primary contests to New Hampshire's own encouraged the belief that the first primary would become irrelevant as candidates campaigned in the larger regional contests. This view was held by some in New Hampshire itself. In February 1995, the *Keene Sentinel* suggested, "Anyone who can't raise $20 million before the first primary shouldn't bother running because even if he wins in New Hampshire there won't be enough time . . . to raise the bucks for the primaries in the big states."[92] The early 1996 schedule threatened a quicker conclusion to the presidential nomination contest than any fought in the 208-year history of the office.

Table 5.1
Republican and Democratic Primary and First-Round Caucus Schedule, January–March 1996

Date	Event	GOP Delegates Selected	Dem. Delegates Selected
Jan. 25–31	Hawaii caucus (GOP)	14	0
Jan. 27–29	Alaska caucus (GOP)	19	0
Feb. 6	Louisiana caucus (GOP)	21	0
Feb. 10	Guam caucus (GOP)	4	0
Feb. 12	**Iowa caucus (GOP/Dem)**	25	56
Feb. 20	**New Hampshire primary (GOP/Dem)**	16	26
Feb. 24	Delaware primary (GOP/Dem)	12	22
Feb. 27	Arizona primary (GOP)	39	0
	North Dakota primary (GOP)	18	0
	South Dakota primary (GOP)	18	0
Mar. 2	South Carolina primary (GOP)	37	0
	Wyoming caucus (GOP)	20	0
Mar. 3	Puerto Rico primary (GOP)	14	0

Mar. 5	**Junior Tuesday**		
	Colorado primary (GOP/Dem)	27	58
	Connecticut primary (GOP/Dem)	27	66
	Georgia primary (GOP/Dem)	42	91
	Idaho caucus (Dem)	0	24
	Maine primary (GOP/Dem)	15	32
	Maryland primary (GOP/Dem)	32	88
	Massachusetts primary (GOP/Dem)	37	115
	Minnesota caucus (GOP/Dem)	33	92
	Rhode Island primary (GOP/Dem)	16	32
	South Carolina caucus (Dem)	0	52
	Vermont primary (GOP/Dem)	12	22
	Washington caucus (GOP/Dem)	18	90
	American Samoa caucus (Dem)	0	6
Mar. 7	Missouri caucus (Dem)	0	93
	New York primary (GOP/Dem)	102	289
Mar. 9	Alaska caucus (Dem)	0	19
	Arizona caucus (Dem)	0	52
	Missouri caucus (GOP)	36	0
	South Dakota caucus (Dem)	0	22
Mar. 9–11	Democrats Abroad caucus (Dem)	0	9
Mar. 10	Nevada caucus (Dem)	0	27
	Puerto Rico primary (Dem)	0	58
Mar. 12	**Super Tuesday**		
	Florida primary (GOP/Dem)	98	177
	Hawaii caucus (Dem)	0	30
	Louisiana primary (GOP/Dem)	9	71
	Mississippi primary (GOP/Dem)	33	47
	Oklahoma primary (GOP/Dem)	38	52
	Oregon primary (GOP/Dem)	23	56
	Tennessee primary (GOP/Dem)	38	83
	Texas primary (GOP/Dem)	123	229
Mar. 16	Michigan caucus (Dem)	0	156
Mar. 19	Illinois primary (GOP/Dem)	69	193
	Michigan primary (GOP)	57	0
	Ohio primary (GOP/Dem)	67	172
	Wisconsin primary (GOP/Dem)	36	93
Mar. 23	Wyoming caucus (Dem)	0	19
Mar. 25	Utah caucus (GOP/Dem)	28	30
Mar. 26	California primary (GOP/Dem)	165	422
	Nevada primary (GOP)	14	0
	Washington primary (GOP)	18	0
Mar. 29	North Dakota caucus (Dem)	0	22
Mar. 30	Virgin Islands caucus (Dem)	0	4

Source: Adapted from: "1996 Presidential Primary and Caucus Calendar," *Congressional Quarterly Weekly Report*, January 13, 1996, pp. 98–99. Republican delegates needed for first ballot win: 996; Democrats: 2,146.

Under the newly compressed system, 70.1 percent of Democratic convention delegates and 62.8 percent of Republican delegates were selected in primaries or caucuses by March 31, 1996 (Table 5.1). New Hampshire had excluded itself from the development of the New England regional primary, nicknamed Yankee or Junior Tuesday. In early 1995, the governors of Vermont, Connecticut and Maine had already signed legislation setting aside March 5, 1996 for their delegate selection contests. Connecticut's move came in reaction to the front-loading of the California primary, which once had been an early June fixture but was now moved up to March 26, Connecticut's own original date. By the end of June 1995, Governor William Weld of Massachusetts and Rhode Island's Governor Lincoln Almond had followed suit. The innovation required passage of primary legislation through the Maine and Vermont legislatures under the guidance of their respective secretaries of state, William Diamond and James Milne. Both states had already scheduled caucuses, not primaries, for March 5.[93] The creation of a northeastern rival to the established southern Super Tuesday was justified by the secretaries as a way not only to attract more attention to their contests but also to direct candidate attention to issues important to the area, a key motivation in front-loading. Such issues included education, energy costs, fishing and conversion of defense facilities to civilian usage.[94] The claim by Rhode Island secretary of state James Langevin that "Our voices will be louder" was received with skepticism by the *Union Leader*, which pointed out that the states in total chose only 264 of 4,290 Democratic convention delegates and 108 of 1,983 Republicans. Florida alone sent 199 and 98 delegates, respectively.[95]

The regional grouping posed no threat to the position of the first-in-the-nation primary. Its sheer size ensured it would not be able to rival New Hampshire's reputation for retail politics. Nevertheless, the new schedule threatened to bring to a head the long-term trend toward wholesale campaigning and permanently bury the hopes of longshot candidates. With large, expensive contests so close to New Hampshire, no time would be left for small candidacies to develop momentum. As Professor John Haskell of Drake University, Iowa, indicates, the front-loading trend, and the intraparty feuding it engenders, exemplifies the way in which the presidential nominating process has spun out of control, serving only to reinforce voter cynicism and apathy. According to Haskell, "front-loading is the greatest threat to the integrity, and perhaps the viability, of the presidential nomination process and the parties."[96] This apparently intractable problem has at least one potential solution, offering a consensual, permanent and, for New Hampshire, a favorable resolution of the first primary question.

In 1995 both Haley Barbour and Democratic National Committee chairman Christopher Dodd acknowledged fears that the compressed campaign season could enable stronger, wealthier candidates to storm to the nomination using a sustained media blitz. Reacting to this nightmare scenario, the National Association of Secretaries of State agreed in February 1996 to form a fifteen-member Commission to Review the Presidential Primary and Caucus Process. The review body, consisting of eight Republicans and seven Democrats, was authorized to work closely with both chairmen in analyzing the mechanics and results of the 1996 nomination process for both parties. The group's mission was to recommend changes to selection procedures in a report to be presented to both the San Diego and Chicago conventions in August 1996. Significantly, Bill Gardner was appointed its chairman. To the secretary himself, this represented a clear sign that a consensus in both major parties had developed in support of New Hampshire's claims. It appeared unlikely that the appointment would have been offered had the intention been to eradicate the primary altogether. Gardner noted, "I think the commission will carry a lot of weight with the parties because they're both panicking now over front-loading and they're looking for a way to calm things down and spread the primaries and caucuses back out again. They would never expect me to condone any plan which nullified our first-in-the-nation primary so I think this appointment is a very positive sign. I certainly won't be a party to any report that undermines what we have fought for all these years . . . and they know it."[97]

In an ironic twist, the challenges of Arizona and Delaware have only served to highlight the grave consequences of front-loading, which drew the states into bitter contention in 1995–96. They may therefore have helped New Hampshire's long-term interests by identifying the state's ongoing battle with the wider problem of timetabling. Mounting concern at the nature of campaigning in the new primary system may increase the appeal of both Iowa and New Hampshire as bastions of retail politics and as essential training grounds for underdog candidacies. The appointment of the new review body indicates the seriousness with which both major parties now regard the problem. With the commission and the national party chairmen now apparently determined to quieten things down, the odds on New Hampshire's retaining its favored status may have improved significantly.

FEDERALIZING THE PRIMARIES

The federal government and courts have traditionally approached the politically charged issues of representation and partisan activity with reluctance and caution. The dividing line between public and private purpose is nowhere more transient than in the realm of electoral organization. Candidate selection, itself only a narrow area within the broader electoral sphere, is fraught with dilemmas involving freedom of speech and the rights of individual states to supervise and direct electoral competition. Since the 1970s, and with increasing pace since the 1980s, a consensus supporting federalization of the presidential nominating process has developed. A comprehensive redesigning of the selection process by the federal establishment is now mooted as an inevitable and necessary step to achieving some measure of balance in the fluctuating dynamics unleashed by McGovern–Fraser.

It is not a new idea. In the twentieth century, strict constructionist interpretations of the Constitution have not prevented government or the courts from intervening in a wide range of ballot-oriented activities, most notably in the 1965 Voting Rights

Act and the 1971 FECA. There are, however, few constitutional provisions explicitly supporting such actions. Article II, Section 2 of the Constitution states merely that the Congress shall "determine the time of choosing the electors, and the day on which they shall give their votes."[98] Landmark rulings, particularly *Nixon v. Herndon* (1927) and *Nixon v. Condon* (1932), established the right of federal authorities to regulate state primaries, despite counterarguments that state parties qualified as private bodies outside the range of federal supervision.[99] Nevertheless, from the early 1900s, the courts have made important decisions affecting state and federal electoral competition in order to combat iniquitous political practices such as "white primaries" (contests held mainly in southern states where only whites could vote), vote-buying, illicit fund-raising and grandfather clauses. Another step forward was made in 1934, when the Hughes Court confirmed the right of Congress to impose guidelines on the reporting of incomes and expenditures of political committees in *Burroughs v. United States*.

The Federal Election Campaign acts of the 1970s laid down rules for fund-raising and related activities in unprecedented detail, prompting the Burger Court to step back from the brink in its 1976 *Buckley v. Valeo* decision, when New York senator James Buckley, aided by Eugene McCarthy, successfully argued that campaign expenditure represented free speech and was therefore protected under the First Amendment. The Court upheld much of the FECA structure, as amended in 1974, but invalidated expenditure limits on the grounds that it was an "indisputable fact that large sums of money are indispensable for the mass media communication that characterizes contemporary political campaigns."[100]

Reform advocates stress the public purpose of elections over their theoretically private character. Although the major national political parties operate as private bodies, their purpose and effect are to direct the affairs of government at all levels and the lives of American citizens. Furthermore, while these bodies may be privately organized and funded, access to the ballot box remains a constitutionally sanctified right. The broader implications of such arguments are clear, and national and state parties have viewed with some trepidation the increasing inclination of Congress to intervene in the scheduling of presidential primaries on these grounds. Ironically, the time for federalization may already be past. During the 1970s, disorganization in the primary system was complemented by a profound weakening of national party structures and their directive influence over state bodies and activists. Former Carter adviser Stuart Eizenstadt believes that party reformers of the post-1968 period were responsible for a dramatic increase in the "aggravation level" of presidential campaigning.[101] Since the mid-1980s, however, both parties have moved to solidify and expand their national operations, opening permanent national headquarters in Washington and augmenting their resources with massive fund-raising drives. The Democratic party in particular has tightened its grip on the lower echelons through procedural reforms. The writ of the DNC now runs far more strongly at all levels of the party than was apparent in the 1970s. At no time since the nineteenth century have national parties been better organized or equipped to administer their candidate selection systems. Nonetheless, primary scheduling, as the preserve of state parties and legislatures, has defied strict party control throughout this period. Disillusionment with the length and cost of presidential campaigns continues to spur reformers. A system of federally mandated regional primaries or some related variant would produce, they argue, much-needed stability, brevity and, above all, coherence in the process.

Understandably, New Hampshire's reception for such proposals has been less than enthusiastic. Having fought hard to preserve its prime position and avoid being drawn into a regional arrangement with neighboring New England states, it regards federalization as anathema not only to the first primary but also to the entire concept of states' rights. New Hampshire is cast once again as the spoiler.

During the mid-1980s, the House of Representatives' Subcommittee on Elections met on numerous occasions to examine proposed legislation for a federally mandated system. Transcripts of these hearings are particularly instructive in examining the role of New Hampshire within the nomination process. Granite State representatives are consistently on the defensive during debates over regional primary formulas since the state always interprets such proposals as an attack on its first-in-the-nation tradition. Both pro- and anti-New Hampshire arguments recognize the pressing need for a more balanced system, but the consensus ends here. New Hampshire and Iowa representatives at the hearings defend their contests as vital to the progress of underdog candidacies and to the survival of the retail politics tradition. Advocates of reform follow two distinct lines of attack. The first is to question the viability of retail in an age of wholesale, media-oriented campaigning; the second is to suggest that, even if viability is established, Iowa and New Hampshire have no prior claim to first place when a rotated state arrangement could distribute that privilege on a more equitable basis—hence, the persistent tendency of the pro- and anti-New Hampshire camps to talk past each other. Both camps agree on the need for change in some form, but neither can be persuaded to accept the other's formula for creating that change.

Five separate legislative proposals are covered in the following discussions. H.R. 6054, examined by the House Subcommittee on September 19, 1984, was introduced by Representative Morris K. Udall with the intent of placing a legally enforceable window on the nomination system. On March 20 and May 8, 1986, four other bills (H.R. 251, H.R. 3542, H.R. 4453 and H.R. 1380) came under congressional scrutiny.[102] The first three of this group provided for the establishment of six, ten and six regional primary groupings, respectively; the fourth mirrored the Udall bill. The proposed groupings of H.R. 4453 are reproduced as Table 5.2.

All five pieces of legislation failed to be enacted into law. The hearings nonetheless provide an interesting perspective on perceptions of New Hampshire's primary at the federal level. Session transcripts reveal the reform advocates' sharp resentment over the state's alleged selfishness and intransigence. They also demonstrate the dilemmas reformers face when they seek to impose uniformity on a process that has developed haphazardly and beyond congressional control.

Table 5.2
Regional Groupings of State Delegate Selection Contests As Specified in H.R. 4453: Inter-regional Presidential Primary and Caucus Act (1986), introduced by Representative Sander Levin (R–MI)

Region 1	(A) Maine, New Hampshire, Vermont; (B) Massachusetts; (C) Connecticut, Rhode Island; (D) Delaware, New Jersey; (E) New York, Pennsylvania
Region 2	(A) Maryland; (B) West Virginia; (C) Missouri; (D) Indiana; (E) Kentucky; (F) Tennessee
Region 3	(A) Ohio; (B) Illinois; (C) Michigan; (D) Wisconsin; (E) Iowa; (F) Minnesota
Region 4	(A) Texas; (B) Louisiana; (C) Arkansas, Oklahoma; (D) Colorado; (E) Kansas, Nebraska; (F) Arizona, New Mexico
Region 5	(A) Virginia; (B) North Carolina; (C) South Carolina; (D) Florida; (E) Georgia; (F) Mississippi, Alabama
Region 6	(A) California; (B) Washington; (C) Oregon; (D) Idaho, Nevada, Utah; (E) Montana, North Dakota, South Dakota, Wyoming; (F) Hawaii, Alaska

Source: H.R. 4453. Under this bill, each regional primary would take place on one of six allotted dates—the second Tuesday in March, the first Tuesday in April, the fourth Tuesday in April, the second Tuesday in May, the fourth Tuesday in May and the second Tuesday in June. Primaries and caucuses of two subregions from each main regional grouping would be held in their allotted order on those dates. The Federal Election Commission was to determine the rota of states by lot for the first presidential election cycle alone.

While the New Hampshire question was not the sole bone of contention in committee hearings, it occupied a considerable amount of time. Representative Al Swift (D-WA) opened the March 20, 1986 session with the debatable observation that national parties had entirely failed in their efforts to regulate their own selection systems and that, consequently, "The vast majority of citizens in this country have little meaningful opportunity to participate in choosing our presidential nominees."[103] Swift maintained that the source of much of the trouble lay in the early contests, which, "with all due respect to the citizens of the great states of Iowa and New Hampshire . . . distort the nomination process."[104]

New Hampshire was repeatedly singled out for its apparently obdurate refusal to cooperate with the efforts of reformers. Morris Udall, recalling the 1983–84 rules controversy, noted that "Chairman Manatt tried very hard to carry out the mandate of the party . . . and he was defied in part by officials in New Hampshire."[105] Manatt himself testified that party efforts to balance schedules were consistently undermined when early states "decide they want to move outside of the agreed-upon time frame."[106] Interestingly, both accusations deliberately steered around, or underplayed, the root cause of the rules dispute—the conflict over the nature of the Vermont contest and the Democratic CRC's refusal to acknowledge the reality of a GOP-dominated state government.

Congressional exasperation at the Granite State surfaced at regular intervals. Responding to claims by Representative Judd Gregg (R-NH) that New Hampshire's primary electorate was especially well-equipped to question candidates on key issues, Swift sarcastically asked whether something had been added to the Granite

State water supply to confer such wisdom.[107] The subcommittee chair proved equally scathing when informed by New Hampshire delegate Norman E. D'Amours that a proposed straw poll in the state of Washington, ahead of the 1988 New Hampshire primary, would meet with no objection from his state. Swift acidly inquired, "You deign to let the state of Washington have a beauty contest, a straw vote or a caucus. As long as we don't have a primary before you, you would let us do that? Damned nice of you."[108] In discussions of H.R. 4453, Representative Sander Levin (D-MI) was advised to locate state party conventions in Michigan safely within his bill's proposed window to prevent the possibility that "the gentleman seated directly behind you (Gregg) would implore his state to put into effect a state convention so New Hampshire could be the first."[109]

Reform advocates, however, had a broader agenda than attacks on New Hampshire. Whatever the implications for the first primary, regionalization of the primary system was widely regarded as the only viable option for introducing stability and fairness into candidate selection. Once freed from the compulsion to chase each other from state to state, candidates would be able to formulate detailed policy programs in an atmosphere of calm deliberation, presenting their platforms to the electorate in a series of regional elections. Bill Nelson (D-FL) believed that such changes would dilute the competition between states and "allow the American people a chance to get to know the candidates."[110]

The emerging consensus thus appeared to endorse regionalization as a cure-all for the ailments of the contemporary system. Charles Bennett (D-FL) attacked the "political psychosis" of reporters, candidates and activists, blaming the phenomenon on "a hodge-podge of decisions being made . . . with no rhyme or reason."[111] Bennett's implication was clear. Media speculation, front-loading of primaries, candidate exhaustion and overexposure, voter apathy and interstate rivalry could all be neutralized or at least modified by a federal tidying up operation. Illustrating this idea was H.R. 4453's proposed rotation in state membership of each primary grouping so that no state would be permanently placed first, last or in any one group.[112]

However broad the agreement over the harmful effects of contemporary practice, there appeared to be no degree of unanimity over proposed solutions. Udall advocated a federally imposed window, against claims from Gregg that such a system would be in violation of states' rights. Georgia secretary of state Max Cleland argued that regionalization would produce consensus candidates, while Dr. Stephen J. Wayne, political science professor from George Washington University, contended that the result would be simply a proliferation of regional and favorite son candidacies leading to a series of brokered conventions. Representatives Swift and Bill Frenzel continued to press for a simple reduction, by some undetermined method, of the clout of early states. Richard Scammon, director of the Elections Research Center, noting this diversity of opinion, bluntly advised: "Frankly, I would just leave it alone. I would respond with Dean Atchison's (sic) comments once to President Truman: 'Have you ever thought, Mr. President, of doing nothing?'"[113]

Pat Caddell, former pollster to the Carter White House, suggested a compromise by which early states could retain pole position but with their influence diluted through the introduction of incremental delegate allocation, permitting greater delegate yields in later states. If apportionment of delegates took place on a proportional basis in early rounds, states in the second stage of primaries would allocate on a winner-take-more basis, leaving states such as California to bring up the rear with massive winner-take-all delegate harvests. Candidates, Caddell suggested, would be encouraged to stay in the race despite early setbacks in the hope of a revival of media interest and substantial later successes.[114] Al Swift appeared to be particularly impressed with the proposal, pressing Caddell to elaborate on the implications for obstructive early states: "In leaving New Hampshire and Iowa outside the system, I presume you're saying just recognize the reality of it and stop worrying about it."[115] Caddell believed that the most effective method of preventing New Hampshire and Iowa from being determinative would be to keep their period of maximum impact a sufficient distance from any states with high delegate yields. He pointed out that New Hampshire would be unlikely to worry since its delegate yield had never been the major factor in its attraction to candidates.[116] This interpretation overlooked, of course, the obvious point that while the first primary's delegate yield has never been a factor, its media impact undoubtedly is. Isolating the primary at the early stage and leaving all important delegate contests until much later would inevitably reduce the state's media impact, possibly triggering a move to a new date closer to the important primaries.

Arguments on both sides throughout these hearings consistently ignored the possibility that New Hampshire and Iowa would not want to hold onto their early positions if those positions held no intrinsic media value. Unsurprisingly, neither state's representatives were quick to point this out. However, a variant of Caddell's solution was to be mooted a decade later by New Hampshire's secretary of state Bill Gardner. The secretary contended in 1996 that New Hampshire simply wished to defend what it had possessed since 1920, "no more, no less" and that the Granite State would not oppose incremental increases in delegate allocation. Indeed, he saw them as a positive development in discouraging further challenges to the state's primary.[117] Proportionate delegate allocation of this type would, of necessity, be left to state parties and legislatures themselves to implement and is one of the more logical and practicable solutions to the Iowa–New Hampshire problem. The front-loading surge was already well underway by 1986, in response to the determinative first primary, yet the sole consequence of this manic rescheduling has been to aggravate the problem it was designed to nullify. While firm indications are not yet available as to the long-term results of the new, compressed schedule, it is reasonable to conjecture that the Granite State will benefit from the proximity of so many other primaries. Since the first primary thrives on the media and depends for its impact on other state contests maintaining the momentum it generates, separation from the rest of the pack or a graded delegate allocation scheme would almost certainly reduce its importance while allowing it to remain a vital aid to small-scale campaigns. Back-loading the system would not prevent the quadrennial media scrimmage in Iowa and New Hampshire but would probably reduce its range and intensity.

Austin Ranney, of the American Enterprise Institute, was openly skeptical of Caddell's submission, arguing that there was no foolproof way in which a system could be engineered to produce certain results in separate rounds, thus arriving at a broadly consensual nominee. Ranney's most severe comments, however, were reserved for Caddell's suggestion that New Hampshire was not as unrepresentative of national voter attitudes as other speakers had claimed. Taking Caddell to task, Ranney oversimplified the pollster's comments in a manner somewhat reminiscent of the vitriolic Royko and Peirce critiques of the 1970s. He commented:

I wish Pat Caddell had stuck around because I wanted to ask him a question. It sounded to me as though he was saying, "Well, we really shouldn't have a national primary, but New Hampshire is so doggone representative and the citizens there are so interested and work so much better than the other states, that if we're going to have a national primary we ought to have one and it ought to be confined to New Hampshire; let New Hampshire vote and whoever wins New Hampshire, let him be the nominee." . . . that did seem to be the logic of what he was saying.[118]

Of the choices at hand, Ranney preferred a rotated regional primary system, particularly for its added virtue of removing New Hampshire's exclusive right to first place. Nevertheless, he stressed his firm conviction that no formula could be relied upon to produce the right nominee or the right president. Ranney concluded, " I suspect that the system we've got now gives us . . . the opportunity to pick a good person, and if we do not use our best judgment to pick a good person, then ultimately the fault, it seems to me, is more with us than it is with the system."[119] Representative William Thomas (R-CA) also cast doubt on the wisdom of imposing structure on the nominating process, rather than simply "letting it flow a little while longer to see what happens."[120] His suggestion that the influence of New Hampshire could be checked simply by permitting California to move its primary to the day immediately after the Granite State poll elicited from Caddell a response that closely foreshadowed the main theme of Judd Gregg's defense arguments. He countered that "you will make sure New Hampshire is not important, I guarantee you that. But if you put a candidate out there . . . and you tell him that the first test is the State of California . . . that candidate, I'm telling you, isn't going to win, even if he's the right person. There's no way."[121]

The dilemma faced by reformers was complex. To deprive New Hampshire of first place in the primary calendar could not be justified purely on the grounds that it was an unrepresentative state if the result would simply be its replacement by another state such as California or New York. However, implementing the popular alternative, a regional system, threatened to stretch candidate funds and physical stamina beyond the breaking point. The impetus for reform lay in the belief that the modern process is too long, arduous and expensive. Reformers aimed for a new structure allowing candidates to allocate time and money on a more cost-effective basis. The weakness of this scenario is immediately apparent. Candidates would be unlikely to spend less time in preparation or less money in campaigning if they were compelled, in a regionalized system, to operate in more states simultaneously. Under a national primary, the problem would, in all likelihood, be intensified to the point at which many candidates, running viable campaigns under current rules, would be compelled to foreclose options on a presidential run months before the first ballot was cast. This problem surfaced for the Wilson and Specter candidacies during the 1996 campaign cycle, the closest so far to approach a regional primary system.

Caddell later issued a strong warning to the House subcommittee that Congress should not, in its eagerness to eradicate the special status of early contests, simply exchange one unacceptable system for another. One possible consequence of ill-judged action would be "30 or 40 states who will decide whose [sic] going to be the new New Hampshire," while another could well be the automatic exclusion of poorly-funded, dark horse candidates from all future presidential races.[122]

These points underpinned the arguments put forward by New Hampshire Representative (later governor and senator) Judd Gregg, who confessed at the outset to feeling like the Japanese representative at an international trade convention. His case comprised the standard recapitulation of the advantages of early, small-state primaries, coupled with a vigorous defense of individual state initiatives in nomination contests and doubts over the future course and nature of a reformed system. Exploiting the image of a small state bullied by larger states and by Washington, Gregg suggested that darker motives lay behind the reform impulse. New Hampshire's unpredictability had made it a source of annoyance to party leaders and media organizations. "What is really being said by the political leadership of this country is, 'Let's take New Hampshire out of the spotlight and keep the process of electing a President in the hands of the few and the powerful.'"[123] This he described as arrogance in its highest form and warned that Congress should not become accustomed to interfering in the internal decision-making mechanisms of state political parties.[124]

Although Gregg inevitably focused on New Hampshire's then-unbroken string of accurate election predictions, he suggested that this did not prove that the Granite State dictated nomination and election outcomes; rather, it pointed to a useful correlation between New Hampshire's political sentiments and those of the nation.[125] Finally, the congressman rejected notions that New Hampshire's insistence on first place in the primary calendar had effectively pushed the start of presidential campaigning back to ever earlier dates. Campaigns, he noted, technically begin from the moment any potential candidate makes a firm commitment to run. Whether New Hampshire's contest came two weeks earlier or later in an election cycle made no substantive difference to this decision.

Gregg had prefaced his comments with the observation that a certain amount of "New Hampshire-bashing" had taken place at the hearings, a comment Frenzel was quick to pick up in his response. "I want to . . . assure him that the authors of some of this wonderful legislation did not (intend) . . . to degrade New Hampshire or its people. . . . I agree that the gentleman never intended to claim for people of New

Hampshire that they had some gift of prognostication."[126] Frenzel then proceeded to ask why the first-in-the-nation privilege, obviously so valuable in New Hampshire's eyes, could not be shared around. Gregg fell back on the standard, and none-too-reliable, defense that past experience with New Hampshire's accuracy in gauging national voter sentiment, combined with the established tradition of pole position, should be sufficient reasons for maintaining the status quo.

New Hampshire's 1975 first primary statute proved still more problematic. As a move to preserve a tradition and a valuable source of state income it could be justified, but reform advocates saw it as little more than a blatant attempt to place the state beyond the reach of national party rules. Gregg and D'Amours could not utilize the tied hands defense effectively employed by Bruno and the state Democrats during the 1983–84 dispute. Swift succinctly summarized the outsider's view of New Hampshire's tendentious law, "It kind of grows out of my daddy can beat up your daddy and then it gets to my daddy's house cost $1 million . . . my daddy's house cost $2 million. And you finally say, well, my daddy's house cost a million more than your daddy's house cost. . . . And you can't top that."[127] Explaining that the rule applied only to primaries, not caucuses, Gregg could only duck Swift's accusation that New Hampshire was preempting the rights of other states and rely on tradition as a justification. The skeptical reformers remained unconvinced.

During the subcommittee hearings, the arguments used for and against New Hampshire in countless regional newspapers over many years were brought finally, and inconclusively, to the national arena. They vividly illustrated the often uncomfortable position occupied by the Granite State as well as the difficulties faced by reform advocates in their attempts to root out what they perceived to be unacceptable quirks and inequities in candidate selection. Theoretical constructs follow an ordered and logical course on paper but are often undermined by conflicting priorities of state and national parties or by disagreements over means and ends within the reform camp itself. These weaknesses can often be effectively exploited by New Hampshire's representatives who argue with some justification that the elimination of one state's tradition should not be the sole underlying purpose of an entire reform bill. The visions encapsulated in the various bills before the subcommittee were seriously questioned by Caddell, Ranney and other speakers, who warned that the law of unintended electoral consequences could not be overcome merely by legislation. Indeed, it is questionable whether they should be overcome at all.

A consistent strand of the reform argument is its dissatisfaction with the system's apparent capacity to produce unsuitable nominees and a tendency to blame the primary process for subsequent weaknesses in presidential leadership. This argument is, of course, badly flawed. Presidential nominees of the post-1968 variety have not, in any real sense, proved less suitable or less representative than their predecessors. The reformed Democratic nomination process has produced, since 1968, three governors, one U.S. senator and a former vice-president; the Republicans, two former vice-presidents and an ex-governor of the country's largest, most populous state. Michael Dukakis, Walter Mondale or Bill Clinton, it could be argued, were no less qualified for the Oval Office than John W. Davis, Alton B. Parker or Horace Greeley. Davis was an obscure former West Virginia congressman, Parker an equally unknown New York lawyer, and Greeley, a celebrated journalist and editor who was singularly ill-suited to the rigors of campaigning and died of exhaustion before the Electoral College had officially ratified his defeat. South Dakota senator George McGovern, often regarded as the unacceptably radical product of a faulty system, was widely-respected as an innovative legislator within the U.S. Senate. The pre-reform system, however, produced Warren G. Harding, an at-best mediocre Ohio senator who reached the presidency only through a deadlocked GOP convention and proved entirely ill-suited to the office. Critics offer the example of Jimmy Carter's meteoric rise in 1976 as evidence that the post-reform process is excessively vulnerable to capture by inexperienced politicians unsympathetic to established party values. Yet the rise of Wendell Willkie in 1940 was a more remarkable feat. Willkie was a successful businessman who, unlike Carter, had held no elective office and had been a convinced New Dealer only a few years before seizing the GOP nomination from an astonished party Old Guard to challenge Franklin Roosevelt. History does not, therefore, offer any clear evidence that post-reform candidates are of an inferior quality to their forerunners.

The tendency among reform advocates has been to compare modern candidates to nonexistent ideals—experienced leaders of integrity, with coherent policy proposals acceptable to a large majority of a party's various regional strongholds and to the national electorate. The size, diversity and federal structure of the United States precludes the emergence of such nominees in all but the rarest cases, and against so lofty a benchmark, most nominees, pre- and post-1968, fall short. Although flaws in the selection process must account for some weaknesses in presidential governance, the bulk of the difficulties facing the modern White House stem from the debilitating experiences of Vietnam and Watergate, reawakened congressional authority, the weakened seniority system, special interest lobbying and a cynical news media. All are factors in the fracturing of American politics since the 1960s and all have played a significant part in increasing hostility to executive authority. The perceived weaknesses of post-imperial presidents must owe more to this damaging environment than to flaws in the leadership selection system.

Nonetheless, most alternative paths to improving the quality of political leadership imply changes in the constitutional relationship between executive and legislature, restrictions on special interest lobbying or media self-restraint. Faced with these choices, nomination rules reform comes to be regarded as a convenient universal panacea. Generalized assumptions linking electoral means to administrative ends lead to hopes that a reformed primary system may produce any number of desirable outcomes—cheaper or shorter campaigns, broader party consensus, higher standards of debate, improved policies, a reduction in media horse race coverage, improved candidate quality or better administrations.

Richard Watson has suggested that rules are seldom neutral and that " they inevitably give an advantage to certain individuals and interests . . . rules both prescribe behavior in political contests and help determine their outcome."[128] Reformers making similar assumptions frequently overstate the potential effect of rules changes on politics in general. Outcomes may certainly be determined by accepted sets of rules, but those outcomes are electoral and limited to the victory of one campaign strategy or calculation over another, to the wider appeal of one type of candidate over another. These are quantitative, not qualitative, outcomes, in which skill in the accumulation of delegate and electoral votes often bears little or no relationship to the candidate's intellectual quality or subsequent performance as president. In a nomination system unlocked to broad, democratic participation via the presidential primary and governed by the battle of interpretations between candidates and media, the premium is set on quantitative skills alone as candidates plot their way through a maze of high-profile popularity contests. While policy detail and coherence are not discounted, their influence is often diminished. In such an environment, efficient or visionary leaders may emerge, but the roll of the dice is in every way as arbitrary as before.

Predictably, such obstacles, and the failure of the 1984 and 1986 bills, did not dent the enthusiasm of campaigners for reform. A brief flurry arose in August 1988 when the Senate Rules Committee reported out S. 1786, a bill requiring five, federally mandated regional primaries and permitting the U.S. attorney-general to instigate judicial action against noncompliant states, a clause clearly inserted with Iowa and New Hampshire in mind. S. 1786 presented another potentially serious threat to New Hampshire's status. Its sponsor, Senator Alan Dixon, proposed that states draw lots to determine the polling order as a way to override the influence New Hampshire and Iowa held over the early nomination period. Secretary Bill Gardner informed the Manchester *Union Leader*, "If we're ever going to lose it, this is the way it can happen."[129]

The Dixon bill, like its 1984 and 1986 predecessors, failed to reach the desk of the president. Yet many legislators remain convinced that the glaring faults of the reformed nomination process must be remedied and that the national parties have demonstrated their inability to effect the necessary changes. Opinion varies as to what form such change must take, although a clear consensus developed in favor of a rotated regional system, but committee transcripts reveal that reform elements in Congress are highly skeptical about the role claimed by New Hampshire for its first-in-the-nation primary. Two main arguments are employed against favored status; first, that the state is unrepresentative of the national electorate; second, that a perennial claim to first position is fundamentally unfair. The primary's defenders appear more than capable of dealing with the first, intellectually flawed, criticism. Apart from reliance on the appeal of tradition, however, there is no effective counter to the second.

CONCLUSION

The troubled history of nomination rules reform, spanning decades of finance reforms, media growth and diversification, primary proliferation, debates over representative equality and timetable battles, increasingly appears to have followed the path pundits predicted for it as far back as the 1970s. Escalating expense and increased participation have not improved the system's capacity for selecting efficient and capable leaders. Indeed, the late-twentieth-century impulse to select candidates running against the Washington establishment, rather than pledging to work with it, has been encouraged by the populist inclinations of primary electorates. It was no accident that the two strongest candidates of the early 1996 GOP nomination race were Patrick Buchanan, a former journalist, and Steve Forbes, a wealthy publisher. Their outsider credentials gained them far more popularity with primary voters than the consummate politician, Bob Dole.

Operating within this perpetually unstable environment, defenders of the first primary have remained committed to preserving its position against challenges from national party organizations and other states. Part of this determination is based on economic self-interest and a certain amount of egotism. Yet New Hampshire officials also voice the fears of many observers that the modern nominating process has run out of control and now threatens to engulf underdog candidacies in a welter of media ads, giant primaries and unpayable bills. Georgi Hippauf, vice-chair of the Republican State Committee, explained to reporters in 1996, "We don't want to see the process of selecting the next president . . . compressed into such a short, media-blitzed period of time that only the major, well-heeled players can get a chance."[130]

The Granite State's ability to protect its primary has been, to date, surprisingly successful. This may be partly due to the transparent weaknesses in the reform case. First, no viable alternative to the status quo has been proposed which does not simply reinforce existing trends or spring purely from state party jealousy of New Hampshire and Iowa. Regional primaries do nothing to help small candidacies; a national primary would push them into extinction. Attacks on New Hampshire's privilege are coupled with demands to share that privilege, an addendum that neatly undermines the original principle. Second, criticisms of the current system are weakened by reformers' evident desire to establish a blueprint of personal and political qualities for future nominees. The conviction that there exists a set of ideal characteristics for party standardbearers and that adjustments to the nomination environment will somehow bring these to the fore is misguided. The caucus and convention systems of past centuries clearly demonstrated that no amount of peer review or nonpartisan sentiment can guarantee the emergence of a successful presidency. Finally, most proposed solutions imply the need for significant federal transgressions in an area previously reserved for adjudication by state parties and legislatures. In an era of revived federalism, such a move would be difficult to justify.

By the close of the twentieth century, front-loading and the intraparty disputes it engenders have pushed state party organizations to the threshold of concerted action. The form this action may take is by no means certain. The DNC made its move, via Rule 10A, to establish a stable basis to the nomination calendar more than a decade ago. But 10A preserves only the prerogatives of Iowa and New Hampshire. Further steps will be needed to encourage states to back-load their events. The Republican party now appears to be awakening to this imperative. The best that the architects of nomination reform can hope to achieve is a balanced system of evenly spaced contests, allowing voters pause for thought and candidates pause for breath, which permits the steady development of media and financial momentum and does not throttle smaller candidacies at birth. Such a task may well prove to be beyond the abilities of the fractious and competitive party system to achieve. For the foreseeable future, however, Congress may be wiser to suspend its own efforts to reform the nomination process until it becomes certain that the parties themselves are incapable of doing so.

NOTES

1. *Delegate Selection Rules for the 1984 Democratic National Convention* (Washington, DC: Democratic National Committee, 1982), pp. 11–12.

2. Gary D. Wekkin, "National–State Party Relations," *Political Studies Quarterly*, vol. 99, no. 2 (1984): 42.

3. Memo, Paul G. Kirk, Jr., to Charles T. Manatt, December 19, 1983, p. 1. All correspondence involving members of the Democratic National Committee, Compliance Review Commission, or New Hampshire First Primary Committee is reproduced in this chapter courtesy of Martin L. Gross.

4. Interview, Robert W. Beckel, Washington, DC, August 25, 1986.

5. Emmett H. Buell, Jr., "First in the Nation: Disputes over Scheduling the Iowa Caucuses, New Hampshire Primary and Other Early Presidential Nomination Contests in 1984 and 1988," Unpublished research draft, 1988. Subsequently published as "First-in-the-Nation: Disputes over the Timing of Early Democratic Presidential Primaries and Caucuses in 1984 and 1988," *Journal of Law and Politics*, vol. 4, no. 2 (Fall 1987).

6. Wekkin, "National–State Party Relations," p. 42.

7. Ibid., p. 43.

8. Interview, Robert Beckel, Washington, DC, August 24, 1986.

9. Wekkin, "National–State Party Relations," p. 44.

10. Interview, William L. Gardner, Secretary of State, Concord, NH, June 5, 1987.

11. Memo, Martin L. Gross to members of First Primary Committee, June 7, 1983, p. 1.

12. Ibid., p. 3.

13. Ibid., p. 4.

14. Memo, Martin L. Gross to Chris Spirou, January 31, 1983, p. 2.

15. Ibid., p. 5.

16. Letter, Martin L. Gross to George Bruno, June 23, 1983.

17. Buell, "First in the Nation," p. 23.

18. Letter, Nancy Pelosi to Edwin Granai, March 14, 1983.

19. Buell, "First in the Nation," p. 16.

20. Letter, Richard Boyer to Charles T. Manatt, March 8, 1983.

21. Ironically, the New Hampshire primary itself, though a delegate selection exercise, functions as little more than a beauty contest due to its low delegate yield. Its media value increases its impact, a fact not lost on Vermont in its 1983 scheduling efforts.

22. *Delegate Selection Rules*, p. 19.

23. Ibid.

24. Letter, Representative Norman E. D'Amours to Senator Alan Cranston, March 23, 1983.

25. Buell, "First in the Nation," p. 23.

26. *New Hampshire Resubmission Evaluation: Initial Finding of Non-Compliance by the Compliance Review Commission* (Washington, DC: Democratic National Committee, October 15, 1983), p. 1. Courtesy William L. Gardner.

27. *Delegate Selection Rules*, p. 19.

28. Joseph P. Kahn, "Quick: What Created Jobs, Filled Hotels, Sold Drinks and Had Very Little to Do with Politics?" *New England Monthly* (April 1984): 38.

29. Ibid.

30. Letter, George Bruno to Nancy Pelosi, November 3, 1983, pp. 2–3.

31. *Legal Aspects of National Convention Delegate Selection Process in the State of New Hampshire*, Document prepared for the Secretary of State, 1983, pp. 1–2. Courtesy William L. Gardner.

32. Ibid.

33. Author Interview, Professor Emmett H. Buell, Jr., Bristol, July 28, 1987.

34. Buell, "First in the Nation," p. 34.

35. Ibid., pp. 35–36.

36. Letter, Martin L. Gross to Charles T. Manatt, December 5, 1983, p. 1.

37. Buell, "First in the Nation," p. 45.

38. Memo, Paul G. Kirk, Jr., to Charles T. Manatt, December 19, 1983, p. 1.

39. Kirk memo, December 19, 1983, p. 7. Kirk cited Gross's letter to Gregory Smith in which Gross pointed out that the Vermont delegate selection threshold of 40 percent had never actually been triggered and that there existed no Vermont party rule binding the preference primary result to the selection of convention delegates. (*Source*: Letter, Martin L. Gross to Attorney-General Gregory Smith, October 4, 1983, p. 2.)

40. Kirk memo, December 19, 1983, p. 9.

41. Ibid., p. 14.

42. Buell, "First in the Nation," p. 48. The claim appears unlikely since Kennedy had withdrawn from the race before December 1983. Mondale had already fixed his signature to the Memorandum of Understanding which supported New Hampshire's case against the DNC, and the former vice-president's chances of defeating President Ronald Reagan were not, even at this stage, highly rated.

43. In an interesting footnote to the episode, Bruno later revealed that he and Nagle had privately met with Kirk in the Virgin Islands in December 1984, when Kirk had already declared his candidacy to succeed Manatt as party chairman. Bruno relates that, while not offering ironclad guarantees for the future saftey of Iowa and New Hampshire, he did assure Nagle and Bruno that "there would be no problem with '88." Kirk subsequently won the chairmanship, and the 1988 election cycle passed without serious compliance problems for either state. (*Source*: Telephone Interview, George Bruno, January 8; 1988).

44. Morris K. Udall, *Testimony Before the House Subcommittee on Elections*, Washington, DC, September 19, 1984. *Hearings Held Before the Subcommittee on Elections of the*

Committee on House Administration, U.S. House of Representatives, Ninety-eighth Congress (Washington, DC: U.S. Government Printing Office, 1984), p. 13.

45. James Ceaser, *Reforming the Reforms: A Critical Analysis of the Presidential Selection Process* (Cambridge, MA: Ballinger Publishing Co., 1982), p. 18.

46. William Crotty and John S. Jackson, *Presidential Primaries and Nominations* (New York: Congressional Quarterly Books, 1985), p. 61.

47. "Many Democrats Cool to Redoing Party Rules," *Congressional Quarterly Weekly Report*, August 24, 1985, p. 1689.

48. Bruno telephone interview.

49. Paul Taylor, "The Way We Choose Our Presidents Is Crazy," in Robert E. DiClerico and Allan S. Hammock, eds., *Points of View: Readings in American Government* (New York: McGraw-Hill, 1982), p. 129.

50. "NH Officials Vow to Fend Off Arizona First Primary Challenge," *Boston Globe*, December 1, 1994, p. 16.

51. "Arizona Governor Angling to Take 1st Primary from N.H.," *Boston Globe*, January 15, 1995, p. 19.

52. Interview, Secretary of State William Gardner, Manchester, NH, February 16, 1996.

53. "Presidential Hopefuls Told to Support NH's Primary," *Union Leader*, January 25, 1995, p. A1.

54. "War on Primary Poaching Is Declared," *Concord Monitor*, January 19, 1995, p. A1.

55. "NH Seeks Help to Defend Primary," *Union Leader*, January 20, 1995, p. A1.

56. Ibid., p. A18.

57. "War on Primary Poaching Is Declared," p. A1.

58. "NH Seeks Help," p. A1.

59. "Arizona Ends Bid for First Primary," *Boston Globe*, January 28, 1995. p. 6.

60. *Union Leader*, February 2, 1995, p. B1.

61. "Delaware Testy on '96 Primary Date, Changes," *Union Leader*, February 3, 1996, p. A1.

62. "Delaware Date Threatens NH's First Primary Rule," *Union Leader*, February 1, 1995, p. A4.

63. Courtesy, William M. Gardner files.

64. "Mucho Macho Pat . . . Bows to NH Gnomes," *News Journal*, Wilmington, April 29, 1995, p. B1.

65. "New Hampshire Fights to Keep Primary First," *Washington Post*, April 30, 1995, p. A12.

66. "To the Barricades, Ye Sons and Daughters of the First State," *News Journal*, Wilmington, February 4, 1995, p. B1.

67. "NH Primary Gaining Protection," *Union Leader*, March 7, 1995, p. A1.

68. "House Passes Presidential Primary Bill," *Union Leader*, March 17, 1995, p. A1.

69. "NH Primary Gaining Protection," p. A1.

70. "Election Dates: Presidential Primary Election," *New Hampshire Election Laws and Political Calendar 1996–1997*, Department of State, Concord, NH, 1996, p. 9.

71. "Delaware GOP Blasts New Hampshire's Candidate Blackmail," Press release, Republican State Committee of Delaware, Wilmington, April 26, 1995, p. 1.

72. Letter, Basil Battaglia to Governor Pete Wilson, May 1, 1995. Courtesy William M. Gardner.

73. "Gramm Vows to Back Early NH Vote," *Boston Globe*, January 16, 1996, p. 3.

74. Press Release, Joseph Keefe, Democratic State Committee of New Hampshire, July 6, 1995, p. 2. Courtesy William M. Gardner files.

75. David Shribman, "Primary Battle of the States," *Boston Globe*, April 28, 1995, p. A15.

76. Interview, Carl Cameron, WMUR-TV, Manchester, NH, June 23, 1995.

77. Letter, Joseph Keefe to William M. Gardner, October 17, 1995. Courtesy William M. Gardner.

78. Interview, Secretary of State William M. Gardner, Manchester, NH, February 16, 1996.

79. Letter, Joseph Keefe to Representative Jim Splaine, December 19, 1995. Courtesy William M. Gardner.

80. Interview, Secretary of State William M. Gardner, State House, Concord, NH, June 19, 1995.

81. "Delaware's Trump," *Keene Sentinel*, January 18, 1996, p. 2.

82. Interview, Secretary of State William M. Gardner, Manchester, NH, February 16, 1996.

83. "Delaware's Primary Expected to Have Full Slate," *News Journal*, Wilmington, January 11, 1996, p. A1.

84. Press release of the Secretary of State. Courtesy William M. Gardner.

85. "Delaware's Primary Expected," p. A1.

86. Derrick Z. Jackson, "In Politics, Who Goes First?" *Boston Globe*, January 5, 1996, p. 19.

87. "Delaware Testy," p. A1.

88. Letter, Edward Shumaker to William M. Gardner, October 20, 1995, p. 2. Courtesy William M. Gardner.

89. Letter, Keefe to Splaine, p. 2.

90. "Merrill Waffles on Primary," *Concord Monitor*, November 16, 1995, p. B1.

91. "GOP May Help End 1st Primary Threats," *Union Leader*, November 21, 1995, p. A6.

92. David Irwin, "Our Primary's Shrinking Justification," *Keene Sentinel*, February 23, 1995, p. 5.

93. "NE Super Tuesday Primary Picks Up Steam Without N.H.," *Union Leader*, February 15, 1995, p. A4.

94. "Region's Secretaries of State Laud 'Yankee Day Primary,'" *Union Leader*, July 15, 1995, p. A4.

95. Ibid.

96. John Haskell, "Don't Rush to Judgement," *State Government News* (Lexington, KY: Council of State Governments, October 1995), p. 37.

97. Interview, Secretary of State William M. Gardner, State House, Concord, February 17, 1996.

98. *Constitution of the United States of America*, Article II, Section 2.

99. Laurence H. Tribe, *American Constitutional Law*, 2nd ed. (New York: Foundation Press, 1988), pp. 1118–19. In *Nixon v. Herndon*, the Taft Court invalidated a Texas statute banning blacks from voting in primary elections. In the followup case, a Texas law permitting party executive committees to set down requirements for voter eligibility, employed as a way to circumvent the *Herndon* ruling, was struck down by the Hughes Court.

100. Tribe, *American Constitutional Law*, p. 1133.

101. Taylor in DiClerico and Hammock, eds., *Points of View*, p. 127.

102. H.R. 6054. *Hearings Held Before the Subcommittee on Elections of the Committee on House Administration*, September 19, 1984, House of Representatives, Ninety-eighth Congress, Second Session (Washington, DC: U.S. Government Printing Office, 1984). H.R.

251; H.R. 3542; H.R. 4453; H.R. 1380; *Hearings Held Before the Subcommittee on Elections of the Committee on House Administration*, March 20, May 8, 1986, House of Representatives, Ninety-ninth Congress, Second Session (Washington, DC: U.S. Government Printing Office, 1986).

103. Representative Al Swift, *1986 Hearings*, p. 50.

104. Ibid., p. 9.

105. Representative Morris K. Udall, *1984 Hearings*, p. 12.

106. Charles T. Manatt, *1986 Hearings*, pp. 98–99.

107. Ibid., p. 47.

108. Representative Al Swift, *1984 Hearings*, p. 17.

109. Representative William Thomas, *1986 Hearings*, p. 39.

110. Ibid., p. 29.

111. Ibid., p. 22.

112. For the state rotation proposal contained within H.R. 4453, see *1986 Hearings*, pp. 15–18.

113. Ibid., p. 112.

114. Ibid., pp. 148–49.

115. Ibid., p. 115.

116. Ibid.

117. Interview, Secretary of State William M. Gardner, Manchester, February 16, 1996.

118. Austin Ranney, *1986 Hearings*, p. 146.

119. Ibid., p. 151.

120. Ibid., p. 123.

121. Ibid., p. 124.

122. Ibid., p. 125.

123. Ibid., p. 46.

124. Ibid.

125. Ibid.

126. Ibid., p. 50.

127. Ibid., p. 48.

128. Richard A. Watson, *The Presidential Contest* (New York: John Wiley & Sons, 1980), p. 9.

129. Gardner files.

130. Paul Peter Jesep, "NH: Of Primary Importance," *New Hampshire Editions*, vol. 6, no. 1 (January 1996): 29.

Conclusion: NASS and Beyond

On May 10 and 11, 1996, a special Committee on Presidential Primaries and Caucuses assembled at Washington's Mayflower Hotel. Established by the National Association of Secretaries of State (NASS), the committee comprised twelve secretaries from states including Delaware, Pennsylvania, California, Massachusetts, Iowa and Minnesota. Assistant secretaries represented the states of Arizona, Maine and Mississippi. The conference was chaired by New Hampshire's secretary of state, William Gardner. For two days, the committee heard representations from its members as well as a variety of party officials, academic observers, journalists and political activists, including Don Fowler, co-chairman of the Democratic National Committee, former presidential contender Lamar Alexander, GOP strategist and former Reagan adviser Lyn Nofziger, Rhodes Cook, senior political writer for *Congressional Quarterly*, and Curtis Gans, veteran of the 1968 McCarthy campaign and now director of the Committee for the Study of the American Electorate.[1]

The meeting's official purpose was to "receive input and undertake deliberations regarding perceived impacts of 'front-loading' of presidential primaries . . . which emerged in the 1996 presidential primary season."[2] The final report, drafted by Arizona's assistant secretary of state Anne Lynch, began by presenting a number of key facts which, it suggested, had created an urgent need for concerted remedial action by state governments and national political parties. Prime among these facts were the chaotic state of primary scheduling, a prospect that was now extending to the 2000 election cycle, and the ongoing efforts by Congress and the Democratic and Republican parties to overhaul the entire presidential nomination system. Furthermore, as Lynch succinctly observed, the candidates themselves "did not like the 1996 process."

The sheer breadth and complexity of the issues under discussion caused initial disagreements concerning the committee's remit. The original intention to debate proposals for reform of a nomination system that all parties agreed was not functioning to the benefit of leadership selection in the United States could not be separated, Assistant Secretary Lynch stated, from wider problems concerning campaign financing and media coverage. Secretary Gardner, supported by the assistant secretary of state for Maine, Chip Gavin, maintained that these issues should be kept distinct and apart. Gavin suggested that the committee would be inviting criticism and perhaps weakening its impact on the major party organizations if it insisted on reaching beyond timetabling reform proposals.[3]

Despite these differences, the committee was rapidly able to establish several major areas of consensus. The two most important of these were that parties, not state legislatures, possessed the main influence in deciding on forms and processes of nomination and that a single, national primary was an unacceptable alternative to the current dysfunction. Both conclusions may prove significant in the long term. The apparent inevitability of a national primary system has always been met by the contention that its size and cost would exclude lesser candidates from seeking the presidency. The 1996 committee's declaration finally makes an official stand against such a proposal and is liable to carry weight with state legislatures and parties, as well as with Congress. The declaration that parties rather than legislatures determine the mode of candidate competition is similarly important. The language of the original Lynch report assigns state legislatures a "secondary role," but its clear intent enables parties to proceed together, or separately, to coordinate caucus and primary dates.[4] The consensus points further admit the importance that is already connected to "a few" small states leading off the primary calendar and call for the continuation of this tradition. These points were subsequently built into the NASS subcommittee's *Draft Initial Proposal* and *Action Plan*. The plan called for draft proposals to be sent to all RNC and DNC officials and to the RNC taskforce on primary elections before its May 30 meeting in Washington. The Committee on Elections and the NASS full body would continue work on the proposals prior to the Association's full meeting in Charleston from July 27 to August 2, 1996.

The committee's six draft proposals made good reading for New Hampshire. Point Two called for cooperation between national and state parties and state legislatures in order to "fix" the broken system. The role of Congress was limited to reviewing finance regulations. A broad consensus beyond the committee on this issue could therefore finally remove the looming threat of what the committee termed "congressional meddling" in state affairs, which would, in all likelihood, have damaged or destroyed New Hampshire's primary tradition. Point Four further reinforces the position taken by Secretary Gardner and New Hampshire's political parties in stating, "The nomination system needs to be spread out to a full three to four months. Political parties should recognize a window from early March or April through June. Any primaries or caucuses outside the window would be subject to party discipline."[5] Since New Hampshire's battles in the 1980s and 1990s had been fought over precisely these issues, the call for a nationally enforced window again implicitly validated the state's position. Finally, Point Three made this validation explicit in calling for a continuation of the Iowa–New Hampshire lead-off tradition.

The NASS subcommittee represents an important, potentially decisive, turning point in the development of the presidential primary and in the life of New Hampshire's benchmark primary. Although the initial report listed possible solutions, including a rotating regional primary system, the firm declaration that small states should lead off the process and that Iowa and New Hampshire should begin this process is the clearest indication yet that the Granite State may be poised to win its long battle. On July 2, 1996, an RNC News Release indicated that the national Republican party was also moving toward a final resolution of the problems bedeviling candidate selection. Party chairman Haley Barbour appointed a taskforce to study the problem in January 1996 in response to growing confusion and disillusionment, coupled with falling voter turnout and rising costs. According to the July 2 release, the taskforce discovered that the truncated 1996 calendar did have a negative effect on turnout: "while the compressed schedule resulted in record-breaking voter participation in the earliest states, it dampened the effectiveness of voters' voices in later states."[6]

Consequently, the RNC taskforce, which included Republican Rules Committee chairman David Norcross, issued recommendations to the Rules Committee comprising a 10 percent increase in delegate allocation for states holding primaries or caucuses between March 15 and May 14 in a nomination year. Those holding contests on or after May 15 would receive a 20 percent increase.[7] The taskforce further recommended that party rules specify July 1 of the preelection year as the deadline for submission of primary and caucus dates and that an official window be established between the first Monday of February and the third Tuesday of June in which all contests should be held. Despite the publicity accorded these proposals by the national party organization, their efficacy remains dubious. It has long been recognized that media publicity and candidate attention are as vital to campaigns as actual delegate numbers and a 10 percent increase in delegates may not be enough to override the temptation for states to opt for an early date. Furthermore, the announcement of official deadlines and windows may in the end prove superficial. It could well shorten the wrangling time for states such as Delaware, New Hampshire and Arizona but would not necessarily decompress the final primary schedule. Therefore, of the two reports of summer 1996, the NASS committee holds out the best prospect for significant, long-term reform.

The mere existence of two high-level committees, however, indicates that the crisis in presidential nomination mechanics is reaching, or has reached, a decisive stage. The fate of the New Hampshire primary will probably now be determined by national party officials and state government representatives acting in concert rather than simply by New Hampshire's own General Court or local party organizations. The Granite State's struggles to preserve its electoral turf have been largely successful, but they have also served to heighten the general impression of discord and paralysis within the presidential selection system which eventually led to the NASS and RNC reports. It is also perhaps ironic that, having used state prerogative so successfully in its defense, New Hampshire's advocates are now prepared to countenance proposals relegating state legislatures to a secondary role in the rule-making process. Such a tactical switch has been made with a set goal in mind—the assurance that the status of Iowa and New Hampshire will be preserved within a new, reformed system. The switch might be regarded as something of a gamble since the consultation procedure is still in its initial stages. The appointment of Secretary Gardner to head the NASS Commission, however, indicates the formation of a fairly solid consensus behind the proposal to leave the two early contests in their time-honored positions.

Throughout its long history, the New Hampshire primary has been shaped and changed by its times, by the currents of party and media development, by changing concepts of democratic participation and altered perceptions of ideal presidential candidates. Its experiences have therefore reflected the turbulence of presidential nominating politics during the twentieth century. Each change in the primary, its popularity, its format, its results and disputes has signaled in microcosm changes in the wider electoral environment. What becomes clear, and what has now been generally conceded in the reform process of the mid-1990s, is that the useful contribution made to the presidential race by the Granite State outweighs its perceived negatives. Taking into account the main arguments against the primary's continuation reviewed in previous chapters, we can establish a series of key points.

First, the New Hampshire primary predated television, a medium that has greatly magnified the effects of its verdicts. Disproportionate primary coverage remains a problem but one that exists before and continues beyond the first primary and that must be addressed and corrected by the media itself, rather than by New Hampshire. Network organizations such as NBC have already begun the process of closely monitoring election news output to balance policy detail with race coverage. Veterans of the primary, including the late John Chancellor, observe that imperatives such as pack and horse race journalism will require careful observation and correction as part of a gradual maturation in media coverage of electoral events over the coming decades. New Hampshire citizens also have a role to play in this process. Although often critical of media coverage of their state, primary supporters have sometimes perpetuated the stereotypes in order to add color to campaigns.

Second, the question of representative contests cannot be applied as an argument against New Hampshire's role. The sheer scope of national candidate selection dictates unrepresentative results at every stage of the process, and only the unacceptable option of a national primary could resolve this issue. Such a resolution would be only partial since primary turnout remains unstable and costs would prevent many candidates from launching a presidential bid. Finally, if representative criteria are to be applied, New Hampshire appears to reflect contemporary American society, its social, political and economic currents, far more closely than is generally realized.

Third, New Hampshire's primary, in tandem with the Iowa caucuses, continues to offer a unique contribution to the presidential selection process. Although modified by new technology, retail politics is alive and well in the Granite State. The size of the state and its demographic spread dictate a town-by-town, door-to-door strategy that is now defunct in larger states such as Ohio or California. This affords ordinary voters the chance to question candidates at close quarters and compels candidates to think on their feet. With the giant regional primaries looming later in the season, this unique environment at the beginning of the selection process is one that should be preserved.

Fourth, New Hampshire aids not only the voter but also the small-scale candidacies of a Kefauver, a McCarthy, a Carter, a Hart or an Alexander. Candidates with little chance of serious attention in regional primaries have two opportunities in Iowa and New Hampshire to improve their financial and polling positions. They find fertile ground in New Hampshire since the state can still be organized on a shoestring budget. In addition, only in the two early states can flaws in the campaigns of front-runners be effectively exploited. By the close of the 1996 electoral cycle, the Democratic National Committee, the National Association of Secretaries of State and veteran activists and reporters had recognized these facts. The Republican National Committee also appears to be moving toward this consensus. The closing of the Iowa–New Hampshire opportunity would signal the complete dominance of wealthy, big-name candidacies. The primary therefore has a role to play and a unique environment to offer in the selection of presidential nominees. Since its verdict is by no means conclusive, either at the conventions or in the November election, it provides a vital platform for lesser known candidates without necessarily terminating the campaigns of more established political figures.

A persistent feature of the post-1968 nomination period has been the demand by reformers that selection processes be ordered, balanced and systematized to reflect national democratic values and practices that existed primarily in the minds of the reformers themselves. The ad hoc, elite-driven process employed during the pre-1968 era felt no need to conform to such high ideals of widespread voter participation, balanced ethnic and gender percentages, proportionate delegate allocation or representative contests. By the 1990s, these values have been largely accepted and adopted, albeit slowly and not without controversy. Yet such reforms spawned new and serious problems. By 1996 the system did indeed appear to be broken as states battled with their neighbors and with national party officials to secure their place in the limelight or to protest against yet more changes in the delegate allocation process.

New Hampshire's primary, at the forefront of the election calendar, has also been at the forefront of these battles and seemed destined, during the 1980s, to become a major casualty. Its fate, however, remains closely linked to the tides of reform, and these tides are now flowing strongly in the Granite State's favor. The first-in-the-nation primary may be preserved; indeed, it must be preserved if the legend is to survive that all Americans, whatever their financial or political status, have a chance to be elected president of the United States.

NOTES

1. Letter, William M. Gardner to Joyce Hazeltine, President, National Association of Secretaries of State, May 20, 1996, p. 3. Reproduced courtesy of William M. Gardner.

2. Report, *National Association of Secretaries of State, Meeting of Subcommittee on Presidential Primaries*, compiled by Anne L. Lynch, Arizona Assistant Secretary of State, May 1996, p. 1. Reproduced courtesy of William M. Gardner.

3. Letter, William M. Gardner to Joyce Hazeltine, p. 4.

4. Lynch report, p. 2

5. Ibid., p. 3.

6. *RNC News Release*, RNC Press Office, Washington, DC, July 2, 1996, p. 2.

7. Ibid., p. 2.

Selected Bibliography

Abramowitz, Alan I., and Walter J. Stone. *Nomination Politics: Party Activists and Presidential Choice*. New York: Praeger, 1984.

Abramson, Paul R., John H. Aldrich, and David W. Rohde. *Change and Continuity in the 1988 Elections*. Washington, DC: Congressional Quarterly Press, 1990.

Adams, Sherman. *First-Hand Report: The Inside Story of the Eisenhower Administration*. London: Hutchinson & Co., 1962.

Aldrich, John H. *Before the Convention: Strategies and Choices in Presidential Nomination Politics*. Chicago: University of Chicago Press, 1980.

Arterton, F. Christopher. *Media Politics: The New Strategies of Presidential Campaigns*. Washington, DC: Healt, 1984.

Barber, James David. *The Pulse of Politics: Electing Presidents in the Media Age*. New York: W. W. Norton, 1980.

Beck, Paul Allen, and Frank J. Sorauf. *Party Politics in America*. New York: HarperCollins, 1992.

Brereton, Charles. *First Step to the White House: The New Hampshire Primary, 1952–1980*. Hampton, NH: Wheelabrator Foundation, 1979.

———. *First in the Nation: New Hampshire and the Premier Presidential Primary*. Portsmouth, NH: Peter E. Randall Publishers, 1987.

Buell, Emmett H., Jr., and Lee Sigelman, eds. *Nominating the President*. Knoxville: University of Tennessee Press, 1991.

Casey, Susan B. *Hart and Soul: Gary Hart's New Hampshire Odyssey and Beyond*. Concord, NH: NHI Press, 1986.

Cash, Kevin. *Who the Hell Is William Loeb?* Manchester, NH: Amoskeag Press, 1975.

Ceaser, James W. *Reforming the Reforms: A Critical Analysis of the Presidential Selection Process*. Cambridge, MA: Ballinger Publishing Co., 1982.

Chester, Lewis, Godfrey Hodgson, and Bruce Page. *An American Melodrama: The Presidential Campaign of 1968*. London: Andre Deutsch, 1969.

Clem, Alan L. *American Electoral Politics: Strategies for Renewal*. London: D. Van Nostrand Co., 1981.

Crittendden, John A. *Parties and Elections in the United States*. Englewood Cliffs, NJ: Prentice-Hall, 1982.

Crotty, William J. *Decision for the Democrats: Reforming the Party Structure.* London: Johns Hopkins University Press, 1978.

———, ed. *The Party Symbol: Readings on Political Parties.* San Fransisco: W. H. Freeman, 1980.

Crotty, William J., and John S. Jackson. *Presidential Primaries and Nominations.* Washington, DC: Congressional Quarterly Books, 1985.

Davis, James W. *Presidential Primaries: The Road to the White House.* Westport, CT: Greenwood Press, 1980.

Diamond, Edwin, and Stephen Bates. *The Spot: The Rise of Political Advertising on Television.* Cambridge, MA: MIT Press, 1984.

Donovan, Robert J. *Tumultuous Years: The Presidency of Harry S. Truman, 1949–1953.* New York: W. W. Norton, 1982.

Donovan, Robert J., and Ray Scherer. *Unsilent Revolution: Television News and American Public Life.* Cambridge: Cambridge University Press, 1992.

Drew, Elizabeth. *American Journal: The Events of 1976.* New York: Random House, 1977.

English, David. *Divided They Stand.* London: Michael Joseph Ltd., 1969.

Foley, J., D. A. Britton, and E. B. Everett, Jr., eds. *Nominating a President: The Process and the Press.* New York: Praeger, 1980.

Gans, Herbert J. *Deciding What's News: A Study of CBS Evening News, NBC Nightly News, Newsweek and Time.* New York: Vintage Books, 1980.

Germond, Jack, and Jules Witcover. *Blue Smoke and Mirrors: How Reagan Won and Why Carter Lost the Election of 1980.* New York: Viking Press, 1981.

Goldman, Peter, and Tom Mathews. *The Quest for the Presidency: The 1988 Campaign.* New York: Simon & Schuster, 1989.

Goldstein, Michael L. *Guide to the 1992 Presidential Election.* Washington, DC: Congressional Quarterly, 1991.

Hadley, Arthur T. *The Invisible Primary.* Englewood Cliffs, NJ: Prentice-Hall, 1976.

Hart, Gary. *Right from the Start: A Chronicle of the McGovern Campaign.* New York: Quadrangle Books, 1973.

Harwood, Richard, ed. *The Pursuit of the Presidency 1980.* New York: Berkeley Books, 1980.

Hastings, Max. *America 1968: The Fire This Time.* London: Victor Gollancz Ltd., 1969.

Heren, Louis B. *No Hail, No Farewell: The Johnson Years.* London: Weidenfeld & Nicolson, 1970.

Hess, Stephen. *The Presidential Campaign.* Washington, DC: Brookings Institute, 1974.

Jewell, Malcolm E., and David M. Olsen. *American State Political Parties and Elections.* Chicago: Dorsey Press, 1978.

Keeter, Scott, and Clifford Zukin. *Uninformed Choice: The Failure of the New Presidential Nominating System.* New York: Praeger, 1983.

Kessel, John H. *Presidential Campaign Politics: Coalition Strategies and Citizen Response.* Chicago: Dorsey Press, 1984.

Key, V. O., Jr., *American State Politics: An Introduction.* New York: Alfred A. Knopf, 1956.

Lengle, James I. *Representation and Presidential Primaries: The Democratic Party in the Post-Reform Era.* Westport, CT: Greenwood Press, 1981.

Lockard, Duane. *New England State Politics.* Princeton, NJ: Princeton University Press, 1959.

Luntz, Frank I. *Candidates, Consultants and Campaigns: The Style and Substance of American Electioneering.* New York: Basil Blackwell, 1988.

Maisel, Louis, and Joseph Cooper, eds. *The Impact of the Electoral Process*. London: Sage Publications, 1977.

Malbin, Michael J., ed. *Money and Politics in the United States: Financing Elections in the 1980s*. Chatham, NJ: Chatham House, 1984.

Manchester, William. *The Glory and the Dream: A Narrative History of America, 1932–1972*. New York: Bantam Books, 1975.

May, Ernest, and Janet Fraser. *Campaign '72: The Managers Speak*. Cambridge, MA: Harvard University Press, 1973.

Mayer, William G., ed. *In Pursuit of the White House: How We Choose Our Presidential Nominees*. Chatham, NJ: Chatham House, 1996.

Mayhew, David R. *Placing Parties in American Politics: Organization, Electoral Settings and Government Activity in the Twentieth Century*. Princeton, NJ: Princeton University Press, 1986.

Moore, Jonathan, ed. *The Campaign for President: 1980 in Retrospect*. Cambridge, MA: Ballinger Publishing Co., 1981.

———. *Campaign for President: The Managers Look At '84*. Dover, MA: Auburn House Publishing Co., 1986.

Moore, Jonathan, and Janet Fraser, eds. *Campaign for President: The Managers Look at '76*. Cambridge, MA: Harvard University Press, 1977.

Nelson, Michael, ed. *The Elections of 1984*. Washington, DC: Congressional Quarterly, 1985.

Orren, Gary R., and Nelson W. Polsby, eds. *Media and Momentum: The New Hampshire Primary and Nomination Politics*. Chatham, NJ: Chatham House, 1987.

Oulahan, Richard. *The Man Who . . . The Story of the Democratic National Convention of 1932*. New York: Dial Press, 1971.

Paletz, David L., and Robert M. Entman. *Media Power Politics*. New York: Macmillan Co., 1981.

Parmet, Herbert S. *Eisenhower and the American Crusades*. New York: Macmillan Co., 1972.

Patterson, Thomas E. *The Mass Media Election: How Americans Choose Their President*. New York: Praeger, 1980.

Patterson, Thomas E., and R. D. McClure. *The Unseeing Eye: The Myth of Television Power in National Politics*. New York: G. P. Putnam's Sons, 1976.

Peirce, Neal R. *The New England States*. New York: W. W. Norton, 1976.

Perry, James M. *Us and Them: How the Press Covered the 1972 Election*. New York: Clarkson & Potter, 1973.

Pierce, John C., and John L.Sullivan, eds. *The Electorate Reconsidered*. London: Sage Publications, 1980.

Polsby, Nelson W. *Consequences of Party Reform*. London: Oxford University Press, 1983.

Polsby, Nelson W., and Aaron Wildavsky. *Presidential Elections: Strategies of American Politics*. New York: Charles Scribner's Sons Ltd., 1980.

Pomper, Gerald M. *The Elections of 1984: Reports and Interpretations*. Chatham, NJ: Chatham House, 1985.

Pomper, Gerald M., and Susan S. Lederman. *Elections in America: Control and Influence in Democratic Politics*. New York: Longman, 1980.

Price, David. *Bringing Back the Parties*. Washington, DC: Congressional Quarterly, 1984.

Ranney, Austin. *Curing the Mischiefs of Faction*. Berkeley: University of California Press, 1975.

——. *Channels of Power: The Impact of Television on American Politics.* New York: Basic Books, 1983.

Reiter, Howard. *Selecting the President.* Philadelphia: University of Pennsylvania Press, 1985.

Robinson, Michael J., and Margaret A. Sheehan. *Over the Wire and on TV: CBS and UPI in Campaign '80.* New York: Russell Sage, 1983.

Rosenstiel, Tom. *Strange Bedfellows: How Television and the Presidential Candidates Changed American Politics.* New York: Hyperion, 1993.

Rosenthal, Alan, and Maureen Moakley, eds. *The Political Life of the American States.* New York: Praeger, 1984.

Schlesinger, Arthur. *Robert Kennedy and His Times.* London: Andre Deutsch, 1978.

Schlozman, Kay S., ed. *Elections in America.* Boston: Allen & Unwin, 1987.

Schram, Martin. *Running for President 1976: The Carter Campaign.* New York: Stein & Day, 1977.

Shafer, Byron. *Quiet Revolution: The Struggle for the Democratic Party and the Shaping of Post-Reform Politics.* New York: Russell Sage, 1983.

Sorensen, Theodore. *Kennedy.* London: Hodder & Stoughton, 1965.

Squire, Peverill, ed. *The Iowa Caucuses and the Presidential Nomination Process.* Boulder, CO: Westview Press, 1989.

Stavis, Ben. *We Were the Campaign: New Hampshire to Chicago for McCarthy.* Boston: Beacon Press, 1969.

Stout, Richard T. *People.* New York: Harper & Row, 1970.

Thompson, Hunter S. *Fear and Loathing on the Campaign Trail.* London: Allison & Busby, 1973.

Trent, Judith S., and Robert V. Friedenberg. *Political Campaign Communication: Principles and Practices.* New York: Praeger, 1983.

Veblen, Eric. *The Manchester Union Leader in New Hampshire Elections.* Hanover, NH: University Press of New England, 1975.

Watson, Richard A. *The Presidential Contest.* New York: John Wiley & Sons, 1980.

Wayne, Stephen J. *The Road to the White House 1992: The Politics of Presidential Elections.* New York: St. Martin's Press, 1992.

West, Darrall M. *Making Campaigns Count: Leadership and Coalition-Building in 1980.* Westport, CT: Greenwood Press, 1984.

White, Theodore. *The Making of the President 1960.* New York: Atheneum, 1961.

——. *The Making of the President 1964.* New York: Atheneum, 1965.

——. *The Making of the President 1972.* New York: Atheneum, 1973.

——. *America in Search of Itself.* London: Jonathan Cape, 1983.

Witcover, Jules. *Marathon: The Pursuit of the Presidency 1972–1976.* New York: Viking Press, 1977.

Wright, James. *The Progressive Yankees: Republican Reformers in New Hampshire, 1906–16.* Hanover, NH: University Press of New England, 1987.

Index

About the Author

NIALL A. PALMER is Lecturer in American Studies at Brunel University in
London, England. He holds degrees from University College, Swansea, and the
University of Bristol.

ISBN 0-275-95569-9

9 780275 955694

HARDCOVER BAR CODE